⑤

Adrian BENNETT

# APPLIED
# Science

## GCSE Double Award

**Editor:**
**Stewart Chenery**

**Tracey Chappell**
**Anna Holmes**
**Beverley Rickwood**
**Steve Unsworth**

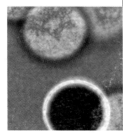

## Hodder & Stoughton

A MEMBER OF THE HODDER HEADLINE GROUP

# Acknowledgements

The publishers would like to thank the following individuals, institutions and companies for permission to reproduce photographs in this book. Every effort has been made to trace ownership of copyright. The publishers would be happy to make arrangements with any copyright holder whom it has not been possible to contact:

Andrew Lambert (1 top right, 64, 95 right, 99 right, 145 top two and bottom, 219); AP Photos (9); Bridgeman Art Library (139 top right); British Automatic Sprinkler Association (22 bottom); British BioGen (187); British Red Cross (24 middle); British Sugar (154 right, 155 top and bottom); Corbis (1 top left, 5 middle and bottom, 6 top left, bottom left and bottom right, 15, 32, 34, 53, 59, 69, 70, 94 all, 108, 111 left, 129 top right and bottom left, 132 bottom, 139 top left and bottom right, 141, 154 left); Ecoscene (126); Geoscience (99 left); Hodder and Stoughton (91 top, 111 right, 113, 159, 190); Holt (6 top middle, 71 top); Lifefile (1 bottom, 25, 134, 140); Medipics (57); Mike Bondy, Close Enough Ranch (67); Photodisc (46); Pilkington Glass (22 top); Science Photo Library (5 top, 6 top right, 11, 18, 35, 36 both, 49 both, 55, 60, 62, 86, 91 bottom, 92 top right, 95 left, 114, 115, 117, 121, 129 top left, 131, 137, 138, 145 second from bottom, 155 middle, 161, 171, 189, 191, 196, 224); Sea Pearls (129 bottom right); Soil Association (71 bottom); St Andrews Ambulance Corp (24 bottom); St Johns Ambulance (24 top); Steve Unsworth (92 top left, 93, 110 all, 119 both, 120, 122, 123, 124 both, 125 both, 132 top); Stewart Chenery (20); Traffic Management Products Ltd (21).

Orders: please contact Bookpoint Ltd, 130 Milton Park, Abingdon, Oxon OX14 4SB. Telephone: (44) 01235 827720, Fax: (44) 01235 400454. Lines are open from 9.00 –6.00, Monday to Saturday, with a 24 hour message answering service. Email address: orders@bookpoint.co.uk

*British Library Cataloguing in Publication Data*
A catalogue record for this title is available from the British Library

ISBN 0 340 84833 2

First published 2002
Impression number    10 9 8 7 6 5  4 3 2 1
Year                 2008 2007 2006 2005 2004 2003 2002

Typeset by Pantek Arts Ltd, Maidstone, Kent

Printed in Italy for Hodder and Stoughton Educational, a division of Hodder Headline Plc, 338 Euston Road, London NW1 3BH.

# Contents

# Contents continued

# Introduction

This book is designed to cover the material leading to Applied Science GCSE Double Award. The course is about what scientists do, the skills they need and the way in which they work. This course will also highlight the skills that are used in many types of work that perhaps you might not normally associate with science.

The course is divided into three units:

**UNIT 1** Developing Scientific skills

**UNIT 2** Science for the Needs of Society

**UNIT 3** Science at Work

Your teachers will assess your work in units 1 and 3 and you will be formally examined in unit 2. Each unit is worth one third of the total marks. It is important that you read the specifications for the course; these will tell you exactly what you have to learn and what you have to do.

In units 1 and 3 you must put together a folder of work. The details are given below:

**For Unit 1 your folder must contain:**

- A report of an investigation carried out into working safely in a scientific workplace.

- Records of one practical activity in each of the **six** areas of microscopy, microorganisms, qualitative analysis, quantitative analysis, electrical properties and other physical properties; each activity should be in a vocational context and include evidence that you:
  - carried out risk assessments;
  - followed standard procedures;
  - used appropriate scientific equipment and/or materials;
  - obtained, recorded and analysed scientific data appropriate to the task.

**For Unit 3 your folder must contain work about the way science is used for the benefit of society. This should include the following evidence:**

- An assignment on science in the workplace, describing the work of scientists and how science is important in a wide variety of jobs.

- Reports on the production of three products that involved different types of chemical reaction.

- A report on making and assessing the effectiveness of one electrical or electronic device.

- A report on how mechanical machines can be used in the workplace.

- A report, including a plan, on your investigation into the growth and/or development and/or responses of a living organism under controlled conditions (you must show appropriate care and consideration when investigating living organisms).

Your teacher will explain each point in detail and also explain when and how your work is to be assessed, but **you** must make sure that every requirement for each unit is completed. (In both cases these are the minimum requirements). Work that you complete for your folders must be kept safely – it may help you if you keep a chart or record of what you have completed, so that you can track your progress easily.

**Unit 2 will be examined under exam conditions and you will be required to answer questions on:**

- Living organisms.
- Obtaining useful chemicals.
- Materials for making things.
- The importance of energy.

Only work from unit 2 will be examined and you will need to revise this carefully in preparation for the examination.

Generally unit 1 helps you develop and learn about scientific skills that you will use during unit 3. Unit 2 contains the knowledge which you must learn to be successful throughout the course.

There are common themes which link all of the units together which means that you may well be studying parts of each unit at the same time. This book will help you link the various parts of the course together, and at the same time will identify the material contained in each unit.

# Introduction continued

The book is divided into five main chapters which follow the themes developed throughout the course. Each chapter is divided into sections, at the beginning of each section you will find an indication of which unit the material refers to.

The outline of the book is shown below:

Throughout this book you will find questions to complete that have been designed so that you may both check and extend your knowledge and understanding. You will also find that key scientific words have been identified and explained throughout.

| | UNIT 1 | UNIT 2 | UNIT 3 |
|---|:---:|:---:|:---:|
| **Chapter 1 Workplace and laboratory science** | | | |
| Science in the workplace | | | ✔ |
| Hazards and risks in the laboratory | ✔ | | |
| The prevention of fire in the laboratory | ✔ | | |
| First aid in the laboratory | ✔ | | |
| The importance of standard procedures | ✔ | | ✔ |
| **Chapter 2 Living organisms** | | | |
| Investigating living organisms | | ✔ | ✔ |
| Cells | ✔ | ✔ | |
| Micro-organisms | ✔ | ✔ | ✔ |
| Agriculture and Horticulture | | ✔ | |
| The Human Body | | ✔ | |
| **Chapter 3 Useful chemicals and materials** | | | |
| Building blocks | | ✔ | |
| Pure substances and mixtures | ✔ | ✔ | |
| Properties and uses of materials | ✔ | ✔ | |
| **Chapter 4 Making useful products** | | | |
| Chemical reactions | ✔ | ✔ | ✔ |
| Chemical calculations | ✔ | | |
| Controlling chemical reactions | | | ✔ |
| **Chapter 5 The importance of energy, instruments and machines** | | | |
| Energy resources | | ✔ | |
| Energy efficiency | | ✔ | |
| Heating systems at work | ✔ | ✔ | |
| Instruments and machines | | | ✔ |

# Chapter One

# Workplace and Laboratory Science

**Chapter 1 is divided into 5 sections:**

**Section 1**    The importance of science in the workplace    Applied Science GCSE Unit 3

**Section 2**    Hazards and risks in the laboratory    Applied Science GCSE Unit 1

**Section 3**    The prevention of fire in the laboratory    Applied Science GCSE Unit 1

**Section 4**    First aid in the laboratory    Applied Science GCSE Unit 1

**Section 5**    The importance of standard procedures    Applied Science GCSE Units 1 & 3

---

## Section 1    The Importance of Science in the Workplace

**Required Knowledge**

Section 1 is divided into two topics:

1 The importance of science      2 The roles of scientists

When completing your Unit 1 assignment work you will need to:

★ Identify local, national and international businesses and service providers that use science.

★ Put employees within these businesses and organisations into one of three classes: major, significant and small users of science.

★ Find out where the organisations are situated and why.

★ Identify the types of scientific activities that are carried out and the job titles and qualifications of the people that perform them.

★ Find out what skills scientists need in addition to their qualifications.

★ Find out what careers are available in science and science related areas.

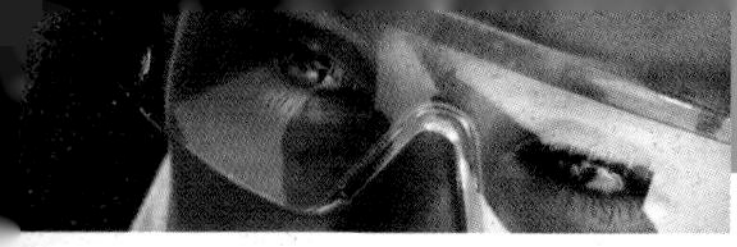

# Topic 1 The importance of Science

The science industry is one of the most important industries contributing to the national economy. The success of the national economy is often judged by the output of the science industry. The science industry contributes to many things that we may take for granted.

Science contributes to everyday life in so many ways, whether you are shopping, playing football, painting your bedroom or watching a film. You may be sitting in a chair which is made of plastic or perhaps filled with fire-resistant foam. Your chair may be covered with a material which is man-made.

You may have a television, hi-fi, or DVD player that has been produced by the science industry.

**Questions**

1 Make a list of the types of industry in which you may find a scientist at work.

Fig 1.1 TVs are produced by the science industry

Fig 1.2 Food and drink is packaged in lots of different types of containers

Perhaps you have just had snack or a drink, these will have been in containers produced by scientists.

As you take a shower, shampoo your hair, or clean your teeth you will be using products that have been developed by scientists.

Fig 1.3

**Questions**

2 a) Look at the car in Figure 1.3. List all the parts that the science industry has helped to produce. b) What type of material has each of these parts been made from?

The chemical industry is one of the biggest users of science in this country. The pie chart in Figure 1.4 gives some idea of the wide range of products that are produced.

**Fig 1.4** Products produced by the chemical industry

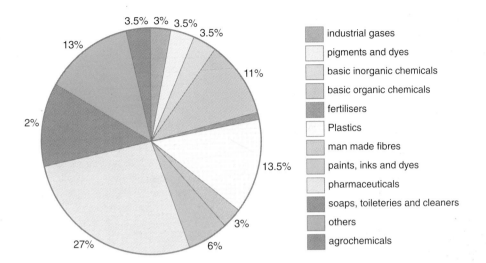

- industrial gases
- pigments and dyes
- basic inorganic chemicals
- basic organic chemicals
- fertilisers
- Plastics
- man made fibres
- paints, inks and dyes
- pharmaceuticals
- soaps, toileteries and cleaners
- others
- agrochemicals

Some of the materials in Figure 1.4 are used as ingredients for chemical products such as pharmaceuticals, paints and personal hygiene goods. However, about half of the chemical materials and products made are purchased directly by other industries and form vital ingredients for the products and services that they provide. All chemicals end up being used in products and services purchased by the consumer, but there may be many stages between the sale of a chemical and the final consumer product. For example, car manufacturers make direct purchases of chemicals, such as paints, but also buy plastic, rubber, textiles and electronic components, which rely upon other chemical materials. On average it is estimated that each UK household either directly or indirectly spends £25 per week on chemicals.

## Questions

3  What does the pharmaceutical industry produce?

4  Suggest reasons why the value of products from the pharmaceutical industry is the highest.

5  What are agrochemicals?

6  Find out the difference between inorganic and organic chemicals and give an example of each.

7  Give four examples of man made fibres that you use.

The chemical industry is a really big business in the United Kingdom. It is the nation's fourth largest industry and the fifth largest industry in the Western world. About two hundred major chemical companies employ 6% of the UK workforce. The map in Figure 1.5 shows the main areas of employment in the chemical industry.

SCOTLAND 6%

NORTH EAST 17%

NORTH WEST 4.5%

MIDLANDS 13.5%

SOUTH EAST EAST ANGLIA 32%

WALES 4.5%

SOUTH WEST 5%

**Fig 1.5** Employment figures for the UK chemical industry

**Questions**

8  Suggest reasons why employment in the chemical industry is highest in the North West, South East and North East of England.

# Topic 2  The roles of scientists

People that work with science and use scientific skills are not necessarily employed in large industries or organisations. There are many others that use science in their work, who are not even considered as scientists. For some of these people science plays a major part in their work such as doctors, nurses, veterinary surgeons, and some types of engineers or architects. Photographers, farmers, gardeners and brewers also use science in their work, but to a much lesser extent.

## Questions

9  Briefly describe how each of the occupations listed uses science in their work.

10  Make a list of the special scientific skills that each of these occupations has.

11  Make a list of the skills that you have learnt in science.

12  Write down any other occupations that you can think of that use science and describe how science helps in their work.

## Practical Work  Investigating local companies that use science

The types of services that use science may include amongst others:

- Those that provide education in science, for example schools and colleges.

- Those that provide and promote the health of individuals, for example doctors, nurses, dentists, pharmacists, midwifes and physiotherapists.

- Those involved in the energy distribution services, for example electricity and gas suppliers.

- Those involved in communication, for example telephone companies.

- Those that provide communications systems, for example telephone systems.

- Those that provide animal welfare.

Other types of businesses and organisations that use science may make or process products for sale. This type of organisation may:

- Produce food and drink products, for example in-store bakeries at the supermarket.

- Produce chemicals, or products from chemicals, for example paints, fertilisers and plastics.

- Produce electrical or electronic equipment.

- Produce mechanical devices, for example lawn mowers or cars.

- Extract or refine materials from natural resources, for example metals, cement or gravel.

## Questions

13  Carry out a survey of your local area in order to discover the type of industries, businesses and services that make use of science. Use the ideas listed here to help you.

Fig 1.6 Services that use science

*continued* ➤

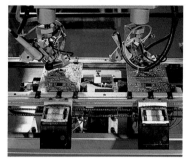

**Fig 1.7** Organisations that use science to make or process products

### Questions

14 The types of scientific activity that are undertaken in the organisations that you identify will of course vary. It is necessary for you to appreciate the skills that may be used by scientists, as you will be using many of these during your course. For all those companies that you have identified, find out what types of scientific activity they carry out.

Scientists and those that use science not only make things but they may also have to:

- Plan carefully how to carry out an activity.

- Carry out research in laboratories, or from books, the internet, or perhaps by undertaking a survey.

- Record accurately the results of their activities.

- Observe what happens during, for example, chemical reactions or biological investigations. Observations are made using the naked eye and by using instruments such as microscopes.

- Make measurements of, for example, mass, volume, temperature or distance.

- Use particular scientific knowledge in their work, for example doctors, nurses and dentists.

- Communicate with other people.

- Use particular practical skills, for example telephone engineers, surgeons, or chefs.

### Questions

15 In the organisations that you have identified, what are the particular skills of those that worked there?

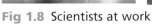

**Fig 1.8** Scientists at work

---

**Practical Work** | **Investigating local companies that use science** continued

Many types of job are available in scientific or related organisations, ranging from research scientist to production manager, or laboratory technician to clerical assistant. The type of job will depend on the qualifications of the person. In addition many organisations run their own training schemes through Modern Apprenticeship Schemes or National Traineeship Schemes.

### Questions

16 Compile a questionnaire which will enable you to find out the responsibilities of some of the people undertaking scientific activities and their qualifications.

Your investigations will only provide you with information on a few of the many employment opportunities that are available within the science sector. You can extend your knowledge in a number of ways:

● By looking at job advertisements in newspapers.

● Visiting a job centre or careers advice centre.

● Asking about job vacancies at a particular workplace.

● Talking to careers advisors.

● Using your work experience placement as a source of information.

● Using the internet to find information on a particular organisation and the type of work that it does.

### End-of-Section 1 Questions

1 Using a local newspaper make a list of all the advertisements which offer jobs that need scientific skills.

2 Produce a poster which gives information about how to find employment which uses scientific skills.

## Section 2 | Hazards and Risks in the Laboratory

Section 2 is divided into three topics

1  Safety regulations
2  Keeping healthy and safe in the laboratory
3  What if an accident happens?

**When completing your Unit 1 assignment work you will need to:**

★  Identify hazard warning signs.

★  Identify biological, chemical and physical hazards, including radioactive substances, and their associated risks.

★  Follow health and safety procedures.

★  Carry out health and safety checks in the work place.

★  Carry out risk assessments for activities carried out in the workplace and laboratory.

## Topic 1 Safety Regulations

Those that work with science are very aware of the hazards and risks involved and as a result have one of the best safety records compared with other types of work.

Unfortunately accidents do happen, in the home, on the road, on the games field, at work and at school. Scientists are very aware of the potential dangers involved in some of the work that they do, in the laboratory, at school and in other workplaces. The news items below illustrate just two examples of the type of accident that can happen and illustrate that the very best plans can sometimes go wrong.

### A school laboratory was evacuated today following an incident during a chemistry lesson

20 students were led to safety by their teacher yesterday, when fire broke out in their laboratory. The local fire brigade arrived minutes later and the fire was quickly brought under control. The fire was believed to have been caused by a chemical spillage during a lesson, where the students were carrying out an experiment into the rate of chemical reactions.

Mr Williams, a spokesman from the school, announced that a full investigation would be carried out into the cause of the accident. He went on to say that two children were being treated for minor burns at the nearby hospital. Mr Williams added that the school had an excellent safety record in its science department, and that staff and students were thoroughly trained in laboratory safety procedure and risk assessment. It is believed that the laboratory will be out of use for the rest of the term.

SCHOOL LAB

**SCHOOL FIRE!**
Special report

### Questions

1   Make a list of all the things that you can think of that may have led up to the chemical spillage in the school laboratory.

# Gas Explosion

A gas worker is in hospital suffering from minor burns after a gas explosion ripped through an office block today. Traffic was brought to standstill towards the end of the morning rush hour.

Firefighters were called to the office block just after 8.45 am, after reports of a loud bang.

Two members of the public, one believed to be an employee, were also taken to hospital with minor injuries.

Several offices in the block were destroyed by the blast, and there was extensive damage to the windows and structure of the building.

Strict regulations control the way in which scientists work and behave in laboratories and other workplaces. It is important for you to be aware of some of these and understand their purpose.

Safety regulations are designed to protect the people who work in potentially hazardous environments. All places of employment are responsible for ensuring that these regulations are followed. Some examples of safety regulations follow.

### Questions

2   Write down as many reasons that you can think of that might have caused this explosion to happen.

## Management of Health and Safety at Work Regulations

These regulations ensure that employers provide their employees with a healthy and safe place in which to work. In particular employers are responsible for:

- Making arrangements for implementing the health and safety measures identified as necessary by a risk assessment for any task undertaken.

- Appointing competent people to ensure that health and safety procedures are carried out.

- Setting up emergency procedures, and ensuring that employees, for example, know what to do in the case of fire.

- Providing clear information and training to employees.

## Control of Substances Hazardous to Health Regulations (COSHH Regulations)

COSHH regulations apply to the storage and use of all substances which are hazardous, for example:

- substances which are toxic, harmful, corrosive or cause irritation;
- substances that may cause cancer or birth defects;
- micro-organisms that may cause disease;
- substances that have minimum exposure limits, for example radioactive substances;
- dust in large concentrations.

COSHH regulations affect many parts of a school, not just the science department, but also design and technology, art and pottery. The regulations also affect many other parts of running a school, such as cleaning, any maintenance work involving chemicals (paints, glues etc), maintenance of swimming pools and pesticide spraying.

## Electricity at Work Regulations (portable appliance testing)

Nearly a quarter of all electrical accidents involve portable equpment. Some of these accidents result in fire, but most cause electric shocks. Portable equipment includes any appliance which is connected to the mains by a cable and plug. The law demands that this equipment is tested regularly. You may have noticed labels attached to the equipment in your school stating when the last test was carried out. The test will detect such problems as a broken earth wire, faulty insulation or use of an incorrect fuse.

## Topic 2 Keeping Healthy and Safe in the Laboratory

No regulation will guarantee the safety of those working in a laboratory or other scientific workplace. It is important that you take responsibility for your own actions and behaviour. You must learn to use all equipment properly. If you are unsure how to use a particular piece of equipment, or carry out an experiment you should always ask. Like many other workplaces your school will have rules and regulations that must be followed when working in the laboratory.

Here is a list of laboratory rules found in a college:

1 Eye protection should be worn at all times.

2 No eating, drinking or smoking in laboratories.

3 Laboratory coats must he worn when handling corrosive, toxic, or flammable materials. Gloves should be worn when necessary, especially when handling corrosive and highly toxic materials.

**Questions**

3 What are your school laboratory rules?

**4** Never work alone.

**5** Do not pipette by mouth.

**6** If you see a colleague doing something dangerous, point it out to him/her and make sure the supervisor is informed.

**7** Know where safety equipment (eyewash, shower, extinguishers) is located and how to use it.

**8** Know how to clean up spills of the chemicals that you use.

**9** Wash your hands after handling chemicals and before leaving the lab.

**10** Open shoes are not to be worn.

**11** Bare legs are not acceptable when handling hot, cold or sharp materials as well as toxic or corrosive chemicals.

**Fig 1.9** Working safely in a laboratory

## Questions

4   Compare your list with the one above and comment on any differences.

Health and safety regulations may seem long and complicated, and together with the rules in your school, difficult to remember. Rules and regulations are based on common sense and sensible behaviour. When working in the laboratory you should take time to think about what you are doing, and be aware of those around you. It may seem that laboratories are very dangerous places in which to work. The purpose of rules and regulations is to minimise the risks, in fact it is because scientists are very aware of the dangers involved, that laboratories are amongst the safest places in which to work.

The theme behind all these rules and regulations is the same:

**STOP, PLAN and THINK before starting**

## Hazards that you may find in workplace and laboratory science

Anything that is potentially harmful may be described as a **hazard**. A laboratory worker must be able to recognise these hazards and be able to deal with them.

## Glossary

**Hazard**
Something that could be dangerous.

## Working with chemicals

Chemical hazards are identified by symbols that have definite meanings. These symbols are universally recognised throughout the world and have very specific meanings.

**Table 1** Hazard symbols

| | |
|---|---|
| <br>CORROSIVE | A substance which may destroy living tissues on contact with the tissue. |
| <br>FLAMMABLE | A liquid may be described as *flammable*, *extremely flammable* or *highly flammable* depending on its flash point. The flash point is the temperature where spontaneous combustion may occur.<br><br>Flammable:<br>A liquid with a flash point greater than 21 °C and less than or equal to 55 °C is said to be FLAMMABLE.<br><br>Extremely Flammable:<br>A liquid with a flash point of less than 0 °C and a boiling point of less than 32 °C is described as EXTREMELY FLAMMABLE.<br><br>Highly Flammable:<br>A HIGHLY FLAMMABLE liquid has a flash point of less than 21 °C.<br><br>Highly flammable is also used to describe substances which:<br><br>• spontaneously catch fire in air;<br>• easily catch fire in contact with flame and continue to burn after the flame is removed;<br>• emit flammable gases when in contact with water or damp air;<br>• are gaseous and flammable at normal pressure. |
| <br>EXPLOSIVE | A substance which may explode when exposed to a flame or heat. This type of substance may also be sensitive to friction or shock. |
| <br>irritant | A substance which may cause irritation to the skin. |
| <br>TOXIC | A substance which if inhaled or taken in through the skin may cause a serious health risk. |
| <br>HAZARD | A substance which could be hazardous if used carelessly. |
| <br>OXODISING | This type of substance gives off a large amount of heat when in contact with other substances. |

# Working with microorganisms

In laboratories where microorganisms are being used, there is always a danger from infection and contamination from bacteria or viruses. Suitable precautions must be taken to ensure that that all specimens are destroyed and disposed of correctly. Microorganisms that are used for experiments should always be stored away from areas where food or drink is consumed, prepared or eaten.

In school laboratories only certain types of micro-organisms may be used. Following any experiments you will be given clear instructions on the procedure to be followed and the material will be carefully destroyed and disposed of for you.

One of the better known hazards arising from the handling of human biological material is HIV (Human Immunodeficiency Virus). Its ease of transfer has made everyone more aware of the need for care when handling any type of material, which has the potential of causing infection.

> **Safety**
>
> **Biohazard**
> Risk of infection or contamination

# Working with radioactive material

Material that emits radiation can damage living cells. The more cells damaged, the greater the danger to the body. The amount of damage done depends on both the intensity of the radiation and the type of radiation.

Gamma radiation is so penetrating that it will pass through the body without much harm, providing the amount is small. Beta radiation is not so penetrating and so more is absorbed by human cells, making it more dangerous. Alpha radiation is even less penetrating and if allowed into the body can cause severe damage. However, because of the low penetrating effect of alpha radiation the layer of dead cells, which form the outer surface of our skin, normally stops it. Alpha radiation is very harmful if inhaled, as there is no outer surface of skin to protect the internal organs.

Radioactive sources used in school laboratories have low levels of radioactivity, but nevertheless should be treated with respect. They are handled with forceps and should not be allowed near the face, and more especially the eyes. They should always be kept in an approved storage cabinet.

In industry, radioactive sources are handled by much longer tongs and transported in thick lead lined containers. Lead and concrete walls are often used to protect those people that work in industry with radioactive sources.

Radioactive sources are only hazardous if handled incorrectly. They are used for a number of purposes in the scientific workplace, such as:

● Food irradiation – to kill infesting insects or prevent potatoes sprouting.

● Medical uses – for killing cancer cells or monitoring bone growth.

● Leak tracing – in pipe work which may be inaccessible.

● Thickness gauging – for thin sheets of paper or aluminium foil during manufacture.

> **Safety**
>
>
>
> **Radiation**
> Risk of radioactive emission

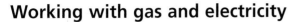

## Working with gas and electricity

Many laboratory activities involve either working with gas or electricity. In the workplace only certain trained people are allowed to replace electrical plugs or fuses (Electricity at Work Regulations). When using electrical appliances in any situation the same good practice should apply.

- Be careful not to spill water or any other type of liquid near an electrical appliance.

- Before using an appliance make sure that there are no loose wires visible.

- Check visibly for any other obvious damage.

- Take care not to allow loose wires or cable to trail across floors or benches.

The Bunsen burner is taken for granted in most laboratories but it is frequently used without much thought. When using the Bunsen burner you should remember to:

- Check that all flammable liquids are securely stoppered and preferably put away in a flame proof store.

- Check that the air hole is shut before lighting the burner.

- Have a lighter ready before turning on the gas.

- Leave a visible flame (yellow) burning whenever the burner is not actually heating, preferably it should be turned off.

- Check that the tubing is not caught around other apparatus in your working area.

- Arrange your working area so that you do not have to lean over the lighted burner at any time.

## Using your knowledge of hazards to make working safer

Before starting any activity in the laboratory you should compile a **Risk Assessment**. A risk assessment should identify the hazards associated with a substance, organism or equipment being used for a particular task and how to minimise them. The risk assessment should consider:

1. The hazardous substance or substances being used or made, and the risks associated with them.

    - The problems that might arise from exposure to the substance.

    - The way that a person might be harmed by the substance (swallowing, inhaling or absorbing through the skin).

    - The particular people who may be harmed (working as a group, in pairs, on your own, etc).

> **Glossary**
>
> **Risk assessment**
> Identifying all risks and hazards associated with e.g. a piece of equipment, a particular substance, or an action.

**2** The precautions that may be taken in order to minimise the risks.

- Find an alternative substance or use smaller quantities.

- Find an alternative method which limits the exposure to the substance if possible.

- Use a fume cupboard if necessary.

- Isolate your working area if necessary.

- Wear protective clothing.

**3** Any other risks.

- Risks from other equipment, such as electrical equipment.

- Risks arising from the environment in which you are working.

Details of hazards associated with particular substances may be obtained from *Hazcards*, which are normally found in the school science department.

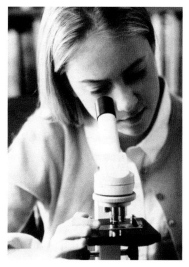

**Fig 1.10** Should you wear goggles when using a microscope?

---

## Questions

**5** Copy the following table and identify the hazards and risks associated with either the material or activity.

| Material or activity | Hazard | Risk |
| --- | --- | --- |
| Sulphuric acid | | |
| Preparing a section of onion to view under a microscope | | |
| Assembling and using a simple electrical circuit | | |

---

# Topic 3 **What if an Accident Happens?**

The most important thing to do if an accident happens is to tell someone, even if the accident does not seem serious. Students working in the school laboratory, or employees working in the workplace might think it is better to keep quiet because the incident seemed very minor. A simple liquid spill in the chemistry laboratory is easily wiped up, but just suppose there was some left and the liquid was hazardous in some way, for example an acid. Someone else may inadvertently get hurt as a result of what seemed like a minor incident.

In the case of major accidents the law demands that these must be reported. The Health and Safety Executive may want to investigate and a report of the accident will always be made. In certain circumstances the scene of the accident may well be preserved (left untouched) to enable a full investigation to be made. Your school and all other workplaces will have a procedure for reporting accidents.

**Safety**

REMEMBER

**Always report accidents**

**Always ask for help if you are unsure of what to do**

## Questions

6  Write a questionnaire that you could use to find out more about essential health and safety measures in your work experience placement or school. You should aim to find out about the main risks involved in your workplace or school, and how these are minimised.

7  In your work experience placement or school find out who is responsible for health and safety, and arrange to interview them using your questionnaire as a basis for the interview. Produce a report, which clearly reflects the potential hazards found in your placement or school, and the health and safety measures taken to deal with these.

Here is a typical checklist of things to do and record if an accident does happen:

### ACCIDENT REPORT CHECKLIST

1  **Identification Information**
  - Class, activity or event in which accident occurred.
  - Date and time of accident.
  - Person in charge.
  - Person injured.
  - Witnesses.

2  **Accident Information**
  - Location of accident.
  - What was the injured person doing? (Just the facts, do not include opinions or determination of cause.)
  - Safety steps taken or not taken. (Do not write the preventative steps the institution could have taken.)

3  **First Aid or Medical Assistance**
  - What type of injury? (Just facts about general nature of injury.)
  - What emergency care was given?
  - Was the injured person taken to the hospital? How?
  - Who did what?

4  **Follow-up**
  - Take notes of communications with the injured or their family and friends.
  - Inform the teacher, risk manager, safety officer and site manager.
  - Do not take immediate steps to make changes without the advice of a supervisor.
  - Save any possible evidence.

## Questions

8  Obtain a copy of an accident report form from your work experience placement or school, and compare it with the checklist above.

## End-of-Section 2 Questions

**1** Explain why regular health and safety checks are important in your school.

**2** Bleach contains two substances that are hazardous:

- Sodium hydroxide – an alkali which is an irritant to the skin and eyes.

- Sodium hypochlorite – a bleach which is an irritant to the skin and eyes and also produces a poisenous gas when mixed wih acids.

Design a safety label suitable to put on a container of bleach.

**3** Design an outline form for writing risk assessments that can be used when carrying out experiments during this course.

**4** In a table make a list of the most common hazards found

a) in the kitchen

b) in the garden shed or garage

c) in the bathroom

For each give an associated risk.

| Section 3 | The Prevention of Fire in the Laboratory |
|---|---|

**Section 3 is divided into two topics:**

1 Causes of fire

2 Dealing with fires

**When completing your Unit 1 assignment work you will need to describe:**

★ What must be done if you hear a fire alarm or smoke alarm.

★ What must be done if you find a fire.

★ How fire doors function.

★ Why different types of fire extinguishers are used on different types of fires.

★ The use of automatic sprinkler systems.

Required Knowledge

# Topic 1 Causes of fire

One of the major hazards particularly in chemistry laboratories and industries that use chemicals is fire.

Fires are best fought by preventing them. Most fires are caused by some sort of human error, incorrect decisions being taken, or the failure to follow instructions. Many fires could be prevented if people were alert and careful at all times.

In the laboratory and scientific workplace, fires may be caused in a number of ways. It is important that you are aware of the possible causes of fire.

**Fig 1.11** Fire crews fighting a large industrial fire

Table 1 Causes of fires

| Chemicals | Many chemicals will combust and must be stored under the correct conditions. Chemicals must also be used correctly, many should not be used near a naked flame in case they catch fire or explode. You should always check a chemical's flammability before using it. |
|---|---|
| Laboratory burners and open flames | Fire may be caused by Bunsen burners being placed too close to where people are working or other combustible material. |
| Hot surfaces | Combustible materials may catch fire if placed on, or too close to, hot surfaces. |
| Spontaneous combustion | Certain types of material, or mixtures of materials, may store heat up and eventually catch fire if stored incorrectly. |
| Static electricity | Static electricity can produce sparks which may start a fire. |
| Electrical equipment | Fires may occur if electrical equipment or machinery is allowed to overheat and not ventilated correctly. |

**Safety**

REMEMBER

Always keep your work area clean.

A major cause of fire spreading in the workplace and laboratory is poor housekeeping, which means not clearing up spillages, scraps of paper and other materials which can easily ignite if allowed too near a flame.

Table 2 shows the cause of accidental fires in buildings other than dwellings between 1994 and 1999.

**Table 2** Causes of accidental fires, 1994–1999

| Year | Faulty fuel supplies | Faulty appliances and leads | Misuse of equipment | Chip/fat fires | Playing with fire | Careless handling of fire or hot substances | Placing articles too close to heat | Other accidental | Un-specified |
|---|---|---|---|---|---|---|---|---|---|
| 1994 | 2200 | 6100 | 4600 | 600 | 300 | 3300 | 2000 | 4300 | 900 |
| 1995 | 2100 | 5900 | 4700 | 600 | 300 | 3400 | 2000 | 5800 | 1100 |
| 1996 | 2200 | 6900 | 4600 | 900 | 300 | 3100 | 2000 | 4900 | 900 |
| 1997 | 2000 | 6800 | 5000 | 1000 | 200 | 2900 | 2100 | 4800 | 700 |
| 1998 | 2000 | 6700 | 4700 | 900 | 200 | 2900 | 1700 | 4700 | 800 |
| 1999 | 2000 | 6700 | 5400 | 1100 | 200 | 2700 | 1700 | 5100 | 700 |

# Dealing with fire

It is important that you know what to do if you discover a fire, hear a fire alarm, or hear a smoke alarm. Look for the instructions in your laboratory and learn them. Typical notices may look like the ones below.

## IF YOU DISCOVER A FIRE

- Raise the alarm immediately.
- If you are carrying out an experiment, make sure your work area is safe by turning off all heat sources.
- Assess the situation from a safe distance.
- If the fire is small and you are able to tackle it make one attempt with an appropriate fire extinguisher or fire blanket.
- Leave the room as quickly as possible making sure all other people have left.

## IF YOU HEAR A FIRE ALARM

- Raise the alarm immediately.
- If you are carrying out an experiment, make sure your work area is safe by turning off all heat sources.
- Close all doors and windows.
- Quickly and quietly evacuate the building via the nearest exit.
- Assemble in the area that has been assigned for your group.

### Questions

1 Which of the causes in Table 2 could be found in the laboratory or scientific workplace?

2 What possible causes may be included in the unspecified category of Table 2?

### Safety

Fire extinguisher

When working in laboratories you should always know where the safety equipment is located and how to raise the alarm.

**Fig 1.12** Students evacuating the laboratory block after the fire alarm has sounded

## Types of fire

There are four types of fire known as classes:

**Class A** is a fire involving solid materials of an organic nature (compounds of carbon) such as wood, paper and cloth, both natural and synthetic.

**Class B** is a fire involving liquids, such as petrol, thinners, solvents, lubricating oils and paint; and liquid based materials or materials that will become liquid when heated, such as cooking fat, waxes and plastics e.g. polystyrene.

**Class C** is a fire involving flammable gases such as propane, butane (LPG), natural gas, acetylene and hydrogen.

**Class D** is a fire involving flammable metals such as magnesium, sodium, aluminium and potassium.

**Questions**

3  Why is it important to turn off all heat sources?

4  Why should you make sure that all windows and doors are closed?

5  Why is it important that you assemble in the area assigned for your group?

## Fire Extinguishers

There are different kinds of fire extinguishers for different types of fire.

| |
| --- |
| Foam extinguishers are **red with a cream colour code** |
| Carbon dioxide extinguishers are **red with a black colour code** |
| Water extinguishers are **red** |
| Dry powder extinguishers are **red with a blue colour code** |

**Class A** fires are best extinguished with a water or foam extinguisher.

**Class B** fires can be extinguished with foam or dry powder extinguishers.

**Fig 1.13** Fire extinguishers

**Class C** – do not extinguish the flame until the fuel supply is turned off or isolated first. Using a fire extinguisher on this class of fire could be tricky, as gas can build up and be explosive. You should always call the Fire Brigade.

**Class D** – these fires need specialist treatment. You should always leave this type of fire to the experts.

Fires involving electrical equipment are best treated with carbon dioxide or powder extinguishers.

> **Safety**
>
> **REMEMBER**
>
> You should never use water to extinguish an electrical fire.

---

**Questions**

6  What are the problems associated with the use of water on electrical fires?

7  Why should you not use water on fires involving fats or oils?

---

Remember that a fire needs fuel, oxygen and heat in order to burn. The first task in fire fighting is to prevent more fuel reaching the fire. The use of the fire extinguisher enables the fire to be cooled down or to be starved of oxygen.

## Fire doors

It is very likely that the door you use to enter and leave your laboratory is a *fire-rated* door. Fire doors are typically made of steel or solid wood. They are provided with specially tested components including closers, latching hardware, and wired fire-rated glass windows. These doors protect the opening created in the 'fire wall' which separates the laboratory environment from the corridor. However, they can only perform their job when used and maintained properly. Some fire doors are found in corridors and automatically shut when the fire alarm sounds, making a 'fire wall' and preventing the fire from sweeping down the corridor.

Fire doors should always be properly used and never abused. The following rules should always be followed:

● Keep the door closed at all times, particularly when the lab is not occupied. The simple action of closing a fire door will help contain the products of a fire, heat and smoke, within the laboratory while protecting adjacent areas and the exit route.

● Never prop open the door with wedges, or by bending the closing mechanism. Aside from possibly rendering the fire door inoperable due to physical damage, propping open fire doors will allow products of combustion to move into other areas and contribute to the spread and severity of the fire.

**Fig 1.14** This glass is used for fire doors. It has been heated to over 920°C for 60 minutes. The glass has not broken and it has stopped heat from passing through it

● Never store equipment or combustibles against the fire door. Placing items of equipment in front of a fire door may result in these materials igniting if a fire were to occur on the other side of the door. This could create hazardous conditions in the corridor, not only for those exiting the building, but also for fire and emergency response personnel entering the building to extinguish the fire.

● You should not nail or screw signs or other items to the fire door. Creating holes or cracks in a fire door will mean that it is no longer secure against fire. Signs may be attached to fire doors provided they are small (less than 5% of the area of the fire door) and attached with adhesive to areas other than the wired glass view panel.

## Automatic Sprinkler Systems

In the UK the number of fires reported in sprinkler controlled buildings over a 12 year period during the 1970s and 1980s was 16 800. Almost half of these were controlled by one or two sprinkler heads.

In Europe over the past 10 years where fires occurred in buildings protected by sprinkler systems:

99% of fires were controlled by sprinklers.
60% of fires were controlled by four sprinklers or less.

Sprinkler systems are a very important aid in the prevention of fires.

### How sprinkler systems work

Automatic fire sprinklers are individually heat-activated, and tied into a network of piping containing water under pressure. When the heat of a fire raises the sprinkler temperature to its operating point, usually around 65°C, a solder link will melt or a liquid-filled glass bulb will shatter to open this sprinkler, releasing water directly over the source of the heat.

**Fig 1.15** A typical sprinkler head found in the ceilings of many public buildings

An automatic sprinkler system does not rely upon human factors such as familiarity with escape routes or emergency assistance. They work immediately to reduce the danger. Sprinklers will quickly prevent fires developing and spreading throughout a building.

The major advantage of a sprinkler system is in the amount of water it uses. Quick response sprinklers release 65–120 litres of water per minute compared to 625 litres per minute released by a fire hose. This makes clearing up after a fire much easier.

## End-of-Section 3 Questions

**1** On a map of your school plan the route that you should take to your assembly point if fire breaks out in the laboratory.

**2** Write a risk assessment which gives the main hazards and risks from fire in your home. For each hazard and risk give a method which may be used as a precaution.

**3** Design tests which compare the effectiveness of different smoke alarms. Your ideas should enable a purchaser of smoke alarms to pick the best value for money product.

## Section 4    First Aid in the Laboratory

Section 4 is divided into two topics:

1   First aid

2   Dealing with injuries

**When completing your Unit 1 assignment work you will need to give details:**

★ About organisations that provide training and qualifications in first aid.

★ About basic first aid to give for:
  ● Heat burns and scalds.
  ● Chemical burns.
  ● Injury caused by breathing in fumes or swallowing chemicals.
  ● Electric shock.
  ● Cuts and damage to the eyes from particles of chemicals.

★ About situations in which it would be dangerous to give first aid.

**Required Knowledge**

## Topic 1 First Aid

When an accident happens in the work place it is important that the people close by know what to do.

In your school and other workplaces there will be people who are trained in giving first aid treatment if an accident occurs.

### Questions

1 Find out who is responsible for first aid in your school.

2 Write a questionnaire that you could use to find out more about essential first aid in a school laboratory or other scientific workplace.

3 Carry out a survey of the first aid equipment kept in your school.

It is important that everyone is aware of some basic first aid techniques that may be required in case an accident happens, whether this be in the home, at school or in the workplace. You may find that those responsible for first aid in your school have first aid qualifications. Three voluntary organisations all run first aid courses.

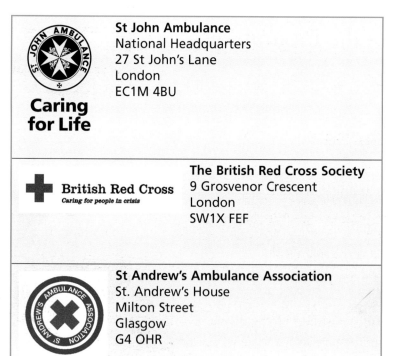

**St John Ambulance**
National Headquarters
27 St John's Lane
London
EC1M 4BU

**Caring for Life**

**British Red Cross**
Caring for people in crisis

**The British Red Cross Society**
9 Grosvenor Crescent
London
SW1X FEF

**St Andrew's Ambulance Association**
St. Andrew's House
Milton Street
Glasgow
G4 OHR

### Questions

4 Use the Yellow Pages to find the address of your local branch of these organisations.

5 Find out about the first aid qualifications that you could obtain in first aid.

## What is First Aid?

First aid is the first treatment given to a person for any injury, before the arrival of a qualified expert. In giving this treatment your responsibility is to help recovery and prevent the condition from becoming more serious. You may be the first at the scene of the accident, so it is important that you know what to do. In laboratories there are a number of common accidents which you should know how to deal with.

Before trying to deal with any situation requiring first aid you must assess the situation carefully. **Emergency Scene Management** (ESM) is the sequence of actions you should follow at the scene of an emergency to ensure that safe and appropriate first aid is given. You should:

## Emergency Scene Management

- Take charge of the situation.

- Call for help. Other people on the scene may be more qualified than you to deal with the situation, if not then ask them for help in assisting with treatment or seeking further assistance. If in school, they may be used to fetch a teacher or health and safety officer.

- Assess hazards. Make the area safe. It is important that you assess if you are in any danger as well as the casualty. It is crucial that you minimise the danger to yourself and guard against further casualties. This is particularly important in some of the examples given later. For instance in the case of gas leaks the source of gas should be cut off if possible. Electricity should be switched off in the case of electric shock. Your own safety is important, after all you have to treat the casualty without yourself becoming a casualty.

- Determine what happened and the type of injury sustained. Try to establish what has happened. You may have to contribute to the accident report form later and give details of the actions that you have taken

## Topic 2 Dealing with Injuries

## Heat burns and scalds

Accidental contact with hot objects frequently causes burns and scalds. In treatment the aim is to reduce the effect of the heat on the affected area, to prevent any infection from entering the wound, and to relieve pain. In order to achieve these aims you should:

- Cool the burn right away. Immerse the burned area in cold water, or pour cold water onto the area, or cover it with a clean, wet cloth until the pain has lessened.

- Loosen or remove anything on the burned area that is tight, such as jewellery or tight clothing, before swelling begins. Do not remove anything that is stuck to the burned area.

> **Glossary**
>
> **Emergency scene management**
> Sequence of actions that should be followed in an emergency, to ensure appropriate first aid is carried out.

> **Safety**
>
> **REMEMBER**
>
> Use your common sense.
>
> Do not attempt to do too much.
>
> Know your own limitations.
>
> Always seek help.

**Fig 1.16**

- Do not break blisters or move any loose skin.

- When the pain has lessened, loosely cover the burn with a clean, non-fluffy dressing. Do not use adhesive dressings. If the burned area is large, use a sheet. Secure the dressing with tape, making sure there is no tape on the burned area.

## Questions

6   What is the purpose of the cold water in treating burns?

7   Why should you not break blisters?

8   Why should you not remove anything that is stuck to the burned area?

## Chemical burns

Many substances that you use in the laboratory are irritating to the skin and may harm tissue even after a short contact time. Common substances found in the home such as bleaches, household cleaners and paint stripper may cause chemical burns. The first sign of a chemical burn is usually when the casualty complains that the skin is stinging or feeling hot. The skin will often appear red. The aim of any treatment is to identify and remove the harmful chemical as quickly as possible. In order to achieve these aims you should:

- Flush the affected area with cool running water for at least 10 to 15 minutes.

- Remember to carefully flush the water away as it may be contaminated with the substance which caused the burn.

- Remove all clothing and jewellery that has been contaminated.

- Monitor the casualty for shock and seek medical assistance.

## Injuries caused by breathing in fumes or swallowing chemicals

Many people may come into contact with potentially dangerous chemicals or gases as a result of the type of work they do. Workplaces using dangerous gas are required to display notices which indicate any action to be taken in case of accidents. Anyone suffering from the effects of gas or toxic fumes needs air, the area should therefore be well ventilated and medical assistance requested.

In cases where chemicals have been swallowed, it is important that the substance is identified if possible and medical help requested. You should never give anything by mouth unless specifically instructed to do so by a medical officer or someone in authority.

# Electric shock

Laboratories, workshops, homes, offices and shops all have electrical appliances which can cause electrical injuries if they develop a fault, or are not used correctly. Water, in particular, is a good conductor of electricity and using electrical equipment with wet hands or whilst standing on a wet floor can often cause electrical injury. Electric shock or injury is caused when an electric current passes through the body.

Before helping a person who has suffered an electric shock it is important to make sure that the person is no longer in contact with the source of electricity. You should always switch off the mains supply and remove the plug from the socket.

Electricity may cause burns to the body at the point of contact, and these should be treated as already described. The person may also become unconscious and suffer from shock, in all such cases further medical help should be sought.

> **Questions**
>
> **9** Why is it important not to touch the casualty until the electricity is switched off?

# Cuts and damage to the eyes from particles of chemicals

Any eye injury can be dangerous as particles may perforate the eyeball, resulting in internal damage and possible infection. The most common problems are caused by small particles of dust and grit. You should not attempt to remove any such particle if it is on the coloured part of the eye, or embedded in the eye.

- If an object is embedded in the eye, you should not remove the object.

- Cover both eyes with sterile dressings to immobilize them. Covering both eyes will minimize the movement of the injured eye.

- DO NOT rub or apply pressure or ice to the eye. If the injury is a black eye, you may apply ice to the cheek and area around eye, but not directly on the eyeball itself.

Normally a person with a particle in their eye will complain of some pain or itchiness of the eye. The eye will often become red and will water intensely. The person's vision may also be affected. In treating the eye to remove any particle you should take great care and seek immediate help if unsuccessful.

If the particle is not embedded it may be removed by washing the eye with a sterile eye wash solution.

### How to flush the eyes

If the chemical particle or foreign body is in only one eye, flush by positioning the casualty's head to the side with the contaminated eye downwards, to prevent flushing any chemical from one eye to another.

Flush with a sterile eye wash solution. If this is not available then tap water should be used. Remove contact lenses after flushing.

## Questions

**10** Why is it important to remove contact lenses after flushing the eye?

## End-of-Section 4 Questions

**1** Imagine that you have to deal with an emergency situation in a laboratory where there is believed to be at least one casualty. Carefully produce a report, which describes the immediate actions you would take in caring for and comforting the casualty. You should remember that it is important to care for yourself as well as for the injured person. You may find it helpful to produce a flow diagram, which shows the steps that you would take.

**2** In some cases following a laboratory accident it may be more appropriate to send for a doctor or ambulance rather than administer first aid yourself.

In which circumstances would it **not** be appropriate to give first aid? Give reasons for your choices.

# Section 5 The use of Standard Procedures

**When completing your practical assignment work for Unit 1 you must be able to:**

★ Read a standard procedure, and check to see if there is anything you do not understand.

★ Carry out a health and safety check of your working area.

★ Carry out a risk assessment for the activity you are doing.

★ Set out your work area and collect together the equipment and materials you need.

★ Follow the instructions one step at a time.

★ Make accurate observations or measurements, selecting instruments which give the appropriate precision.

★ Identify possible sources of error, and repeat observations and measurements when necessary, to improve reliability

Much of the work that is done in laboratories and other scientific workplaces is carried out using a **standard operating procedure**. A standard procedure describes exactly how to carry out a procedure or experiment. It also ensures that whoever carries out an experiment does it in exactly the same way, and that results are gathered in the same way.

The standard procedure used for a particular task will also deal with health and safety issues that may arise during the operation, and will include a risk assessment. Particular companies may have their own standard procedures for carrying out certain investigations to ensure a consistent approach by all those that work within that company.

Standard procedures that are important during this course include:

● The correct techniques when using particular measuring instruments such as pipettes and burettes.

● **Aseptic** techniques when working with microorganisms.

● Preparing solutions that have a specified concentration.

● Carrying out chemical analysis, which includes **qualitative** and **quantitative** techniques.

● The use of particular pieces of equipment such as the microscope.

● The calibration of particular pieces laboratory equipment.

These represent only a very small example of standard operating procedures. All types of industries and organisations, not just those which are science based, have their own standard procedures. Many of these are published, some as policies or charters, but many as just procedures. For example the British Pharmacoepia is a book containing the standards (formulae) for commonly used medicines.

## Glossary

**Standard procedure**
The approved method of completing a task.

**Aseptic**
Free from any living organism.

**Qualitative analysis**
Analysis to find which substances are present.

**Quantitative analysis**
Analysis to find the amounts of a substance present.

Many industries and organisations subscribe to standards published by the International Organisation for Standardisation (ISO). In the UK many firms also belong to the British Standards Institute. You may have seen the Kitemark on many products. The Kitemark is a sign that the products that carry this logo meet certain British standards.

**Fig 1.17**

## End-of-Section 5 Questions

1   Produce a poster which illustrates one of the standard procedures that you have carried out in the laboratory.

2   Write a paragraph which explains the importance of standard procedures in hospital laboratories.

3   Make a list of as many products that you can find at home which carry the Kitemark.

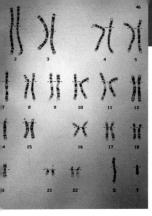

# Chapter Two

# Living Organisms

Chapter 2 is divided into 5 sections:

| | | |
|---|---|---|
| Section 1 | Investigating Living Organisms | Applied Science GCSE Units 2 & 3 |
| Section 2 | Cells | Applied Science GCSE Units 1 & 2 |
| Section 3 | Micro-organisms | Applied Science GCSE Units 1, 2 & 3 |
| Section 4 | Agriculture and Horticulture | Applied Science GCSE Unit 2 |
| Section 5 | The Human Body | Applied Science GCSE Unit 2 |

## Section 1 — Investigating Living Organisms

Section 1 is divided into four topics:

1 Useful animals
2 Useful plants
3 Useful micro-organisms
4 Investigations using living organisms

**When completing your assignment work for Unit 3 you will need to:**

★ Understand that in order to maximise the amount of product obtained, scientists must provide organisms with the most suitable conditions.

★ Give examples of what these suitable conditions might be.

★ Give examples of how organisms can be monitored.

**In the Unit 2 written examination you will be expected to know:**

★ That useful products can be made from plants, animals and micro-organisms.

★ That living organisms are made up of chemical compounds.

★ A range of examples of where living things are useful.

**Required Knowledge**

All living things are made up of the chemical compounds that we ourselves need in our diets: carbohydrates, proteins and fats. Carbohydrates and fats are composed of the **elements** carbon, hydrogen and oxygen. Protein is made up of carbon, hydrogen, oxygen and nitrogen. These are the elements of life, required by all living things in order to carry out the processes necessary for life. These are the elements we take into our bodies when we eat other animals and plants.

Perhaps food, then, is the most vital material that we obtain from other living organisms. However, many other useful products can be obtained from living things. These include fabrics, building materials, medicines and dyes, to name but a few.

Living things can be classified into three main groups: animals, plants, and micro-organisms. All three of these groups provide us with useful products. We will look at examples of useful products from each of these groups. We will also look at how scientists can maximise the amount of product they produce by investigating the conditions needed.

**Glossary**

**Elements**
Substances that cannot be broken down into simpler parts.

# Topic 1  Useful Animals

Animals are a good source of protein in our diet. Protein is essential for building muscles, for growth and for the repair of cells in our bodies.

Animals are also a source of many of the essential vitamins and minerals that we need to stay healthy. For example, animal liver is a good source of iron, which we need for our blood.

Some animals, such as cows and goats, also provide us with milk, which is another good source of protein. Milk is also a good source of the mineral calcium, which we need for healthy bones and teeth.

Animals are also useful to humans for their skins or coats. We use the wool from sheep to make clothes to keep us warm. We also use the skins from cows to make the leather for shoes and bags.

## Case Study  The cow – a very useful animal

Cattle are particularly useful to humans. There is evidence, in ancient wall paintings and on pottery, that cattle have been domesticated by humans for over 8000 years. Cows produce milk, they can be eaten as beef, and their skins can be used to make leather. In days gone by, they were also used to pull carts and ploughs, their bones were used to make weapons and tools, and their dung was burnt to give heat or was made into bricks for building. Very useful animals indeed!

**Fig 2.1** Picture of the cave paintings of cows (bison, ox) from Lascaux caves

In Britain today, cows are bred for two main purposes: for beef and for milk. Farmers usually only rear their herd of cattle for a single purpose. For example, cattle raised to produce beef are not used for milk production. This is because the best conditions to raise beef cattle in, are not the same as for milk cattle. Beef cattle require high levels of protein from cereals, and they are usually kept housed throughout their lives. This ensures that the cows gain weight quickly (about 1.25kg per day) and are ready to be slaughtered when they are about 11 months old.

Milk cows on the other hand are raised on a high carbohydrate diet. The more carbohydrate they eat, the more milk they produce. These cows graze on grass in the summer and are fed hay and root vegetables during the winter.

Farmers are now finding that cattle can be even more useful thanks to modern technology. Beef cows can now be given steroid injections to increase the amount of muscle they produce, and so give the farmers more meat to sell. In addition, a hormone extracted from bacteria, can now be given to milk cows to increase their milk production.

Farmers that breed cows are now aided by 2 modern methods called artificial insemination and embryo transplantation. Artificial insemination is where farmers remove sperm from bulls and inject the sperm into the female cows. The sperm can be frozen and easily transported to many herds of cows, so that more calves are born from one bull. Embryo transplantation involves fertilising eggs from one cow, and placing them into the wombs of other cows to grow – a bit like test-tube babies in cows!

**Questions**

1 Why do farmers usually only rear one type of cattle?

2 What different conditions are needed by beef cattle and milk cattle?

# Topic 2  Useful Plants

Plants are a source of carbohydrate. We use carbohydrate to give us energy. All plants are made up of carbohydrate in the form of starch or sugars. We digest these sugars and starches, breaking them down into glucose, which we need for respiration.

Some plants are particularly good sources of carbohydrate and we eat a lot of them in our diets, for example potatoes, rice and sugar cane.

Some plants, such as beans and pulses, are also a good source of protein. Fruits and vegetables also provide us with some vitamins and minerals that help to keep us healthy. For example, oranges are a good source of vitamin C. A substance called cellulose, which is found in the **cell walls** of plant cells, forms the part of our diet that we call fibre. This fibre helps our **digestive system** to work properly.

Plants have other uses too. The cotton plant is used to make fabric for our clothes and homes. Some plants have been found to help treat diseases and the useful ingredients within them are extracted and made into medicines. Other plants can be used to make colourful dyes, although the bright colours we see in the fashion world today are all man-made. Onion skins, red cabbage and beetroot were used to make the coloured dyes in medieval times.

**Glossary**

**Cell wall**
A rigid layer around the outside of plant cells and that holds the cell together.

**Digestive system**
The part of the human body that breaks down food.

# Topic 3  Useful micro-organisms

Micro-organisms include bacteria, fungi and viruses. They have been found to have a whole range of uses to humans, most of which are in the food and drink industry.

**Case Study** | **Plants – Ancient Remedies and New Technologies**

**Fig 2.2** The Pacific yew tree, source of Taxol

A relatively new drug called Taxol is fast becoming one of the world's leading anti-cancer treatments. The substance that it is made from originally comes from the bark of the yew tree. There are numerous references in ancient folk law about the healing properties of the yew tree. Taxol was discovered in 1962 when Dr A Barclay of the US National Cancer Institute collected bark from the pacific yew tree and found that it reduced the activity of cancer cells in a number of leukaemias and tumours of the breast, ovary, brain and lungs. After much research as to why this happened it was found that Taxol stops cells dividing and so prevents cancer growth.

Trials of Taxol began in 1983, but the drug was in very short supply. Unfortunately, it requires the sacrifice of a one hundred year old yew tree to provide a cancer patient with a single dose of Taxol! Environmentalists were concerned about endangering the ancient yew tree forests of North America. This led to research to discover whether Taxol could be made chemically in the laboratory. This was finally achieved in 1993, using new high-tech methods that include computer modelling. Taxol is now becoming a lifesaver for thousands of patients with cancer.

Did you realise that the aspirin tablets that we take as painkillers originally came from a plant? Bark from the willow tree has been used as a herbal remedy for hundreds of years. People used to chew the bark to relieve mild pain, fever and swelling. In 1897, Felix Hoffmann, a German chemist, used a simple chemical reaction on an extract from this bark to make aspirin. This was the first-ever manufactured drug and, to this day, remains the most commonly taken medicine in the world.

**Questions**

3   Aspirin and Taxol were both originally extracted from plants. How did ancient people first discover their benefits as medicines?

4   Why is it better for the environment that these drugs are now made chemically in the laboratory?

A type of fungus, known as yeast, is used in brewing, wine making and baking. All involve a process called fermentation. Fermentation is where yeast cells convert glucose into carbon dioxide, alcohol and energy.

$$\text{Glucose} \xrightarrow{\text{yeast}} \text{carbon dioxide} + \text{alcohol} + \text{energy}$$

In brewing, sugars from barley are converted into alcohol by the yeast. Changing the type of yeast, the fermentation time and adding other ingredients, can make different types of beers.

In wine making, the yeasts that grow naturally on the skins of grapes are used to ferment the sugars within the grapes. Different types of grapes produce different wine flavours.

In baking, yeast is used because it produces carbon dioxide, making the bread rise. The alcohol, also made during fermentation in baking, evaporates away as the bread is baked in the oven.

Different kinds of bacteria are used to produce butter, yoghurt and cheese, from milk.

Some micro-organisms are used in the production of medicines. The best known example is the fungus *Penicillium*, which produces a substance called penicillin. Penicillin can kill many types of bacteria and is known as an antibiotic.

## Case Study | A story of Antibiotics

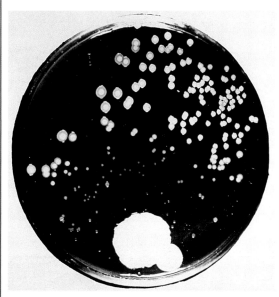

**Fig 2.3** Fleming's agar plate, showing growths of *Penicillium* (white areas)

In 1928, a scientist called Alexander Fleming accidentally discovered that a mould called *penicillium* could kill certain bacteria. It took scientists 12 years to obtain the substance in a form that could be used. The substance was said to have antibiotic properties, and was named penicillin. Penicillin was produced in laboratories and made into tablets or injections. In 1940 it was first tried out in hospitals to treat people with certain bacterial diseases and was thought to be a miracle cure. Other antibiotics, that kill different bacteria and are also obtained from micro-organisms, have since been discovered. Pharmaceutical

companies (drug companies) now manufacture antibiotics on a massive scale.

Diphtheria used to be a major cause of death among children. It is caused by a bacteria which produces a life-threatening poison in the nose and throat of those infected with it. In England and Wales, the number of people who died from diphtheria in the 1910s was almost 5000 per year. By the 1960s the number of deaths had fallen to less than 10 per year. This fall was due almost entirely to the introduction and increased use of antibiotics.

Unfortunately, new forms of bacteria keep evolving that the antibiotics cannot kill. This is thought to be because antibiotics have been over-used, which has resulted in bacteria becoming resistant to the antibiotics. This means that diseases tend never to be wiped out completely. For this reason doctors prefer not to give you antibiotics unless they are absolutely necessary.

### Questions

5   In addition to the introduction of antibiotics, can you think of any other reasons why deaths from diphtheria dropped so drastically between the 1910s and the 1960s?

6   Why should you not take antibiotics unless you really need them?

# Topic 4 Investigations Using Living Organisms

Living organisms need to be grown in the most suitable conditions, to ensure that they grow healthily and that the maximum amount of product is obtained.

Scientists investigate what conditions living organisms need to function properly, by monitoring both the organism and the conditions under which it is growing. This enables them to understand how the organism works. Here we look at how you would undertake your own investigation.

## Practical Work | Investigating a living organism

### How to select an organism for investigation

There are several factors to consider when selecting an organism for investigation:

- The timescale of your experiment. If you have only got a day to complete your investigation then it would be useless to try to investigate growth in plants.

- The conditions that you will be providing. You must have the equipment, time, and money to provide these conditions for the length of the investigation.

- The particular activity you want to monitor. You must make sure that you have the equipment to make the necessary measurements.

- The care of the organism. You must ensure that you can give the appropriate care and consideration needed to the living organism during the investigation.

- The cost of your experiment. You must set a budget and stick to it. Living organisms and their requirements can be expensive, so you must find out the cost before you plan the rest of your investigation.

### Conditions needed

These will depend on the actual organism chosen. The following factors should be considered:

- Nutrients needed,
- Temperature,
- Light,
- Water,
- Exercise/performance (can be considered in human investigations).

Usually you vary one of these factors to see what effect it has on the organism. The rest of the conditions need to be kept constant. It is important in planning your investigation that you think about how you will change one of the conditions, and how you will keep the other conditions the same.

## Questions

**7** Many investigations involve humans. Explain why you might select this particular organism for investigation.

*continued* ➤

## Activities to be monitored

What you are able to measure will again depend on the organism chosen for investigation.

When using animals you could monitor the following:

● Growth – by measuring height or weight (most animals grow too slowly for you to measure this, but scientists could measure this over a longer period of time).

● Response to a stimulus – by recording behaviour when a stimulus such as light or touch is applied.

● Heart rate and breathing rate – can be measured in human investigations.

When using plants, you could monitor the following:

● Growth – by measuring the height of plants.

● Yield – by measuring the amount of useful product obtained, for example weight of fruit or vegetable.

● Response to light – by measuring the amount of bending the plant makes towards the light.

When using micro-organisms you could monitor the following:

● Yield – by measuring the amount of useful product obtained, for example volume of beer or antibiotic.

● Growth or reproduction – by counting the number of micro-organisms or colonies grown.

**Case Study** **Investigating turnips**

*Brassica rapa* is the name of a member of the turnip family that has been much investigated by scientists, you may even do some experiments with it at your school. It is sometimes called 'rapid cycling brassica' which gives you a hint as to why it is used so much in investigations – it grows very quickly.

You can buy the seeds from any garden centre, they are cheap and the seeds are easy to grow in a basic compost soil. In about a week the seedlings may need to be potted into larger containers. After about 3–4 weeks the plants will have reached about 20 cm in height and will start to produce tiny yellow flowers. To actually get turnips to form the plants must be grown for longer, but this is not usually what scientists use these plants for. The whole of the life cycle from seed to producing new seeds is very quick – a matter of a few weeks, hence the name 'rapid cycling brassica'.

It is clear to see the reasons for selecting this living organism for investigation, but what can you investigate and what conditions are needed?

The plants require nutrients, in the form of fertiliser, water, light and a reasonable temperature. It is common to investigate what effect changing one of these conditions has on the plants, while keeping the rest of the conditions constant to ensure a fair test. The heights of the plants can be measured over a period of 3–4 weeks.

*continued* ➤

## Case Study   Investigating turnips continued

A good example involves having several sets of plants that are each grown with a different essential nutrient missing. One set of plants would be grown with nothing missing and used as a control to compare the others to. This would show what happens when plants don't have certain nutrients, you can then work out what these nutrients are needed for by the plant.

### Questions

8   Why is *brassica rapa* a suitable organism for doing investigations on in school?

9   Make a list of the conditions that you would need to consider in your investigation.

10   Why would you use 'sets' of plants rather than single plants to make sure you get good results?

## End-of-Section 1 Questions

1   a)   Give the names of three animals that we eat.

   b)   Give two examples of how we use animals to obtain products other than food.

2   We eat plants to get carbohydrates like starch and sugar, proteins, vitamins, and the more complex carbohydrate called cellulose. Give one reason why we need each of these different types of food.

3   Give three types of products, other than foods, that can be obtained from plants.

4   Micro-organisms are used for many different purposes, several of which involve yeast and the process known as fermentation.

   a)   Explain what fermentation is.

   b)   Give two examples of the use of fermentation in the food and drink industry.

   c)   What other products can we obtain from micro-organisms?

5   When investigating living organisms, what factors must be considered before deciding which organism to choose for your investigation.

6   Select an organism that you might like to study.

   a)   State your reasons for choosing this organism.

   b)   What activity are you going to monitor?

   c)   What conditions have you got to consider for this organism?

   d)   Which of these conditions are you going to investigate, in other words which condition will you be changing throughout your experiment? How will you change it?

   e)   Why must you keep the rest of the conditions the same? How will you do this?

## Section 2    Cells

Section 2 is divided into four topics:

1   Animal and plant cells
2   The microscope

3   Standard Operating Procedures
4   Special features of cells

**Your Unit 1 portfolio should include evidence that you have:**

★   Set up a light microscope.
★   Prepared a temporary slide.

**In the Unit 2 written examination you will be expected to know:**

★   That living organisms are made up of cells.
★   The similarities and differences between animal and plant cells.
★   How substances move in and out of cells by diffusion and osmosis.
★   How cells divide by mitosis during growth.
★   How cells divide by meiosis to produce gametes.

# Topic 1   Animal and plant cells

All living things are made up of cells. A cell is the basic unit of life – the smallest part of an organism that can function independently. Cells are the building blocks of organisms in the same way that bricks are the building blocks of houses. In order for scientists to understand how living things work, it is important for them to know what cells look like and how they behave.

The human body is made up of millions of cells, each one being about 0.001 cm wide. These cells are organised into **tissues** and **organs**. The cells are so small that you cannot see them with the naked eye but must use a **microscope**.

There are 2 main types of cells, animal cells and plant cells, although some micro-organism cells are unlike either of these and are discussed in a later section. A typical animal cell and a typical plant cell are shown in Figure 2.4.

> **Glossary**
>
> **Tissues**
> Groups of similar cells that have the same function (e.g. skin, muscle).
>
> **Organs**
> A part of an organism, made up of different tissues (e.g. heart, liver).
>
> **Microscope**
> A piece of equipment that scientists use to view things invisible to the naked eye (e.g. cells).

**a. Animal cell**

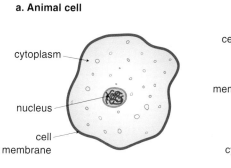

cytoplasm

nucleus

cell membrane

**b. Plant cell**

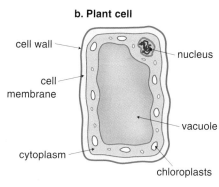

cell wall

cell membrane

cytoplasm

nucleus

vacuole

chloroplasts

**Fig 2.4**  A typical animal cell (a cheek cell) and a typical plant cell (a leaf cell).

The features labelled in the cell diagrams are known as **organelles**. Some of these organelles are the same in both animal and plant cells and some of them are only found in plant cells. Table 1 summarises the similarities and differences between plant and animal cells.

| Similarities | Differences |
|---|---|
| ● Both have a cell membrane | ● Only plant cells have a cell wall |
| ● Both have a nucleus | ● Only plant cells have chloroplasts |
| ● Both have a cytoplasm | ● Plant cells have one large vacuole, while animal cells have many small vacuoles |
| | ● Plant cells often have a regular shape, while animal cells are often irregular in shape |

**Table 1** The similarities and differences between plant and animal cells

# Organelles

It is important to know the **structure** and the **function** of the main features of plant and animal cells.

### Cell membrane

The **cell membrane** is a thin boundary surrounding the cell. It holds the cell together and controls the movement of substances into and out of the cell.

### Cytoplasm

The **cytoplasm** is a clear, jelly-like watery liquid. It contains the smaller parts of the cell (organelles) and dissolved substances.

### Cell wall

The **cell wall** is a thick, flexible and porous layer outside the cell membrane in plants. It is made up of a complex carbohydrate called cellulose. It supports and protects the cell.

### Nucleus

The **nucleus** is the densest part of the cell. It contains chromosomes, which are thin strands of DNA. The nucleus controls the reactions that occur in cells – it is the cell's 'brain'.

### Chloroplasts

**Chloroplasts** are small, spherical structures containing a green pigment called chlorophyll which absorbs sunlight. The energy from the sun is used to make food (photosynthesis).

**Glossary**

**Organelles**
The parts that make up a cell.

**Structure**
This is what the organelle, cell, tissue or organ *looks like*.

**Function**
This is what the organelle, cell, tissue or organ *does*.

## Vacuole

The **vacuole** is a bag of fluid, known as cell sap, surrounded by a membrane, which enables the cell to store dissolved sugars and salts. The vacuole also puts pressure on the cell wall, helping to keep the cell rigid.

---

### Questions

1 Copy and complete the following table for the features of plant and animal cells listed on page 40.

| Feature | Structure | Function |
|---------|-----------|----------|
|         |           |          |
|         |           |          |
|         |           |          |

---

# Topic 2  The Microscope

Cells are too small to be seen with the naked eye, so a microscope can be used to magnify them so that we can see them. Some organisms, such as yeast, are made up of only one cell, so you can see the whole organism under the microscope. But most organisms are made up of lots of cells and under the microscope you would see a group of cells, known as a tissue.

The kind of microscopes that you use in school are called **light microscopes**, because they shine light through the cells you are looking at, and then use glass lenses to magnify and focus the image. Most light microscopes can magnify cells up to 400 times, but a really good microscope can magnify up to about 1500 times.

### Glossary

**Light microscope**
A microscope that uses rays of light to view objects.

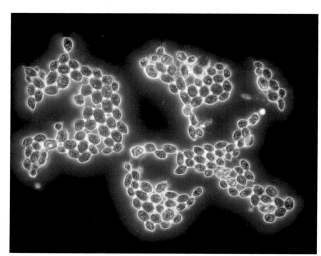

**Fig 2.5** Yeast cells seen through a light microscope (magnification = × 600).

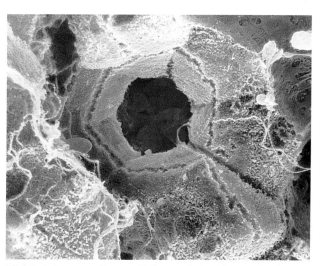

**Fig 2.6** Human liver cells seen through an electron microscope (magnification = × 1600).

A special kind of microscope, called an **electron microscope**, can be used to look at the tiny organelles inside a cell. Electron microscopes use a beam of **electrons** instead of light, and can magnify up to 500 000 times. They therefore allow much more detail to be seen. Photographs taken of images on an electron microscope are called electron micrographs. These enable close examination of cells and are used widely in modern medical science.

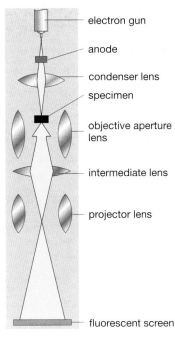

**Fig 2.7** An electron microscope

> ### Glossary
>
> **Electron microscope**
> A very high powered microscope that uses beams of electrons.
>
> **Electrons**
> The negatively charged parts of an atom.

> ### Questions
>
> **2** What are the advantages of using an electron microscope rather than a light microscope?
>
> **3** Why don't we use electron microscopes in school?

## Topic 3  Standard Operating Procedures

There are two important **standard operating procedures** (SOPs) relating to cell biology. One SOP is used for setting up the light microscope, and one for preparing a slide of cells to look at under the microscope.

> ### Glossary
>
> **Standard operating procedure**
> A set of instructions to follow to ensure that everyone always performs certain procedures in the same way.

> ### Practical Work | Setting up a light microscope
>
> Look at the diagram below to learn the names of all the parts of the microscope before you begin.
>
>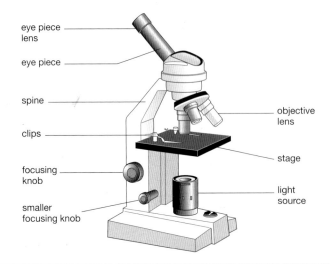
>
> **Fig 2.8** A light microscope

**Practical Work** | **Setting up a light microscope** continued

1  Place the microscope in front of you with the 'spine' of the microscope towards your body.

2  Wind the stage of the microscope down to its lowest point.

3  Place the slide to be viewed on the stage with the clips holding the slide in place.

4  Starting with the lowest objective lens (usually ×4) look through the eye piece and slowly turn the main focusing knob until the image comes into view.

5  Use the smaller focusing knob to bring the image into focus. Decide which part of the image you would like to look at further and carefully move the slide on the stage until this part of the image is in the centre of the image viewed.

6  Using the more powerful objective lenses in size order (usually ×10 and then ×40) continue to re-focus on the desired part of the image until you have a view of your cells at the highest magnification (×400 with a ×10 eyepiece and a ×40 objective lens).

7  Draw a sketch of what you can see at this highest magnification. If you cannot get a clear image because the lens cannot get close enough to the cells without touching the slide, (take care whenever the objective lens is close to the slide as the slide may break), go back to the previous smaller lens, re-focus and draw the image at this lower magnification.

8  Ensure that you write the total magnification next to your drawing (look at the size of the eyepiece and multiply this by the size of the objective lens).

**Practical Work** | **Preparing a slide of onion cells**

1  Cut a section of onion tissue approximately 1 cm² and peel from the underside of it the transparent, paper-thin layer using tweezers.

2  Place this thin layer, which is only one cell thick, onto a clean slide.

3  Add 2 or 3 drops of iodine onto the onion to stain parts of the cells and enable them to be viewed more easily.

4  Add a cover-slip to the onion, in order to seal it. This is done by placing the cover-slip in the drop of iodine on one side of the onion sample and lowering it down at an angle using a mounted needle (as shown in Figure 2.9).This will make sure that no air is trapped under the cover-slip.

5  If necessary, blot any excess iodine off the slide (make sure that you don't suck it out from under the cover-slip and dry out the onion cells).

**Questions**

4  Why do we add iodine to the cells when we want to look at them?

*continued* ➤

**Practical Work** | **Preparing a slide of onion cells** continued

**6** The slide can now be placed on the stage of the microscope, ready to look at the onion cells.

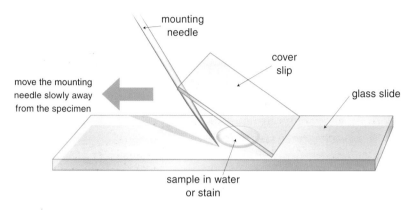

mounting needle

cover slip

glass slide

move the mounting needle slowly away from the specimen

sample in water or stain

**Fig 2.9** Lowering a cover-slip onto onion tissue

## Hints on how to research a topic

Throughout the Applied Science course you will be asked to research various topics. If you were asked to 'research cells' you would not necessarily be given a list of questions to answer but you would be expected to include the following:

● How big are they?

● How can we see them?

● How is the equipment used to see them in big labs and hospitals different from that used in schools?

● How do we prepare cells for viewing?

● What do animal and plant cells look like (draw them)?

● What are the similarities and differences between animal and plant cells?

● What is the general name for the parts inside a cell? Give examples and say what they look like (their structure) and what they do (their function).

All the answers to these questions can be found in this section, but you should practise your research skills by using wider sources to check your information. Always pay particular attention to the dates of publication, remember that advances in technology are constantly updating our knowledge of science. Ensure that your sources of information are up-to-date and therefore reliable.

When researching any topic, a quick scan through a few sources of information usually enables you to establish what the key points are.

# Topic 4  Special Features of Cells

Cells are important because they are the building blocks of all living things. There are some processes that occur within cells that are particularly crucial to the survival of the whole organism. These include diffusion, osmosis, and cell division.

## Diffusion and Osmosis

The cell membrane controls the movement of different substances into and out of cells. This is because the cell membrane is **selectively permeable**, it allows some substances to pass through but not others. Those substances that pass through, such as water, have **particles** that are small enough to fit through the tiny holes in the cell membrane. Other substances, such as sugar, do not pass through because their particles are too big. In living organisms both diffusion and osmosis occur across the cell membrane.

## Diffusion

**Diffusion** is the movement of particles from where there is a high concentration of particles to where there is a low concentration. It occurs because all particles are moving and the more particles there are, the more they collide with each other. The particles move further apart and spread out as far as possible, they diffuse out across an area. Examples include digested food diffusing from the **gut** into the blood, oxygen diffusing from the lungs into the blood, and carbon dioxide diffusing from cells into the blood.

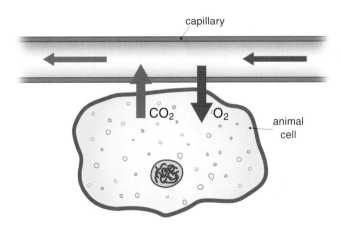

**Fig 2.10** A cell takes in oxygen and gets rid of carbon dioxide by diffusion

## Osmosis

**Osmosis** is a type of diffusion which involves the movement of water molecules, for example across cell membranes. Water moves from where there is a high concentration of water to where there is a low concentration. The flow of water will continue until the concentration of water molecules on each side of the cell membrane is equal.

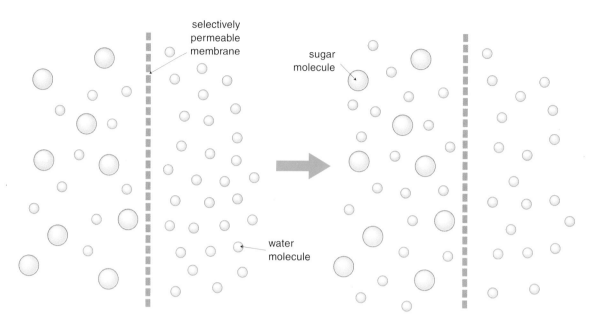

**Fig 2.11** Water moves from where there is a high concentration to where there is a low concentration.

## Cell division

### Chromosomes

Chromosomes contain instructions to make many different types of protein within cells. Chromosomes are made up of DNA in a sequence of genes, and are found in the nucleus of a cell. Each gene, by controlling the production of a particular protein, determines a charcteristic of the organism. For example in humans one gene determines a person's eye colour.

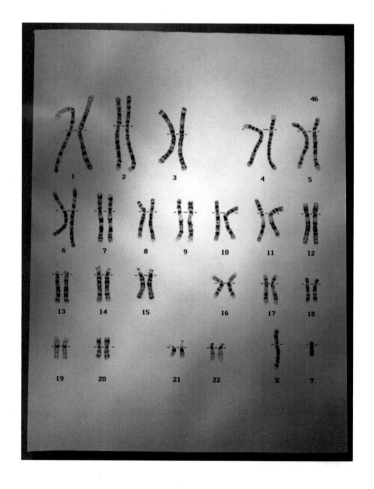

**Fig 2.12** Human chromosomes

All human cells, excluding the sex cells, contain 46 chromosomes, arranged in 23 pairs. Chromosomes play an important role when cells divide. There are two types of cell division, called mitosis and meiosis.

## Mitosis

Mitosis is the name given to the way in which cells divide to provide new cells for growth, or for repairing a damaged part of the organism. As mitosis begins, the 46 chromosomes within a cell are copied to produce two identical sets. Each set then moves to opposite ends of the cell. The cell membrane begins to pinch in the middle, dividing the cell into two. There are now two identical cells, each containing an identical set of 46 chromosomes.

Some organisims, such as bacteria, reproduce using mitosis, producing offspring identical to themselves.

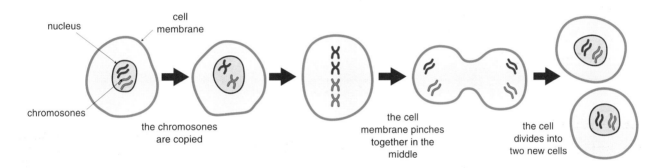

nucleus

cell membrane

chromosones

the chromosones are copied

the cell membrane pinches together in the middle

the cell divides into two new cells

**Fig 2.13** Mitosis

## Meiosis

Meiosis is the name given to the way in which cells divide to form the sex cells or gametes. These gametes are the male sperm and the female egg in animals, and the male pollen and the female egg in flowering plants. The gametes are made by ordinary body cells dividing, but unlike with mitosis the resulting gamete cells have only half the number of chromosomes as the original cell. This is to ensure that, when the two gametes fuse together during fertilisation, the new offspring will have the full set of 46 chromosomes. In humans this means that the sperm and the egg both have 23 chromosomes so that the baby can have the normal 46.

Meiosis begins in much the same way as mitosis. The chromosomes are copied and the cell divides producing two cells. But unlike mitosis these cells now undergo a second division without the chromosomes being copied again. So meiosis produces four cells in total, each with 23 chromosomes. When the gametes join together at fertilisation the resulting offspring receives half its chromosomes from one parent and half from the other, so it is not identical to either of its parents.

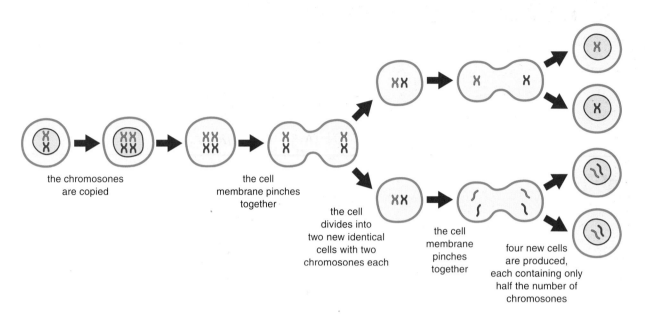

the chromosones
are copied

the cell
membrane pinches
together

the cell
divides into
two new identical
cells with two
chromosones each

the cell
membrane
pinches
together

four new cells
are produced,
each containing only
half the number of
chromosones

**Fig 2.14** Meiosis

## Questions

7  Explain why it would be a problem if egg
and sperm cells were formed by mitosis
instead of meiosis.

## Case Study   Diagnosing disease

The study of cells and tissues is important in helping doctors to find out what is wrong with their patients. They need to make a diagnosis before they can decide on the correct treatment. In addition to looking at the patient's symptoms, sometimes the doctor needs a better idea of what is going on inside the body. Samples of cells or tissues, such as blood cells or lung tissue, are taken from the patient and sent off to the pathology department of the hospital to be looked at under the electron microscope. When the photographs (electron micrographs) have been taken they can be compared with others taken from healthy individuals and from patients with known diseases.

Look at electron micrograph A in Figure 2.15. It shows a tissue sample taken from the lungs of a healthy person. You can see that there are lots of tiny projections on the membranes, these create a large surface area in the lungs. This ensures that the

maximum amount of oxygen can get across the lungs and into the blood. It also enables the maximum amount of carbon dioxide to pass from the blood and into the lungs for removal from the body. If a sample taken from your lungs looked like this then the doctor would know that your lungs were healthy.

Now look at electron micrograph B and compare it to A. You can see that the membranes are smoother and the total surface area much smaller. This would be likely to cause a problem with breathing, as not enough of the gas exchange mentioned above could take place. This lung tissue has come from a patient with a lung tumour, which can lead to death if not diagnosed and treated early.

*continued* ➤

**Case Study**   **Diagnosing disease** continued

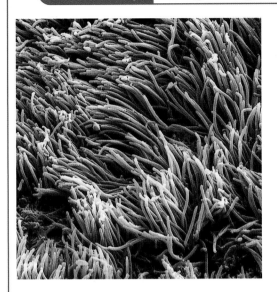 

**Fig 2.15** Electron micrographs A-normal & B-tumour

**Questions**

8  Explain how having electron micrographs taken of tissue samples help doctors find out what is wrong with their patients.

9  Describe the differences that you can see between diagrams A and B, and explain the problems that the patient with emphysema would have with breathing.

**End-of-Section 2 Questions**

1  State the differences and similarities between animal and plant cells.

2  a)  What does the term organelle mean?

   b)  Give the name of an organelle that is present in both animal and plant cells.

   c)  Name two organelles that are found only in plant cells.

3  a)  What are the differences between how a light microscope works and how an electron microscope works?

   b)  What are the advantages of using an electron microscope?

   c)  What is the main disadvantage of an electron microscope?

4  Explain what a standard operating procedure is and why it is important that scientists follow them.

5  Define diffusion and explain why it is important in living cells.

6  a)  How many chromosomes are there in normal human body cells?

   b)  How many chromosomes will there be in cells that have undergone division by
       (i)  mitosis?
       (ii)  meiosis?

## Section 3    Micro-organisms

**Section 3 is divided into five topics:**

1 Types of micro-organisms
2 Useful micro-organisms
3 Harmful micro-organisms

4 Protection against harmful micro-organisms
5 Growing micro-organisms

**In this section you will learn that:**

★ Aseptic techniques are used when culturing micro-organisms (Unit 1).

★ Scientists that grow useful micro-organisms can improve their yield by providing them with the best possible conditions (Unit 3).

**In the Unit 2 written examination you will be expected to know that:**

★ Micro-organisms are classified as bacteria, fungi and viruses.

★ Micro-orgamisms play an important role in the production of foods, drinks and medicines, with some specific examples.

★ Bacteria, fungi and viruses may cause disease, with some examples of each.

★ A range of methods are used to protect against infection in food production, with some specific examples.

★ Immunisation is used to protect humans and other animals from infection, with some specific examples.

★ Anti-microbial agents are used to kill micro-organisms and, specifically, antibiotics kill bacteria but not viruses.

There are many different micro-organisms, some of which are harmful and some of which are harmless, or even useful, to humans. They are almost all microscopic. A single microbe cannot be seen with the naked eye, although a collection of them, usually known as a colony, can sometimes be seen.

## Topic 1  Types of Micro-organisms

There are millions of microbes in the atmosphere, soil, oceans and our bodies. They are classified into three main types: bacteria, fungi and viruses.

### Bacteria

Bacteria are believed to be the oldest type of organism on earth. Fossils of bacteria have been found which date back further than any other living organism. They are **single-celled organisms**, and differ from other animal and plant cells in that they have no nucleus.

> **Glossary**
>
> **Single-celled organisms**
> Organisms made up of only one cell.

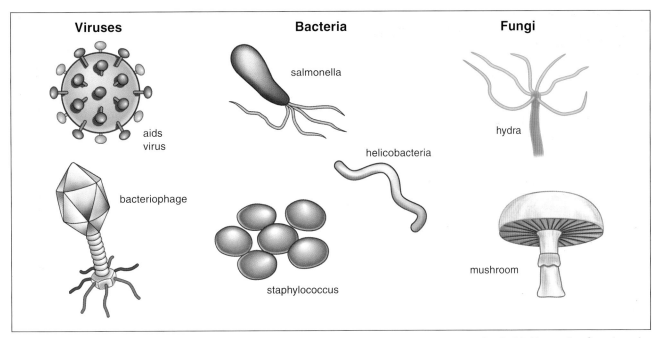

**Fig 2.16** Bacteria, fungi and viruses

Bacteria occur in air, dust, water, soil and inside other organisms. They can even be found in hot springs at temperatures of 60 °C. One gram of soil may have up to 100 million bacteria within it, and 1 cm³ of fresh milk has 3000 million bacteria in it! Bacteria, along with fungi, are vital to all other organisms because they cause the decay of organic material and the subsequent recycling of nutrients in the environment.

Bacteria reproduce by splitting into two in a process called binary fission, which is a form of **asexual reproduction**. Examples of bacteria include salmonella, streptococcus and E-coli.

## Fungi

Fungi are often wrongly classified as plants as they are **multicellular organisms** and have a cell wall. They do not, however, have chlorophyll within their cells and so do not photosynthesise.

Fungi live in soil or inside other organisms and obtain their nutrients by absorbing organic nutrients from dead plants and animals, so recycling the nutrients. Fungi reproduce rapidly by producing spores. Examples include mushrooms and toadstools, moulds and yeast.

## Viruses

Viruses are the smallest living organisms, but they do not really classify as cells as they have no nucleus, cytoplasm or cell membrane. They are about 50 times smaller than bacteria, with an average width of ten thousandth of a millimetre.

Early scientists knew of the existence of viruses from their experiments, even though they were too small to see with a light microscope. In 1898 they were named 'virus' after the Latin word for poison. Viruses were one of the first biological structures to be studied when the electron microscope was developed in the 1930s.

### Glossary

**Asexual reproduction**
Reproduction involving only one parent, where the offspring are identical to the parent.

**Multicellular organisms**
Organisms made up of many cells.

### Questions

1  Describe how the three types of micro-organisms reproduce.

2  Put the three types of micro-organisms into order of size, starting with the smallest.

Viruses have a very simple structure, with a coil of **DNA** wrapped up in a protein coat. They can only survive outside the cells of another organism for a very short time, because they use the materials from the cells of their host to reproduce. Viruses inject their DNA into host cells. Once inside the cell the viral DNA uses the products within the cell to produce new viruses. Eventually the host cell bursts, releasing all these new viruses, which go on to infect more host cells. Examples include the AIDS virus and the influenza virus.

> **Glossary**
>
> **DNA**
> Made up of genes and wound into chromosomes, it controls the way an organism develops.

# Topic 2  Useful Micro-organisms

## In the food industry

Micro-organisms can be used by humans for a variety of purposes. Bacteria are used in many economically important processes, such as making butter, yoghurt and cheese. These are all made from milk. Different micro-organisms are added and the milk is treated in different ways, depending on whether butter, yoghurt or cheese is being made. For example, in yoghurt making, bacteria change the sugar in the milk to a substance called lactic acid. This makes the milk go thicker and slightly sour.

Genetically engineered bacteria, along with certain fungi, are also used in the food industry to make proteins that humans can eat. These kinds of proteins may be important in developing countries where food is in short supply. They are a cheaper and quicker means of feeding many people than with animal or plant protein. For example, in 1971 research began on harvesting a protein, called mycoprotein, made by a fungus called *Fusarium*. In 1985 the name 'Quorn' was chosen as the trademark for this product and it is now eaten as a high-protein alternative to meat in the UK. Its sales have increased as more people have chosen to become vegetarians.

Fungi have also traditionally been used in the fermentation process in baking and producing beer and wine. This has been briefly mentioned already in Section 1. When fungi make energy for themselves they convert sugar into alcohol. This is a type of **anaerobic respiration**. As part of this process they also give off carbon dioxide as a waste product. The word equation for fermentation is:

> **Glossary**
>
> **Anaerobic respiration**
> This is where organisms obtain energy without using oxygen. It is used by many yeasts and bacteria.

$$\text{glucose} \rightarrow \text{energy} + \text{alcohol} + \text{carbon dioxide}$$

The process of fermentation can be used to produce alcohol, which can be drunk by humans. The type of alcohol made depends on which plants the original sugar came from and which extra ingredients have been added. Different types of beers can be made using different yeasts, changing how long the beer ferments, and adding other ingredients. In wine making, the sugars from grapes are fermented by the yeasts that grow naturally on the skin of the grapes. Different types of grapes produce different wine flavours.

In baking, fermentation is used because the yeast produces carbon dioxide which makes bread rise. The alcohol, which is also produced during baking, evaporates away as the bread is baked in the oven.

Fermentation using yeast can also be used to produce alcohol for use as a fuel. This kind of fuel is known as a bio-fuel because it is produced by living things. The advantage of making this kind of alcohol is that it can use waste sugars from the food industry, as the food source for the yeast. These waste sugars could not be used if the alcohol was being made for humans to drink.

**Fig 2.17** Yeast is added to vats of barley to produce whisky

## In the pharmaceutical industry

The pharmaceutical industry develops and makes medicines. Many of these medicines come from living organisms. Both bacteria and fungi have been found that have antibiotic properties. This means that they kill other bacteria. As already mentioned in Section 1, penicillin was the first antibiotic to be discovered and remains the best known. However, antibiotics have no effect on viruses.

Bacteria that have been genetically engineered are used in the pharmaceutical industry, to make drugs and human hormones. The most well known example of this is the production of human insulin, also mentioned in Section 1.

Viruses have never really been used for any useful purpose. This is because scientists know less about viruses than they do about bacteria and fungi. However there has been a recent development in this area of science. Viruses are being investigated as a possible cure for diseases like cystic fibrosis. Viruses survive by mixing their DNA with that of the host cell. They are being used as a way of inserting genes into cells that have faulty genes. This is the first time viruses have been thought of as useful in any way, and they could play a big part in the future of an expanding area of medicine known as **gene therapy**.

> ### Glossary
> **Gene therapy**
> Altering genes to treat diseases or genetic disorders.

28 million pints of beer are brewed each day in the UK and the population spends £13 500 million on beer each year! Brewing is a good example of the usefulness of living organisms as it involves not only micro-organisms, but plants as well. The micro-organism used in brewing, yeast, is a fungus too small to be seen with the naked eye. Plants provide the sugar for fermentation, as barley, and the bitter flavour, as hops.

Scientists have carried out much research into the process of fermentation and the conditions required by yeast to make beer. The basic ingredients of brewing, however, are the same today as those used when yeast was discovered in the seventeenth century. Even earlier than that, as far back as the Middle Ages, beer was made using yeast without actually knowing what yeast was. At this time, beer was drunk instead of water because there was no supply of clean drinking water and the beer was safer and more pleasant to drink!

The basic ingredients of beer are:

- **Malted barley** – the main source of sugars that are fermented by the yeast. This provides the yeast with food.

- **Water** – makes up the bulk of the beer and makes beers brewed in different parts of the country taste different.

- **Yeast** – the key component in brewing, changing sugar into alcohol during the process of fermentation.

- **Hops** – provide the characteristic bitterness and contribute to the aroma of the beer.

water + barley + yeast + hops $\rightarrow$ heat + yeast + beer + carbon dioxide

Brewing is an environmentally friendly process. The heat and yeast can be recycled, and the carbon dioxide used to add fizz to other drinks.

Brewers must carefully monitor the flavour of the beers they are producing. When necessary, they must alter the conditions in which the yeasts are grown, in order to perfect their product and ensure that it competes with its rivals. All this to find the perfect pint!

**Questions**

3   What is the name of the process that is used in brewing, where yeast converts sugar into alchohol?

4   Why do beers brewed in different parts of the country taste different?

5   What makes beer taste bitter?

6   Why is brewing seen as an environmentally friendly process?

# Topic 3 Harmful micro-organisms

Bacteria, fungi and viruses can cause diseases in other living organisms. Bacteria mainly affect animals. They cause diseases such as food poisoning, caused by the *salmonella* bacteria, diphtheria and tetanus. Fungi affect mainly plants and cause diseases such as Dutch elm disease and mildew. Fungi are also responsible for some food spoilage, such as moulds, and for skin diseases, such as athlete's foot and ringworm.

Viruses affect both animals and plants. Despite their incredibly small size, viruses cause some of the worlds most serious diseases. In recent years, the most notable human virus has been the HIV virus that causes AIDS. This virus attacks the white blood cells that help us to fight disease, and so AIDS is described as a disease of the **immune system**. Viruses also cause less serious diseases such as the common cold, 'flu and chicken pox. However, these viruses still cause global problems because **immunisation** is made difficult by the constantly changing outer structure of the virus. This makes it difficult for the immune system to recognise the virus.

**Glossary**

**Immune system**
The part of the body that destroys a disease-causing micro-organism that has entered the body.

**Immunisation**
Defending the body against disease by giving a vaccination injection.

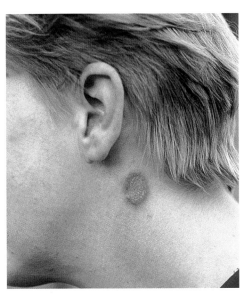

**Fig 2.18** Ringworm is caused by a fungus

Some examples of bacterial, fungal and viral diseases are shown in Table 1.

Table 1

| Type of organism affected | Bacterial diseases | Fungal diseases | Viral diseases |
|---|---|---|---|
| humans | tetanus cholera tuberculosis (TB) | athlete's foot ringworm eczema | common cold 'flu measels rubella mumps polio AIDS |
| other animals | tetanus anthrax foot rot tuberculosis | ringworm eczema | foot and mouth rabies |
| plants | | mildew potato blight soft rot dutch elm disease | alfalfa mosaic disease rose mosaic disease tomato spotted wilt |

## Protection against harmful micro-organisms

Micro-organisms that cause disease are known as pathogens. Pathogens infect other organisms in a number of different ways:

- by air,
- by **contaminated** water,
- by contaminated food,
- by direct contact,
- by insect bites.

By knowing how these organisms are spread, we can work out the best ways of protecting ourselves from infection.

**Glossary**

**Contaminated**
Food or water that contains harmful micro-organisms, known as pathogens.

# Harmful micro-organisms in food production and how to prevent infection

Since micro-organisms can get inside the body most easily by being taken in through the mouth, protecting against micro-organisms in food is the best way to avoid infection.

Foods provide perfect breeding grounds for micro-organisms. Bacterial diseases that are spread by contaminated food include *Salmonella* food poisoning, botulism, cholera and typhoid. It is important to ensure that all possible steps are taken during the production of food to eliminate or reduce the risk of infection. In addition, some simple precautions can also be taken in the home.

- Don't buy food which has gone past its sell-by date, as micro-organisms may already be growing in the food.

- Don't refreeze frozen food that has thawed out, as micro-organisms may now be growing in the food.

- Do keep perishable food in the fridge, as the cold temperature restricts micro-organisms' growth.

- Do wash vegetables thoroughly to remove any micro-organisms from the soil.

- Do wash hands before handling food to prevent any micro-organisms from getting on to food.

- Do keep your food preparation area clean to reduce the risk of contaminating one food with the micro-organisms from another food.

- Do keep hot food hot and cold food cold until it is eaten, to reduce micro-organisms multiplying, which they do at warm temperatures.

- Do reheat food thoroughly to kill micro-organisms that have already started to grow.

## Questions

7  Why should cooked food be reheated thoroughly if it is not eaten straight away?

8  Why does keeping perishable food in the fridge help protect us from micro-organisms?

9  What is the name of a bacteria that causes food poisoning?

### Personal hygiene

For individuals, personal hygiene is probably the most significant way of ensuring that pathogens are not passed from person to person. Washing your hands after going to the toilet, after blowing your nose and before preparing food, is important for everyone. However, personal hygiene is absolutely vital for anyone working in the food industry and coming into direct contact with food.

In addition to these basic precautions workers in the food industry must wear hats over their hair and they must wear gloves if they directly handle food. These high standards of personal hygiene will minimise the spread of micro-organisms from person to person and also from people into the food being prepared.

### Antiseptics and disinfectants

There are also some chemicals that can be used in the food industry and at home to ensure that surfaces and equipment used for food preparation are thoroughly clean and do not have micro-organisms on them. These are antiseptics and disinfectants.

Antiseptics are chemicals that prevent bacterial growth. These can be used to clean wounds on the skin. In the preparation of food, antiseptic soaps can be used to wash the hands and make sure they are bacteria free. Disinfectants are bacteria-killing chemicals that are too strong to be used on human skin. They are used to clean floors and surfaces where food is prepared. It is important that food does not come into contact with the disinfectant as it is a very strong and quite nasty chemical, that we would not want to consume.

### Sterilisation

Equipment that comes into contact with food in the food industry must be cleaned very carefully. The best way to ensure that all the micro-organisms have been removed or killed is to sterilise the equipment. Sterilisation involves heating the equipment to very high temperatures. Equipment to be treated in this way is placed in an **autoclave** and heated under pressure with steam to about 115°C for 20 minutes. The high temperature kills the micro-organisms and the equipment is then said to be sterile.

Sterilisation can also be used as a way of ensuring that there are no bacteria present in some of the foods we eat. Milk can be sterilised to remove the possibility of any micro-organisms being present, although this has now been widely replaced by pasteurisation. Sterilisation destroys more micro-organisms than pasteurisation. Sterilisation also extends the shelf-life of milk by several months, whereas with pasteurisation it is only extended by several days. However, sterilisation affects the flavour of the milk, and most people prefer the taste of milk that has been pasteurised.

Foods cooked in a pressure cooker are also effectively sterilised. In school laboratories, pressure cookers or autoclaves can be used to sterilise equipment, especially those used in micro-organism experiments.

> ### Glossary
> **Autoclave**
> A large pressure cooker used to sterilise equipment.

**Fig 2.19** An autoclave

---

### Questions

**10** What are the advantages and disadvantages of sterilised and pasteurised milk?

**11** How does personal hygiene help protect us against harmful micro-organisms?

**12** Antiseptic and disinfectants are both chemicals that kill micro-organisms. How are their uses different?

## Immunisation against harmful micro-organisms

Diseases caused by micro-organisms are spread from person to person in the many ways already listed. However, certain people do not get diseases while those around them do. This was noted as far back as mediaeval times. These people are said to be immune to the disease. It was discovered that if you had had a mild dose of the disease already you were not likely to get the disease again in a more serious form.

Scientists have spent years investigating why this happens. This research began in 1796 when a doctor called Edward Jenner first realised that exposure to a disease known as cowpox seemed to stop some of his patients from contracting the much more serious disease, smallpox.

The body produces substances called antibodies that destroy micro-organisms. Different antibodies are made to destroy different micro-organisms. The body can remember how to make antibodies to a particular microorganism. This means that if the same microorganism enters the body again, the same antibodies are made immediately and kill the micro-organism before it causes a problem for the body a second time. This is called natural immunity.

Due to much scientific research, immunity can now be achieved without actually ever having the disease. This artificial immunity is given in the form of a vaccination. Vaccination is where a substance containing a pathogen is injected into the body. The pathogen that is present in the vaccine has been made harmless beforehand, but the body still makes the antibodies to fight the particular disease.

Vaccination is now available against influenza. The injection contains the influenza virus that has been made harmless. After this vaccination the body makes antibodies against influenza virus. Vaccination against influenza is recommended by doctors for those in susceptible groups, including the very old and those suffering from respiratory problems such as asthma. Unfortunately, vaccines can only be developed against individual strains of the virus but because the virus constantly changes, a further injection against the new virus is needed the following winter.

**Fig 2.20**

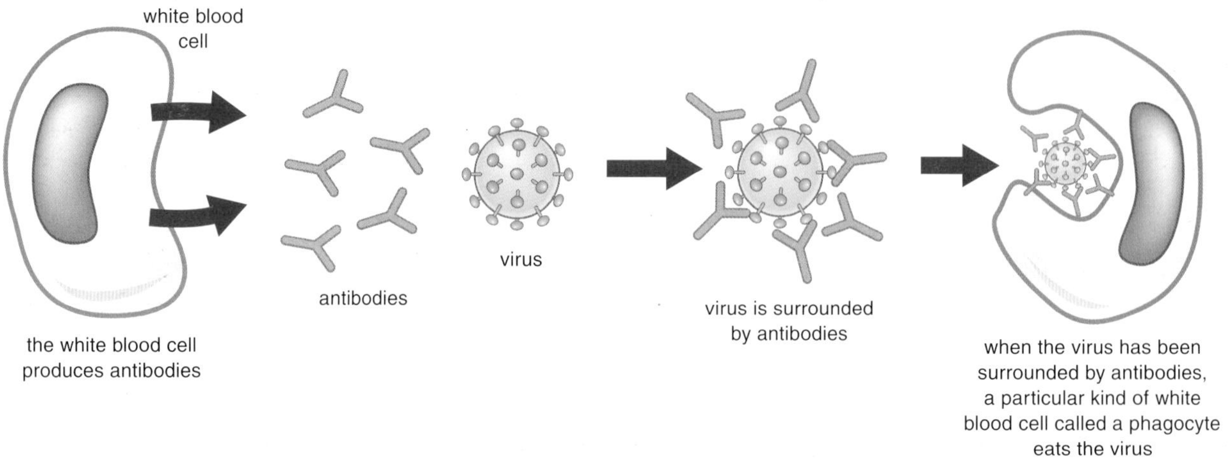

white blood cell

antibodies

virus

the white blood cell produces antibodies

virus is surrounded by antibodies

when the virus has been surrounded by antibodies, a particular kind of white blood cell called a phagocyte eats the virus

## Case Study | Influenza

Influenza is the proper name for 'flu. The influenza virus spreads from person to person through the droplets in human breath and by mucus when sneezing. It can also be passed on to humans by animals such as pigs, ducks and chickens.

'Flu epidemics occur almost annually, usually in the winter in the UK, and the disease can be fatal. The most recent epidemics occurred in 1993 and 1976, but the worst worldwide epidemic ever was in 1918. This was the year that the First World War ended.

Over 22 million people caught 'flu that year, and more people died than had been killed in total throughout the war.

### Questions

**13** Why is personal hygiene important in preventing the spread of the influenza virus?

## Case Study | Poor James Phipps

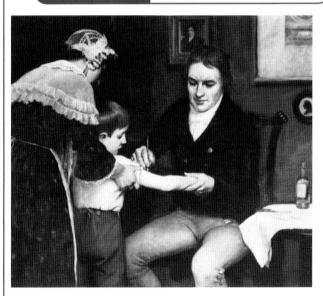

**Fig 2.21** Jenner vaccinating James Phipps against smallpox

In 1796 Edward Jenner, a young country doctor from Gloucestershire, first established the principle of vaccination against a disease called smallpox. Smallpox is caused by a virus and was a major killer in the eighteenth century. Between 20% and 40% of those who contracted the disease died from it. Those who survived the disease were usually left disfigured and blind.

Jenner noticed that milkmaids and cowmen who had contracted cowpox never developed smallpox. Cowpox was a mild disease, caused by a virus very similar to the smallpox virus. Milkmaids and cowmen caught cowpox from the cattle that they looked after. Jenner developed an hypothesis that a recent dose of cowpox caused these people to become immune to smallpox.

Jenner tested his idea on an 8 year old boy called James Phipps. He scratched James' arm and rubbed into the scratch pus from a pustule on the arm of a milkmaid suffering from cowpox. A small sore developed on James' arm but otherwise he remained healthy. Later, after the sore had disappeared, Jenner infected James with smallpox using the same method of scratching his arm and rubbing smallpox pus into the scratch. James survived and showed none of the symptoms of smallpox.

From his experiments, Jenner concluded that if you had already had a disease, or in the case of cowpox and smallpox, a very similar disease, then your body was already prepared to fight this disease. If you came into contact with the disease again then the body was prepared for an attack and the disease could not establish itself. Jenner had also found that it was possible to prepare for attack by a disease by introducing the pathogen into the body artificially. This led to the development of a vaccination against smallpox.

Vaccinations against many other serious diseases followed. In 1840 a law was passed making vaccination against smallpox compulsory. The last case of smallpox in the world was in 1977.

*continued* ➢

**Case Study** | **Poor James Phipps** continued

Poor James Phipps would probably have died if Jenner had been wrong. Fortunately, for James and for all of us today who have vaccinations, Jenner was right. Today Jenner's experiment, on a human subject, would not be allowed. It takes years of research before products can be tested on humans. Modern medicine does, however, owe Jenner and James a big thank you for a very bold experiment!

**Questions**

14 Explain why James did not develop smallpox after being infected with the smallpox virus.

15 What is a vaccination?

16 Why do you think an experiment like this could not be done in this way today? Is this a good or a bad thing?

## Antibiotics

Antibiotics are substances that kill bacteria, but do not destroy human cells. This means that they can be taken into the human body to fight off a disease that you have already got. Sometimes your body can fight a disease on its own, but your doctor might prescribe antibiotics if you have a disease that will need some help to get rid of.

Antibiotics are produced naturally by some micro-organisms. The most well known example of an antibiotic is penicillin. It is made by the fungus *Penicillium* (see Section 1).

Antibiotics are very successful against bacteria, but unfortunately they cannot kill viruses. Many people are surprised when they go to their doctors with a cold or 'flu and are not given antibiotics. This is because colds and 'flu are caused by viruses. The cold must be allowed to run its course as the body begins to fight it itself. Sometimes other drugs such as painkillers may help, for example to reduce swelling, until you get rid of the infection.

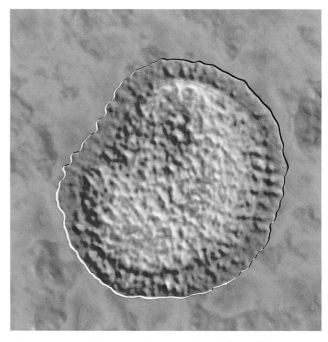

**Fig 2.22** An electron micrograph of the influenza virus

If antibiotics are so good at killing bacteria, then why are bacterial diseases still around? Although much success has been had with antibiotics, they are no longer the wonder drug they once were. This is because bacteria can change due to random **mutations** within their DNA, and sometimes when they change they become **resistant** to the antibiotics. If one **bacterium** mutated and became resistant to an antibiotic, it would survive when the antibiotic killed all the other bacteria. This new bacteria would then rapidly reproduce, producing lots of this new bacteria. This could lead to an individual developing a bad case of the disease, which the usual antibiotic could not treat. A new, improved antibiotic would have to be found.

**Glossary**

**Mutations**
This is a sudden change in the DNA of a cell that gives the cell different characteristics.

**Resistant**
The micro-organism is unaffected by antibiotics or other drugs.

**Bacterium**
The name of one single cell of bacteria.

Some bacteria have been found to be resistant to many of the usual antibiotics. They are referred to as multi-resistant bacteria. These bacteria are often found in hospitals where antibiotics are widely used for very serious diseases and only resistant bacteria can survive. The wider the use of antibiotics, the more likely resistant bacteria are to grow. This means that doctors no longer prescribe antibiotics unless they think it absolutely necessary.

# Topic 5  Growing micro-organisms

Scientists now know a lot about micro-organisms. They have worked out how micro-organisms can be used to make products that are useful to humans. They have also learnt how harmful micro-organisms infect other organisms, and how to prevent or treat infection. This study of micro-organisms is called microbiology. None of this knowledge could have been gained without doing experiments with the micro-organisms themselves. Since micro-organisms cause disease, these experiments can be very dangerous if scientists do not take certain precautions. Even when growing useful and harmless micro-organisms it is possible that you are providing the correct conditions for other harmful micro-organisms to grow as well.

**Microbiologists** grow micro-organisms in what they refer to as a nutrient medium. This is usually a liquid or jelly, such as agar, that contains all the nutrients that the micro-organisms need for maximum growth. The micro-organisms themselves are called a culture.

By investigating what the ideal conditions for micro-organisms are, microbiologists, like those scientists that work on animals and plants, can try to make sure that the useful micro-organisms are provided with the conditions to achieve the most growth. The maximum amount of product will then be produced. In the case of harmful micro-organisms, scientists want to know the ideal conditions for growth so that these can be avoided and so minimise infection.

Scientists who work in microbiology laboratories must be sure of 2 things during an experiment with micro-organisms:

1  Micro-organisms from the experiment must not get out into the environment, as this contaminates the environment and may cause infection of the scientists or others.

2  Micro-organisms from the environment must not get into the experiment, as this contaminates the experiment. It may affect the results and prevent proper conclusions from being made because unknown micro-organisms may change what would have happened to the micro-organisms being investigated.

Special techniques are used to stop either of the above from happening. These are laboratory practices that aim to reduce the risk of contamination or infection and are called aseptic techniques.

> **Glossary**
>
> **Microbiologists**
> Scientists working with micro-organisms.

These aseptic techniques are standard operating procedures (SOPs) because they should always be done in the same way. Although you do not need to know the fine details about how each individual technique is carried out, you need to know that these would always be carried out in a way that is standard to all laboratories.

## Aseptic techniques

**Fig 2.23** Using aseptic techniques

To avoid contamination of the environment:

● Always work in a draught-free area.

● Flame the tops of bottles containing micro-organisms in a bunsen burner.

● Do not use unknown cultures (micro-organisms) in experiments.

● Incubate all cultures in a sealed container.

To avoid contamination of the experiment:

● Again always work in a draught-free area.

● Sterile gloves, masks and hats or hairnets must be worn at all times.

● Clean lab coats must be worn.

● Benches must be washed with antiseptics.

● Sterile pipettes or sterile metal loops must be used to transfer cultures.

● Culture mediums must be sterile before use.

---

### End-of-Section 3 Questions

1 a) What are the three types of micro-organism?

   b) Which of these are
   (i) the smallest
   (ii) the largest?

   c) Which type of micro-organism has until recently been the least useful to humans?

   d) How is the micro-organism in c) now being used by humans?

2 Give a list of the main useful products that can be obtained from micro-organisms. You should be able to name at least six.

3 All three types of micro-organism can cause diseases. Name three diseases of either animals or plants that are caused by each type of micro-organism.

4 Personal hygiene and the use of antiseptics, disinfectants and sterilisation are all important in the food industry in protecting us from infection from harmful micro-organisms. Give a brief description of what each of these involve and say how they protect us.

5 Humans can gain immunity to disease using two different methods. Name the two methods and state how they make us immune.

6 Why does your doctor not prescribe antibiotics for you when you have 'flu?

## Section 4 | Agriculture and Horticulture

**Section 4 is divided into eight topics:**

1 Photosynthesis
2 Minerals needed by plants
3 Selective breeding
4 Genetic engineering

5 Intensive farming
6 Organic farming
7 Intensive versus organic farming
8 Monohybrid inheritance (higher only)

**In the Unit 2 written examination you will be expected to know:**

★ That wool, silk, cotton and leather are obtained from living organisms.

★ How plants make food by photosynthesis.

★ That plants use the process of respiration to release energy.

★ That plants need certain minerals, which they obtain from the soil, for healthy growth.

★ That nitrates are needed by the plant for proteins, which are needed for cell growth.

★ That magnesium is required for chlorophyll.

★ How selective breeding is used to produce the desired characteristics in organisms.

★ How genetic engineering can be used to produce organisms with the desired characteristics.

★ How intensive farming increases crop yields and meat production.

★ How organic farming uses more natural methods.

★ The advantages and disadvantages of intensive and organic farming.

★ How monohybrid inheritance works.

★ What dominant and recessive alleles are.

Farming is usually the production of animal and plants for use by humans as food. There are a few examples of where farming is used to produce fabrics such as cotton, wool and leather. Modern methods of farming include intensive and organic farming, selective breeding and genetic engineering technology. Knowledge of how living organisms work is necessary for both farmers and scientists, before these methods can be used effectively to ensure top quality products with the highest possible yields. In particular, it is necessary to know about photosynthesis and nutrition in plants.

## Topic 1 Photosynthesis

All living organisms need energy in order to stay alive. They produce this energy during respiration. Glucose is needed for respiration to take place. Here is a reminder of the word equation of respiration.

glucose + oxygen → energy + carbon dioxide + water

Animals get the glucose needed for respiration from eating and digesting food. Plants do not get their glucose in the way that we do. They make their own glucose using energy from the sun. This process is known as photosynthesis. The equation for photosynthesis is shown here.

carbon dioxide +water + light energy → glucose + oxygen

You will notice that this equation is similar to that of respiration, only backwards. This may help you to remember the equations.

Plants can only photosynthesise if they have a green pigment called **chlorophyll** in their cells. In particular they must have plenty of chlorophyll in the cells of their leaves. This enables the plants to absorb the sunlight needed for photosynthesis. Plants photosynthesise and respire during daylight, and only respire during darkness.

In order to photosynthesise as much as possible, and so produce as much glucose as possible, plants must have the correct conditions. Plants need the correct amounts of carbon dioxide, water and light, and an appropriate temperature. When the plant has produced glucose it uses some of it in respiration, and converts the rest into starch for storing until it is needed.

We can do an experiment to show that plants need light. We do this by testing the leaves for starch, in plants that have been kept in the light and the dark. This experiment is always done in the same way and so is referred to as a standard operating procedure (SOP).

### Glossary

**Chlorophyll**
The green pigment found in structures called chloroplasts in plant cells. It is chlorophyll that enables plant cells to photosynthesise by absorbing light energy from the sun.

## Practical Work | Testing leaves for starch – SOP

1  Put two similar plants in the dark for several days, geranium plants are good plants to use, to remove all the starch already in their leaves.

2  Take one plant out and place it in the light for several days. Leave the other in the dark.

3  Remove a leaf from each plant and test each for starch as follows:

- Dip the leaf in boiling water for 30 seconds, to kill it and soften it.

- Then place the leaf in boiling ethanol for 10 minutes to remove the chlorophyll (green colour).

- Now wash the leaf in hot water to remove the ethanol.

- Place the leaf on a white tile and add a dilute solution of iodine.

Fig 2.24 Iodine test on a leaf

The leaf that was placed in the light will turn a blue/black colour showing starch is present. The leaf that was kept in the dark will be the pale brown colour of the iodine.

### Questions

1  In this experiment, what is the purpose of

(i)  the boiling water?
(ii)  the boiling ethanol?
(iii) the iodine solution?

A similar experiment to this can be used on variegated leaves, where the leaves are green and white. Ivy and spider plants have variegated leaves. This experiment shows that only the green parts of leaves produce starch, as these are the parts that contain the pigment chlorophyll. Photosynthesis will not take place without chlorophyll.

**Fig 2.26** a) This plant is lacking magnesium b) The same plant once fertiliser has been added

## Topic 2 Minerals needed by plants

As well as needing glucose for respiration, plants also need other nutrients, known as minerals, in order to grow properly. They obtain these minerals from the soil, by absorbing them through their roots. The most important of these minerals are nitrogen in the form of nitrates, phosphorous in the form of phosphates, potassium and magnesium.

Nitrates ($NO_3^-$) contain the chemical elements nitrogen and oxygen. Plants need nitrates so that they can make proteins. Cells need these proteins so that the plant can grow and repair itself when damaged.

Phosphates ($PO_4^-$) contain the chemical elements phosphorus and oxygen. They are needed so that the reactions inside the plant's cells can work properly.

Plants need the chemical element potassium so that their cell membranes can work properly.

Magnesium is needed so that the plant can make chlorophyll for photosynthesis.

a)

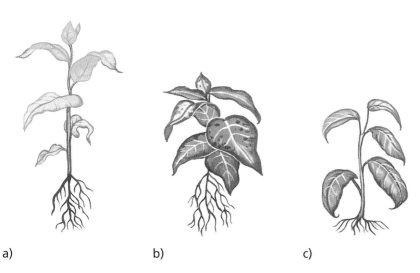

a)                    b)                    c)

**Fig 2.25** Plants lacking a) nitrogen, b) potassium and c) phosphorus

b)

# Topic 3 Selective Breeding

Selective breeding is a method used by farmers to improve the quality of their animals or crops, and sometimes to also improve the **yield**. Selective breeding involves selecting particular individuals with a characteristic that the farmer wants, and only breeding them and not others. By doing this over several generations, it is possible to get more desirable animals or crops.

A good example of this can be seen in cows. If a farmer only breeds cows that have a high milk yield, then the chances are that most of the calves will also have a high milk yield. When these calves are older, the farmer will choose the ones with the best milk yield to breed again. After several generations most of the farmer's cows will have a high milk yield.

Selective breeding has also been used to produce sheep with better quality wool, fruit with better flavour, and crops, such as wheat, that are **disease-resistant**.

Dog breeders have also used selective breeding for hundreds of years to produce the great variety of different breeds and to enhance certain characteristics within a breed. For example, bulldogs have, over many generations, been bred to have a short, squat face to enhance their facial wrinkles. Breeders saw this as a desirable feature, and people were prepared to pay more money for a bulldog with more wrinkles.

Gardeners use selective breeding to develop new varieties of plants and to improve a particular feature of a plant. Examples of improved features could be flower colour, number of petals, height of the plant, or the ability to grow in different conditions.

In all of these cases there are great financial benefits to the farmers, breeders or growers who use selective breeding. They produce animals or plants with features that people want, and so make more money from them.

**Glossary**

**Yield**
The amount of useful product produced.

**Disease-resistant**
Organisms that are immune to certain diseases.

**Questions**

2 Why do farmers use selective breeding?

## Case Study The Wool-less Sheep

Breeders in Ontario, Canada have produced a new breed of sheep using the technique of selective breeding. Sheep with less wool were selected and bred. From the offspring, those with the least wool were bred again. After many generations, there was no wool left on this particular breed. This wool-less Katahdin Hair Sheep has been bred as a meat breed. The breeders are promoting the many advantages of this kind of sheep to farmers who want to produce meat rather than wool:

● low-fat meat,
● requires no shearing,
● take less barn space,
● deer-like coats that shed rain and snow,
● not susceptible to lice or parasites,
● adaptable to hot and cold climates,
● extended breeding season,
● rapid lamb growth.

Since the important factor to farmers is that they get the maximum return on their money, the Katahdin's biggest selling point is the fact that they require no shearing. Shearing sheep is a time-consuming and costly process for farmers who are not breeding their sheep for wool.

*continued* ➢

## Case Study | Cloning – the way forward?

**Fig 2.29** Dolly the sheep

In 1996 people the world over were astounded when a team of scientists from the Roslin Institute in Edinburgh finally announced the birth of 'Dolly the sheep', the first ever cloned mammal. Dolly was cloned by taking a cell from a 6 year-old sheep and removing the nucleus. This nucleus was then placed in a fertilised egg that had already had its own nucleus removed. This egg was then implanted into another sheep. When Dolly was born she was an exact copy of the sheep that the original nucleus had been taken from.

Since then many other mammals have been successfully cloned by the same technique of genetic engineereing. Not so humans! Not that is, until November 2001, when an American biotechnology company made headline news with their claim that they had cloned the first ever human embryo. The scientific community was in uproar. Some thought this the greatest scientific development ever. Others, even those involved with Dolly, were reluctant to admit this to be a major breakthrough, since no actual human baby was produced. Most of the general public felt this to be an unnatural act that ought not to be investigated further.

The company, however, maintained that this was a major new aspect of medical research. They were forging ahead to develop treatments for diseases of the nervous system such as Parkinson's disease and spinal cord injurys. Damage to the nervous system cannot normally be repaired, but cloned nervous tissue may be the much looked for solution. Many countries, including the UK, have banned reproductive cloning, whereby a cloned embryo is implanted into a womb and allowed to develop into a human.

Within the first few days of 2002, however, came a major set back to cloning technology. Dolly had been found to be developing arthritis. Scientists were not able to determine whether this was related to the cloning methods. They stated that it was unusual, but not unheard of, for a five year old sheep to develop arthritis. Since Dolly was the oldest cloned mammal, they had no other animals to compare her to. Dolly was cloned from a six year old sheep so perhaps she was actually behaving like an 11 year old? Scientists began to worry about the impact of cloning on animal health. Many experiments were put on hold until further investigations could be done and further information on the effects of cloning found, by looking at other, younger cloned animals, as they got older. Everyone wondered what future there was for cloning technology.

### Questions

5  Explain how Dolly was cloned.

6  Why would Dolly be an exact copy of the sheep she was cloned from?

7  In January 2002, what happened to cause people to doubt the success of the cloning methods?

8  What is your own opinion about the future of cloning technology?

# Topic 5  Intensive Farming

Farmers can improve their yields by controlling the conditions in which their animals and crops are grown. Rearing animals or growing crops in this way is known as intensive farming. The methods used make financial sense for farmers. A lot of money is spent when the farmer is setting up his intensive farm, but the cost of maintaining the farm is usually much less than with other types of farming.

## Intensive farming of animals

The animals are almost always kept inside purpose built housing, that initially costs the farmer a lot of money to build. Often there are also costs involved in setting up machinery that allows the system to be **automated**. The food that the farmer feeds his animals can also be expensive, as he wants to make sure the animals gain weight quickly. However, the advantages of intensive farming usually outweigh the disadvantages. The biggest advantage of intensive farming is the low labour cost. Many animals are kept close together inside the buildings, saving space, and only a few people are needed to look them after.

For example, by using modern battery farms, a million chickens can be reared by only one or two people. These people usually operate the machinery that feeds the chickens and collects the eggs. Keeping the chickens in cages means that they move around very little, putting almost all their energy into gaining weight and egg laying. The food supply can be regulated, so that the chickens get just enough, but not too much, food of the correct type. The temperature can also be controlled so that the chickens grow and lay eggs at the best possible rate. Since these ideal conditions are easy for the farmer to maintain, he will soon be selling lots of eggs and plump chickens. This means that it is usually worth the initial investments.

> **Glossary**
>
> **Automated**
> A system where machines do the work instead of humans.

**Fig 2.30** A battery chicken farm

## Intensive farming of plants

Plants require certain minerals for healthy growth. They take in these minerals from the soil through their roots. The most important minerals are nitrogen, phosphorus and potassium. Land that is being used to produce crops on a regular basis must have these minerals added to the soil to stop the soil running out of them. Only by doing this can the farmers make sure that they are getting the best yields. The cheapest way of adding these minerals to the soil is in the form of inorganic fertilisers. These are man-made chemicals and contain all the minerals that plants need to grow. They are produced as either pellets or granules and can be spread over large areas of land quickly and easily by machinery. Obviously the farmer has to buy this machinery when he first sets up his intensive farm, which can be expensive. There is also a disadvantage to using inorganic fertilisers, which is that they can be washed away by the rain and cause problems in ponds and lakes. This problem, known as **eutrophication**, occurs when nitrates get into the water, causing large growths of bacteria and suffocating fish.

In addition to the use of inorganic fertilisers, intensive farms also use chemical pesticides. These can be of several kinds, insecticides, fungicides and herbicides are the main ones. Insecticides are sprayed onto the plants to kill insect pests that eat the crops. Fungicides can be applied to the seeds, roots or leaves of crops, to protect against and destroy fungi that can cause diseases in plants. Herbicides (weed

> **Glossary**
>
> **Eutrophication**
> When large amounts of nitrates and phosphates are washed into streams and lakes, causing nutrient levels to rise and rapid growth of algae, which then die, starving the water of oxygen.

killers) are sprayed around the area of the crops to kill other plants that are growing in the wrong place (weeds).

The advantages of pesticides are that the crops are protected and their survival chances are higher. But the disadvantages are that, when the crops are sprayed, the crops themselves are covered with the chemical. It is important that these crops are washed well before we eat them. The chemical may pass into the soil and nearby plants and animals may also be contaminated. The pesticides must be sprayed carefully and in as small amounts as possible to reduce the risk of affecting other organisms.

**Fig 2.31** A farmer spraying herbicide onto a field of wheat

# Topic 6  Organic farming

Living organisms are made from organic compounds such as carbohydrates, fats and proteins. The elements in these organic compounds are constantly cycled between living organisms and their environment as the living organisms respire, photosynthesise, excrete and die. This cycling of nutrients is happening all the time in natural **ecosystems**.

Organic farming is so-called because it uses methods and compounds that fit in better with the natural environment. This is farming without the use of man-made chemicals. Traditional systems of farming were almost totally organic and in some parts of the world farming has continued in this way. In the UK, organic farming has become increasingly popular since the 1960s, as consumers are made aware of some of the environmental problems of intensive farming methods. Modern organic farming is seen not as a step back in time, but as a way of combining the more traditional natural methods with new advances in science.

Less money is spent setting up housing, foods tend to be cheaper and no chemicals need to be bought. However, both animals and plants require more looking after using organic methods, and so more people need to be paid, so labour costs are higher.

Foods that are grown organically carry the Soil Association symbol if they satisfy the standards set by the association, which is the largest organic certifying body in the UK. This symbol on food labels assures the consumers that the food has been produced in a way which prioritises environmental considerations and animal welfare issues. It also shows that the use of chemical inputs, such as synthetic fertilisers and pesticides, has been avoided where possible.

**Glossary**

**Ecosystem**
The particular environment where organisms live, and all the organisms that live there.

**Fig 2.32**

## Organic farming of animals

Animals that are reared by organic farming methods have more space per animal and eat more natural foods than those in intensive farming systems. They are usually only housed during cold weather and spend the rest of their time outdoors where they can graze and move around as much as they want. These animals take longer to gain weight under these conditions, and so the farmer has to keep them for longer before he can sell them. The final product, be it beef, chicken or lamb for example, is more expensive for us to buy because of this.

## Organic farming of plants

In organic crop production, manures or composts are used to fertilise the soil. Manures are the waste products of animals, such as cow dung. Composts are made by allowing micro-organisms to break down any dead matter, such as vegetable peelings and fallen leaves. Both of these fertilisers are natural and do not involve the use of man-made chemicals.

Pests are treated by what is known as biological control. Weeds are removed mechanically. This involves actually pulling them up rather than adding chemicals to kill them. How crops are planted may also help avoid pests. Planting certain crops together often means that one crop benefits the other. For example, with insect pests, one crop may attract natural predators that eat the pest of the other crop. A small number of naturally occurring chemicals are used as pesticides in organic farming. The best example of this is the insecticide called pyrethrum. This comes from the dried flowers of the chrysanthemum plant. It is considered to be 100% natural and environmentally friendly. It kills insects, but has no effect on animals and breaks down naturally in the presence of sunlight (it is biodegradable) so it does not build up in the ecosystem.

# Topic 7  Intensive versus organic farming

The advantages and disadvantages of each type of farming are summarised in Table 2.

| | Intensive farming | Organic farming |
|---|---|---|
| Advantages | • High yield per area.<br>• Requires less space.<br>• Low labour costs. | • Better conditions for animals.<br>• No pollution of environment from chemicals.<br>• Chemical-free foods.<br>• Low set up costs for farmer. |

Table 2 Intensive versus organic farming

| | Intensive farming | Organic farming |
|---|---|---|
| Disadvantages | • Poorer conditions for animals.<br>• Possible pollution of environment from chemicals.<br>• Chemicals may be present on foods.<br>• High set up costs for farmer. | • Low yield per area.<br>• Requires more space.<br>• High labour costs. |

# Topic 8  Monohybrid inheritance

We have already looked at how farmers use a method called selective breeding to produce offspring with desirable characteristics. In order for farmers to apply this method, it is necessary for scientists to understand how certain characteristics are inherited. Much is now known about **inheritance**, which has enabled scientists to apply the methods of genetic engineering. The passing of characteristics from parents to **offspring** is called monohybrid inheritance.

In 1865, an Austrian monk called Gregor Mendel published the results of his studies on the way in which characteristics were passed on from one generation to the next. By 1900 other scientists were beginning to think that he had the right idea and people began to take notice.

As a result of Mendel's work the following conclusions were drawn, which form the basis of what you need to know:

● An organism gets its characteristics from its **genes**.

● Genes come in pairs, one from the mother and one from the father.

● Sometimes one particular characteristic is controlled by a single pair of genes, this is known as **monohybrid inheritance**.

● Genes can be **dominant** or **recessive**. If a dominant gene is present then that characteristic will always be expressed. Recessive genes only express themselves if both genes in the pair are recessive.

● Dominant genes are represented by a capital letter and recessive genes by a lower case letter.

● The genes that control a particular characteristic can come in different forms, these different forms are known as **alleles**. For example, the alleles that control eye colour are **B** for brown eyes (dominant) and **b** for blue eyes (recessive).

## Glossary

**Inheritance**
Characteristics that are passed from parents to their offspring. For example eye colour is inherited.

**Offspring**
The children produced by any living organism.

**Genes**
Parts of the chromosomes inside cells, that control the characteristics of an organism.

**Monohybrid Inheritance**
One particular characteristic controlled by a single pair of genes.

**Dominant**
The allele that is expressed in the phenotype, even if only one of the pair of genes is dominant.

**Recessive**
The allele that is only expressed in the phenotype when both of the genes are recessive.

**Alleles**
Different forms of a particular gene.

- Since the genes come in pairs, an individual could have any of three different combinations of the genes. For example, with eye colour they could have **BB**, **Bb** or **bb**. Which of these possible combinations an organism has is called its **genotype**.

- The outward appearance of a particular characteristic in the organism is called its **phenotype**.

- When an organism has a genotype with two genes that are the same for a particular characteristic, it is said to be **homozygous** ('homo' means 'the same'). When an organism has two different genes for the same characteristic, it is said to be **heterozygous** ('hetero' means 'different').

| Genotype | BB | Bb | bb |
|---|---|---|---|
| Phenotype | brown eyes | brown eyes | blue eyes |
| Type | homozygous | heterozygous | homozygous |

**Glossary**

**Genotype**
The genetic make-up of an organism. The sum total of all the genes, even those that are not expressed.

**Phenotype**
The characteristics of an organism based on its genes and the environment in which it lives.

**Homozygous**
Inheriting either two dominant alleles, or two recessive alleles for a particular characteristic.

**Heterozygous**
Inheriting one dominant allele and one recessive allele for a particular characteristic.

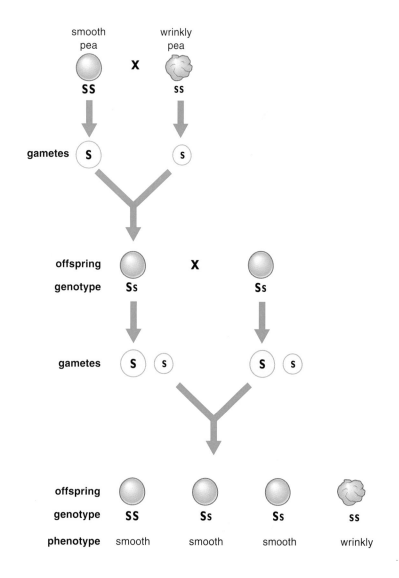

**Fig 2.33** Mendel studied pea plants which produced either wrinkled or smooth peas. Pea plants which were homozygous recessive for pea shape produced wrinkled peas

# How to show inheritance

Inheritance is best shown by looking at an example using the inheritance of a characteristic such as eye colour in humans. **B** represents the gene for brown eyes and **b** represents the gene for blue eyes. Remember that there is a pair of genes for each characteristic. A person with the phenotype 'brown eyes' may have the genotype **BB** or **Bb**. Since **B** is the dominant gene, the fact that this person has brown eyes means that one or both of their genes must be **B**. A person with the phenotype 'blue eyes' can only have the genotype **bb**, because if there were a **B** he/she would have brown eyes.

One of the genes is passed on to the offspring from each parent. In other words, the gametes will only have one of the two genes. The gametes are the sperm and egg in animals, and the pollen and egg in plants. There is an equal chance of either of the genes in the pair being passed on each time the individual has a child. The child will also receive one of these genes from the other parent, ensuring that the child also has a pair of genes for the particular characteristic. The inheritance of a characteristic such as eye colour can be shown in the form of a genetic cross.

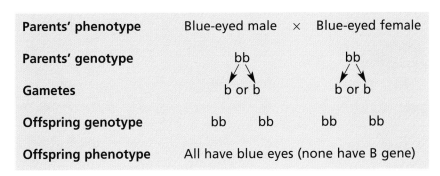

The above genetic cross shows that two parents with blue eyes will have children that all have blue eyes. There is no **B** gene in the parents, therefore none of the children will have brown eyes. Where an individual has brown eyes, showing the inheritance of eye colour is more difficult. This is because the brown-eyed person could have one of two different genotypes, **BB** or **Bb**. You must do the genetic cross showing both possibilities if you do not know which genotype they are.

First possibility:

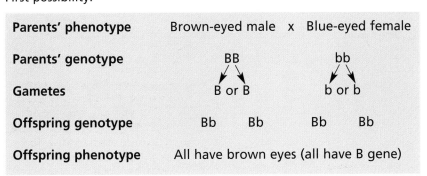

Second possibility:

| Parents' phenotype | Brown-eyed male x Blue-eyed female |
| Parents' genotype | Bb | bb |
| Gametes | B or b | b or b |
| Offspring genotype | Bb  Bb | bb  bb |
| Offspring phenotype | 50% brown and 50% blue eyed |

These genetic crosses enable you to work out the chances of having offspring with certain phenotypes, if you cross parents with certain phenotypes. It is very useful to be able to work this out when farmers, breeders and growers are trying to perfect the characteristics of the offspring. In humans, it can be used in 'paternity suits' to help work out who the father of a child might be.

## End-of-Section 4 Questions

1  a)  State the word equation for photosynthesis.

   b)  How is this equation similar to that for respiration?

   c)  How does the plant store the glucose formed during photosynthesis?

2  Explain how you would test a leaf for starch to show that the plant had been photosynthesising.

3  Plants need the nutrients nitrates, phosphates, potassium and magnesium. What are each of these minerals needed by the plant for?

4  a)  What is meant by 'selective breeding'?

   b)  Give two examples of the use of selective breeding.

5  How is genetic engineering used in the production of human insulin?

6  a)  Discuss the advantages and disadvantages of intensive and organic farming.

   b)  If you were a farmer which method of farming would you use? Explain why.

7  If the dominant gene for red petals in pea plants is represented by R, and the recessive gene for white petals is represented by r, show the genetic cross between plants with the genotypes RR and rr.

# Section 5 | The Human Body

Required Knowledge

**Section 5 is divided into five topics:**

1 The circulatory system
2 The respiratory system
3 Respiration

4 Keeping things constant
5 Monitoring performance

**In this section you will learn:**

★ That by monitoring their bodies' activities during training, athletes can improve their performance (unit 3).

★ How to monitor the performance of a person during an activity (unit 3).

**In the Unit 2 written examination you will be expected to know:**

★ The structure of the human circulartory system, the function of the heart, and the composition and function of the blood.

★ How the structure of the thorax enables ventilation of the lungs.

★ That respiration may be aerobic or anaerobic depending on how much oxygen is available.

★ That oxygen debt occurs in the muscles during vigorous exercise.

★ That humans operate best within a range of conditions.

★ How humans maintain a constant body temperature.

★ How the blood glucose levels are controlled by the hormone insulin.

It is important for scientists to have a good knowledge of the human body. Some scientists are involved in medical research and so they must know a great deal about how the body works. All scientists must know enough about the body to be able to apply basic first aid in the event of an emergency.

Figure 2.34 shows the internal structure of the human body.

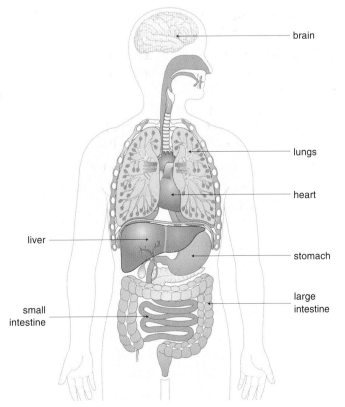

brain

lungs

heart

liver

stomach

small intestine

large intestine

**Fig 2.34**

# Topic 1 The Circulatory System

The circulatory system is made up of the heart, the blood and blood vessels. We describe the circulatory system as a double circulatory system because, on its way once around the body, blood passes through the heart twice. A diagram of the circulatory system can be seen in Figure 2.35

There are three main functions of the circulatory system. These are:

- Transport – the movement of digested food, oxygen and waste products (such as carbon dioxide).

- Protection against micro-organisms.

- Control of body temperature.

By looking at the structure of the heart, the blood and the blood vessels, we will see how these functions are achieved.

## The Heart

The heart is a pump, made of muscle, which keeps blood flowing around our bodies at all times.

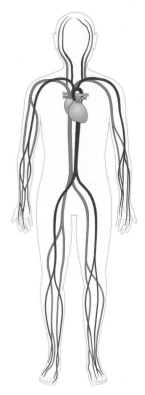

**Fig 2.35** The circulatory system

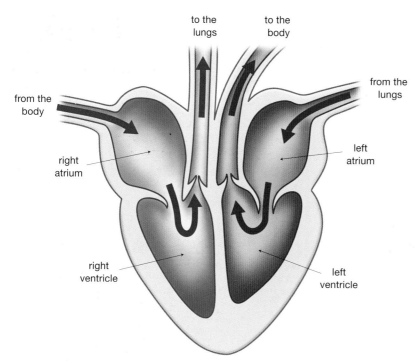

**Fig 2.36** The human heart

You can see from Figure 2.36 that the heart has four chambers. The top two chambers, where blood flows into the heart, are called **atria**, the left atrium and the right atrium. The bottom two chambers, where blood flows out of the heart, are called **ventricles**, the left ventricle and the right ventricle. Between the atrium and ventricle on each side there is a valve that stops blood flowing backwards through the heart.

### Questions

**1** Why is our circulatory system called a 'double circulatory system'?

### Glossary

**Atria**
The two upper chambers of the heart that receive blood from the veins.

**Ventricles**
The two lower chambers of the heart that pump blood into the arteries and around the body.

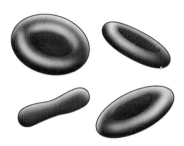

The muscular walls of the ventricles contract and relax continuously, pushing blood out of the heart when they contract, and allowing more blood in when they relax. It is this surge of blood that causes your heartbeat, which you can feel as a pulse in your wrist or neck. A normal heart rate for a person at rest is between 60 and 80 beats per minute. Your pulse is taken by doctors and nurses to check that you are healthy and that your heart is beating normally.

## Blood

Blood is made up of four things:

- plasma,
- red blood cells,
- white blood cells,
- platelets.

## Plasma

Plasma is the liquid part of the blood. It is a pale yellow solution which contains substances dissolved in water. The dissolved substances are nutrients (the foods that we have digested), carbon dioxide (which is being transported to the lungs for breathing out), and hormones (which are being transported around the body to where they are needed).

## Red blood cells

Red blood cells carry oxygen to our cells for respiration. They contain a pigment called haemoglobin that combines with oxygen to form oxyhaemoglobin, and this is how oxygen is carried to the cells.

You can see from Figure 2.37 that red blood cells have no nucleus, this means that the whole cell can be filled with haemoglobin for carrying oxygen. They also have a very thin cell membrane that covers a large surface area, so that oxygen can be easily absorbed.

## White blood cells

White blood cells protect us from disease. One type of white blood cell, phagocytes, eat harmful micro-organisms. Another type, lymphocytes, produce **antibodies** that help to kill harmful micro-organisms and neutralise poisonous chemicals.

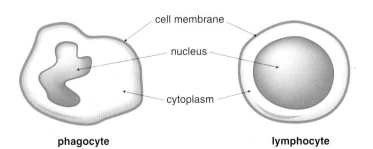

phagocyte                    lymphocyte

**Questions**

2   The muscle in the walls of the left ventricle is much thicker than that in the walls of the right ventricle. Why do you think this is?

**Fig 2.37** Red blood cells

**Questions**

3   One of the important functions of the circulatory system is transport. How are dissolved foods, oxygen and carbon dioxide transported around the body?

**Glossary**

**Antibodies**
Chemicals made by white blood cells that kill harmful micro-organisms. Different antibodies are needed for different micro-organisms.

**Fig 2.38** White blood cells

## Platelets

Platelets are small parts of blood cells without a nucleus (Figure 2.39). They help the blood to clot when we have a cut, and stop us from bleeding to death. They do this by forming a mesh of fibres where the skin is cut, which traps red blood cells and forms a clot. As the clot dries out it becomes a scab, which stops further bleeding and stops harmful micro-organisms from getting in.

**Questions**

4  Why are red blood cells the shape they are, with no nucleus?

## Blood vessels

Blood vessels are the tubes which blood passes through on its way around the body. They also help us to control our body temperature because those in the skin can contract and expand to allow more or less blood through them. In cold weather, the blood vessels in the skin contract, so less blood flows to the body surface and less heat is lost. In warm weather, the vessels expand, allowing more blood to the surface and more heat to be lost.

There are three types of blood vessels, arteries, veins and capillaries (Figure 2.40).

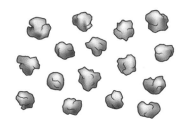

**Fig 2.39** Platelets

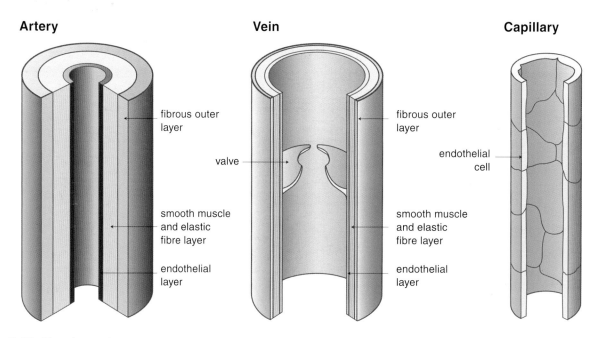

**Fig 2.40** Blood vessels

## Arteries

Arteries carry blood away from the heart. They carry blood that is at a high pressure which forces it around the body, and therefore they need to have thick muscular walls. With the exception of the artery that takes blood from the heart to the lungs, the pulmonary artery, all arteries carry **oxygenated blood**.

**Glossary**

**Oxygenated blood**
Blood that is carrying oxygen.

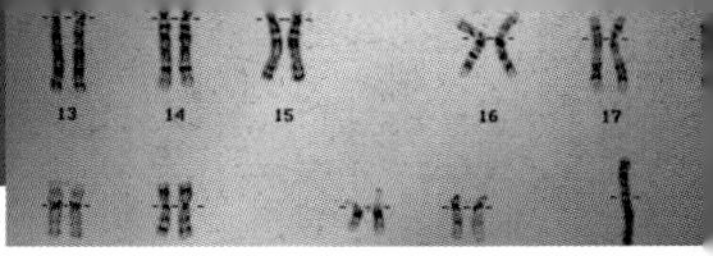

## Veins

Veins return blood to the heart. They carry blood that has a much lower pressure so the walls are thinner and much less muscular than the arteries. Veins contain valves to stop the blood from flowing backwards. With the exception of the pulmonary vein that brings blood back into the heart from the lungs, all veins carry **deoxygenated blood**.

## Capillaries

Capillaries are the smallest kind of blood vessel. They branch off from arteries and join together again to form veins. They have walls which are only one cell thick, to allow substances, such as digested foods, oxygen and carbon dioxide, to pass easily in and out.

# Topic 2  The Respiratory System

There is often confusion about the difference between breathing and respiration. Breathing is the actual movement of air into and out of the lungs by the actions of the ribcage and **diaphragm**. Respiration is what happens in the cells when oxygen and food are burnt to produce energy. All living things must respire but they do not all breathe. To avoid confusion between these two terms, breathing is sometimes referred to as ventilation of the lungs, as the term ventilation is also used to describe the movement of air into and out of buildings and you will be more familiar with it.

### Glossary

**Deoxygenated blood**
Blood that is carrying very little oxygen.

**Diaphragm**
A sheet of muscle underneath the ribcage that contracts and relaxes to help the movement of air into and out of the lungs.

### Questions

**5**  What are the differences between arteries and veins?

### Questions

**6**  What is meant by the terms breathing and respiration?

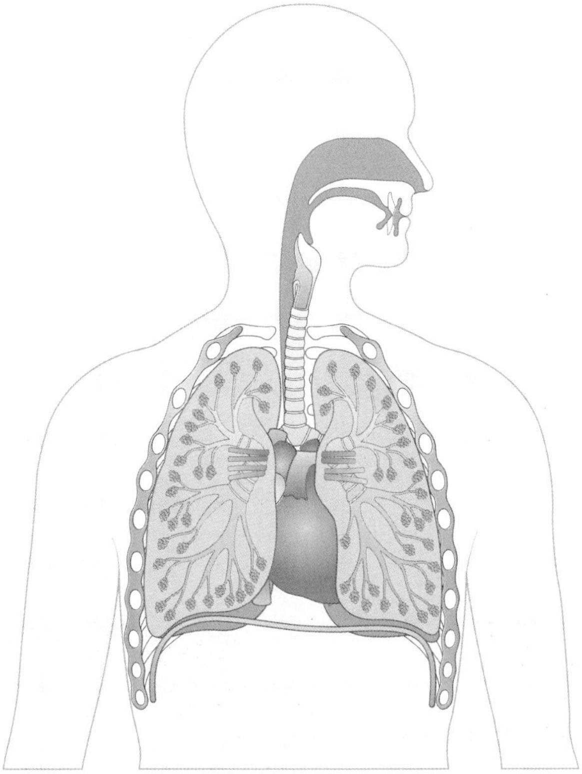

**Fig 2.41**  The respiratory system

## Ventilation of the lungs

This can be described in two parts, as breathing in and breathing out, and can be represented in flow charts.

### *Breathing in (inhaling)*

Rib and diaphragm muscles contract

↓

Ribcage pushed up and out, diaphragm is pulled flat

↓

Volume inside chest increases

↓

Pressure inside chest decreases

↓

Air flows into lungs

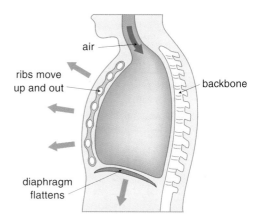

### *Breathing out (exhaling)*

Rib and diaphragm muscles relax

↓

Ribcage drops down and in, diaphragm resumes its dome shape

↓

Volume of chest decreases

↓

Pressure inside chest increases

↓

Air is pushed out of lungs

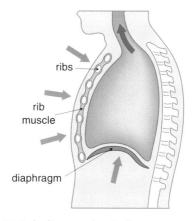

**Fig 2.42** Inhaling and exhaling

# Topic 3  Respiration

Every activity we take part in requires energy, from running and dancing, to other activities that we don't think about, such as excreting waste and growth. This energy comes from respiration. Respiration is a chemical reaction that occurs in cells. There are two types of respiration, that which requires oxygen, **aerobic respiration**, and that which does not require oxygen, **anaerobic respiration**.

## Aerobic respiration

This is the most common form of respiration. Glucose reacts with oxygen to form energy, carbon dioxide and water. This can be represented in the form of a word equation:

glucose + oxygen → carbon dioxide + water + energy

**Glossary**

**Aerobic respiration**
Respiration that occurs in the presence of oxygen.

**Anaerobic respiration**
Respiration that occurrs in the absence of oxygen.

This is very similar to when fuels are burnt to release energy. The carbon dioxide and water are waste products. Carbon dioxide must not be allowed to build up in the body, as it is poisonous and so must be removed from the body as soon as it is formed.

The glucose and oxygen needed for respiration are brought to the cells by the blood. The glucose and oxygen pass through the thin walls of the capillaries by a process called **diffusion**. Carbon dioxide produced by respiration diffuses back from the cells into the blood. It is carried by the blood to the lungs where it is removed by breathing out.

## Anaerobic respiration

Sometimes respiration occurs without oxygen. This is called anaerobic respiration. Some organisms respire in this way when they run out of oxygen. For example, yeast respires in this way during fermentation:

$$\text{glucose} \xrightarrow{\text{yeast}} \text{carbon dioxide} + \text{alcohol} + \text{energy}$$

Muscles in the human body respire without oxygen when they have been exercising for some time and have run out of oxygen. This happens when the oxygen available to the muscle cells is being used up more quickly than the body can breath more in and transport it around the body. This anaerobic respiration in the muscles during vigorous exercise causes a build up of a substance called **lactic acid**.

$$\text{glucose} \rightarrow \text{lactic acid} + \text{energy}$$

The muscles require more oxygen to remove this lactic acid. This means that the muscles are owed oxygen, they are said to be in **oxygen debt**. This oxygen debt is repaid once the exercise is over and the muscles can go back to respiring normally, in otherwords with oxygen.

### Questions

**7** What is the difference between aerobic and anaerobic respiration.

## Topic 4 Keeping things constant

There are certain factors within our bodies that must be kept at a fairly constant level if we are to function properly. In the human body we refer to this as **homeostasis**.

The most important factors that we need to look at are body temperature and the amount of sugar in the blood. Both of these must be kept as constant as possible. If either of them rise or fall outside of the normal range, it can cause major problems, and possibly lead to death. Our bodies must, therefore, have ways of keeping these factors constant, and we will look at each factor in turn.

### Glossary

**Diffusion**
The movement of a substance from where there is a lot of it, to where there is not as much of it. It usually involves gases or substances dissolved in water.

**Lactic acid**
A waste product that builds up when our muscles are short of oxygen. It is this build up of lactic acid that makes our muscles feel 'wobbly' after vigorous exercise.

**Oxygen debt**
The oxygen needed to remove the lactic acid that has built up in muscles from anaerobic respiration during exercise.

**Homeostasis**
The way in which the body maintains a constant internal temperature.

### Questions

**8** What is homeostasis? Why is this necessary?

## Controlling body temperature

The normal temperature of the human body is 37 °C, but it will operate properly over a range of temperatures from 36.5 °C to 37.2 °C. If the body temperature rises above 37.2 °C the person could develop a fever or heat stroke, and if it falls below 36.5 °C, the person will suffer from hypothermia. In both of these situations, the body is not functioning normally because it is either too hot or too cold, and the normal chemical reactions are not taking place as they should. The body has its own ways of making sure that its temperature does not go outside of the normal range.

The most important part of the body involved in the control of body temperature is the skin. Figure 2.43 shows the structure of the skin. **Receptors** in the skin send messages to the brain to say that the temperature is rising or falling. The brain sends messages back to the skin to tell the skin how to respond.

> **Glossary**
>
> **Receptors**
> The end part of a nerve that detects a stimulus, such as heat or touch.

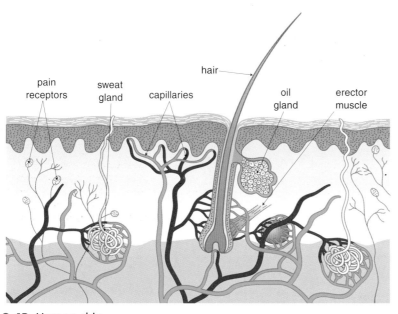

**Fig 2.43** Human skin

## What happens if the body temperature starts to rise?

- Capillaries in the skin expand allowing more blood flow near the surface of the skin. This enables some heat to be lost from the body.

- The sweat glands secrete sweat (water and salts) onto the skin. As the sweat evaporates, it takes heat from the body. This sweating cools the body down.

- The erector muscles, which raise and lower the tiny hairs on the skin, relax if the body is warm. This causes the hairs to lie flat and stops them from trapping air next to the skin. This means that heat loss is not prevented.

- In addition to all these strategies, we can help our bodies to lose heat by wearing less clothes, or lighter, thinner clothes. White clothes also help as they reflect heat.

## What happens if the body temperature starts to fall?

- Capillaries in the skin contract, allowing less blood flow near the surface of the skin. This reduces heat loss from the body.

- We begin to shiver. This contraction of the muscles produces heat and starts to warm the body up on the inside.

- The erector muscles contract, raising the tiny hairs on the skin. This traps a layer of air next to the skin, this acts as an insulator and reduces heat loss.

- We can also help by wearing warm clothes. Fleeces trap lots of air because of the way the fabric has been designed, and so keep us warm. Lots of thin layers will also have the same effect.

## Controlling the blood glucose level

During the process of **digestion**, the human body breaks sugars and starchy foods down into the simple sugar, glucose. This glucose is then absorbed into the blood and transported around the body to the cells. The cells use it for respiration in order to produce energy.

Too much glucose in the blood at any one time can damage the kidneys, and too little can make us feel faint. It is a good job then that our bodies have their own ways of keeping the amount of glucose in the blood fairly constant. They do this using a hormone called insulin. Insulin is produced in an organ called the pancreas. The way in which insulin is used to control the blood glucose level is an example of **feedback control**, because it involves the feedback of information to the pancreas about glucose levels in the blood.

### What happens when the blood glucose level rises?

This happens after a meal. The pancreas releases more insulin into the blood. Insulin causes glucose to be converted to **glycogen** in the liver. This reduces the level of glucose in the blood back to the desired level.

### What happens when the blood glucose level falls?

This happens if you haven't eaten for some time. The pancreas releases less insulin into the blood. Glucose is no longer converted to glycogen, in fact some glycogen is converted back to glucose in the liver, and the blood glucose level rises to normal again.

### Sometimes this control mechanism doesn't work

Sometimes a person doesn't produce enough insulin to keep their blood glucose level constant. This could be because they have a faulty pancreas. These people are called diabetics and the condition that they suffer from is diabetes. If this condition is not treated the blood glucose level can become too high, making the diabetic person dizzy at first. This can then lead to coma and possibly death.

> ### Glossary
>
> **Digestion**
> The process of breaking down complex food substances into simple molecules, so that the body can use them for energy or growth.
>
> **Feedback control**
> A system where the outputs affect the inputs.
>
> **Glycogen**
> A carbohydrate made in the liver and muscles by joining lots of glucose molecules together. It is used to store glucose for later use.

Diabetics must control their own blood glucose levels, since their bodies cannot. They must take great care with their diet, eating regular meals containing the right amount of sugar and starch. In addition, insulin injections may need to be taken to keep the glucose at a normal level. To find out if they need insulin, diabetics are taught how to take samples of their own blood and test it for glucose.

# Topic 5  Monitoring performance

How well the body works can be called its 'performance'. This term is most commonly used when talking about athletes. Athletes train their bodies to achieve the maximum performance they can and hopefully win their races or events. Athletes monitor their body to find out how well it is working, and what they need to do in order to improve. Factors such as heart rate, breathing rate and blood pressure can all be monitored.

## Measuring heart rate

Heart rate is measured by pressing an artery against a bone with your fingers. The easiest place to take this pulse is either in the wrist or the side of the neck. Once the pulse is found, the number of beats felt in one minute can be counted. When a person is resting, a normal heart rate is between 60 and 80 beats per minute.

When you exercise, your heart rate automatically goes up so that more blood can be pumped around the body. This happens so that more oxygen and glucose can be transported to the cells, so that more energy can be produced by respiration. However, when you stop exercising, your heart rate should go back to normal within a few minutes.

You can use your heart rate, and the time it takes for your heart rate to return to normal, as an indicator of your fitness. The fitter you are the lower your resting heart rate is likely to be, and it will also return to normal very quickly. When an athlete is preparing for a race or other event, he wants to build up his muscles and make them work better. He does this by training, where he practises his event, does fitness exercises in a gym and runs to build up his stamina.

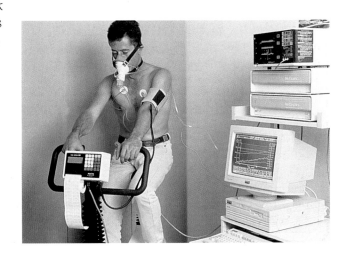

**Fig 2.44** A fitness test

## Measuring breathing rate

This is taken by simply counting the number of breaths taken in one minute. It is recorded in breaths per minute. The fitter you are the more efficient your lungs are. This means that the muscles of the diaphragm and those between the ribs are good at contracting, so the lungs can take in plenty of air in each breath and you don't need to breathe in as many times each minute to get the required oxygen. You can make your lungs more efficient by taking regular exercise, so that they get used to being worked harder.

The total amount of air your lungs can hold is called your **vital capacity**. This increases over a period of time, with regular exercise.

> **Glossary**
>
> **Vital capacity**
> The maximum amount of air that the lungs can hold after a deep breath.

## Measuring blood pressure

This is taken using a special meter called a sphygmomanometer. This measures the pressure of blood in the arteries and involves wrapping a special sleeve around the upper arm, pumping air into it until the blood in the arm stops flowing, and then releasing the pressure and measuring when the blood starts flowing again. The measurements are compared with expected values to make sure your blood pressure is not too high or too low.

### Case Study | The marathon runner

A marathon is a 26 mile run. Anybody can enter a marathon provided that they are healthy. It is, however, almost impossible to complete a run over this distance without a good level of fitness and some very serious training.

Dave is a 45 year old teacher. He is the head of sixth form in a large comprehensive school. He considers himself to be a reasonably fit as he manages the school's under-18s football team and runs coaching sessions twice a week. Dave is also a referee in the local Sunday league.

The football team are sponsoring Dave to complete the London Marathon to raise money for a local charity. He has been offered lots of advice from both the Science and PE departments about preparing himself for this event, and has devised the following training shedule, which begins 16 weeks before the race:

| | |
|---|---|
| Weeks 1–3 | 30 minutes run/walk every other day<br>A long walk at the weekend |
| Weeks 4–6 | 30 minutes run every other day<br>30 minutes swim twice a week<br>Longer walk/run at weekend |
| Weeks 7–9 | 45 minutes run every other day<br>45 mintues swim twice a week<br>Longer run at weekend |
| Weeks 10–12 | 45 minutes run or other exercise every day |
| Weeks 13–15 | 45 minutes run or other exercise every day<br>Up to 2 hours run at weekend |
| Weeks 16 | No more than 20 minutes per day of gentle exercise |

### Questions

9 Why does Dave not immediately start with a 45 minute run every day?

10 Why does Dave reduce his exercise the week before the race?

11 What else must Dave think about besides exercise during his 16 weeks of training?

## End-of-Section 5 Questions

1 Veins and arteries carry blood around the body. Which of these carry blood

   a) towards the heart?

   b) away from the heart?

2 Why must all cells in the body be close to a supply of blood?

3 Why does the heart have valves?

4 Describe what happens when we breathe in.

5 a) What is respiration with oxygen called?

   b) What is the word equation for this type of respiration?

6 a) What is respiration without oxygen called?

   b) What is the word equation for this type of respiration in yeast?

   c) What is the word equation for this type of respiration in exercising humans?

7 State two factors that must be kept constant in the body.

8 a) What is the body's normal temperature?

   b) What are you suffering from if the body temperature is:
   (i) too hot?
   (ii) too cold?

   c) What does the body do to try to conserve heat if the body temperature drops too low?

# Chapter Three

# Useful Chemicals and Materials

Chapter Three is divided into three sections:

**Section 1**    **Building Blocks**   Applied Science GCSE Unit 2

**Section 2**    **Pure Substances and Mixtures**   Applied Science GCSE Units 1 & 2

**Section 3**    **Properties and Uses of Materials**   Applied Science GCSE Units 1 & 2

## Section 1    Building Blocks

Section 1 is divided into six topics:

1  The Chemical Elements
2  Metals and Non-metals
3  The Structure of the Atom

4  Compounds
5  Ionic Bonding
6  Covalent Bonding

In the Unit 2 written examination you will be expected to:

★ Know the chemical symbols for 20 common elements.

★ Classify materials as elements (metals and non-metals).

★ Give examples of elements used straight from the ground.

★ Describe the structure of the atom in terms of protons, neutrons and electrons.

★ Classify materials as compounds.

★ Name some simple compounds, given their formulae; and state the formula, given the name of the compound.

★ Classify chemical compounds as inorganic or organic, given their formula.

★ Give an example of a compound used straight from the ground.

If you are entered for the Higher Tier examination paper you need to:

★ Have a basic understanding of ionic bonding.

★ Have a basic understanding of covalent bonding.

Required Knowledge

# Topic 1 The Chemical Elements

We obtain useful chemicals from the natural raw materials present on Earth. **Elements** are the building blocks from which all materials are made, but few of them exist as the pure element naturally. Most are chemically combined with one another to form **compounds**.

About 90 elements occur naturally on Earth. Each one has been given a name and a **symbol**.

Twenty common elements and their symbols are listed in Table 1. You need to learn the symbols for these elements.

| Element | Chemical Symbol | Element | Chemical Symbol |
|---|---|---|---|
| Aluminium | Al | Magnesium | Mg |
| Barium | Ba | Nitrogen | N |
| Bromine | Br | Oxygen | O |
| Calcium | Ca | Phosphorus | P |
| Carbon | C | Potassium | K |
| Chlorine | Cl | Silicon | Si |
| Fluorine | F | Silver | Ag |
| Hydrogen | H | Sodium | Na |
| Iron | Fe | Sulphur | S |
| Lead | Pb | Zinc | Zn |

**Table 1** Twenty of the most common elements

Elements can be found in the Earth's crust, in the atmosphere and in the ocean.

For example:

- Nitrogen is present in the atmosphere as a gas.
- Bromine can be extracted from compounds dissolved in the ocean.
- Copper can be obtained directly from the Earth's crust.
- Potassium is extracted from a compound present in the Earth's crust.

## Oxygen

The element oxygen is present in the atmosphere, in the ocean and in rocks. In the atmosphere, oxygen exists as an uncombined element.

**Questions**

1  Which symbols of the elements listed in Table 1 come from the Latin name for the element?

**Questions**

2  Approximately what proportion of the Earth's atmosphere is made up of oxygen?

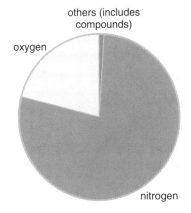

**Fig 3.1** Composition of the Earth's atmosphere

others (includes compounds)

oxygen

nitrogen

In the oceans, oxygen is combined with the element hydrogen to form water ($H_2O$), a liquid compound that is so plentiful that it covers approximately 70% of the Earth's surface.

In the Earth's crust, oxygen is combined with the element silicon to form silicon dioxide ($SiO_2$). This is a solid compound that forms quartz, one of the most common types of rock.

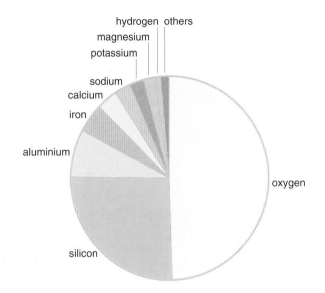

**Fig 3.3** Composition of the Earth's crust (Mass per cent)

**Fig 3.2** The Earth from space

**Questions**

3 Approximately what proportion of the Earth's crust is made up of oxygen?

Although oxygen is the most common element found in the rocks of the Earth's crust and there are vast quantities of it in the ocean, it is much easier to obtain the element from the atmosphere. This is because, in rocks and water, oxygen is chemically combined with other elements to form compounds. It is hard to obtain pure elements from compounds because energy must be supplied to break the **chemical bonds**.

In the atmosphere, oxygen is mixed with other gases such as nitrogen. It is easy to separate elements that are just mixed with other substances and not chemically combined.

Oxygen is separated from the air by **fractional distillation**. The air is cooled to –200 °C to turn it into a liquid. As the liquid air is heated the nitrogen (boiling point –196 °C) and other gases evaporate to leave pure oxygen (boiling point –183 °C).

Oxygen is essential for burning and of course for all living things. However, pure oxygen is also required in large quantities for industrial and medicinal uses.

For example, oxygen is used in oxy-acetylene welding and cutting. When acetylene (ethyne) burns in oxygen the flame is hot enough to melt most metals.

**Glossary**

**Chemical bond**
The force of attraction that holds the elements together in a compound.

**Fractional distillation**
The separation of a mixture of liquids into fractions. This process relies on the liquids in the mixture having different boiling points.

**Fig 3.4** The flame is hot enough to melt steel

Fig 3.6 Testing for oxygen in the laboratory

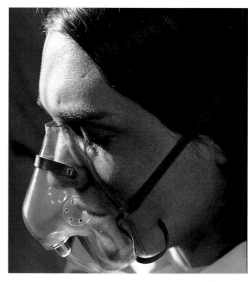

Fig 3.5 Oxygen helps patients to breathe

Oxygen is also used to help patients with lung disease to breathe. Pure oxygen from a cylinder is supplied to a facemask in order to increase the percentage of oxygen in the air that the patient is breathing in.

There are, however, hazards in the handling and transporting oxygen. Whatever burns in air, burns much better in pure oxygen.

## Questions

4   What hazard symbol should be attatched to a vehicle transporting liquid oxygen?

A glowing splint will relight when it is placed in oxygen. This can be used as a simple test for the gas in the laboratory.

## Topic 2  Metals and Non-metals

Different elements have different **physical properties** and **chemical properties**.

Elements can be classified as metals or non-metals based on major differences in their properties. The typical physical properties of metals and non-metals are shown in Table 2.

| Metals | Non-metals |
|---|---|
| Usually have high melting points and boiling points | Usually have low melting points and boiling points (some are gases) |
| They are shiny, strong and dense | They are dull and less dense than metals |
| They are good conductors of heat and electricity | They are poor conductors of heat and electricity |
| They are **malleable** and bendable | They are brittle |

### Glossary

**Physical properties**
Melting point, boiling point, electrical conductivity and density are examples of the physical properties of an element.

**Chemical properties**
The ways in which a chemical reacts with other substances.

**Malleable**
Capable of being hammered into shape.

Table 2  The typical physical properties of metals and non-metals

The melting points and boiling points of some common elements are shown in Table 3.

| Element | Melting point (°C) | Boiling point (°C) |
|---|---|---|
| Aluminium | 660 | 2470 |
| Bromine | −7.2 | 58.8 |
| Calcium | 850 | 1487 |
| Chlorine | −101 | −34.7 |
| Fluorine | −220 | −188 |
| Hydrogen | −259 | −252 |
| Lead | 327 | 1744 |
| Phosphorus | 44.2 | 280 |
| Silver | 961 | 2210 |
| Zinc | 420 | 907 |

**Table 3** Melting points and boiling points of some common elements

One of the best ways of checking whether an element is a metal or a non-metal is to see how well it conducts electricity.

A simple experiment to test electrical conductivity is shown in Figure 3.7.

**Fig 3.7** Metals are good conductors of electricity

## Metal or non-metal?

Carbon and silicon are not as easy to classify as some other elements. They are non-metals, but they have some metallic properties.

Carbon, in the form of graphite, is a soft and slippery solid. It will conduct electricity and it has a high melting point and boiling point.

Fig 3.8  Carbon in the form of graphite

Silicon is a brittle grey solid. It is a semiconductor with a high melting point and boiling point.

## Gold

In some ways gold is a typical metal:

- It has a high melting point and boiling point;
- It has a high density;
- It conducts electricity well;
- It is shiny;
- It is malleable.

However, because gold is very unreactive, it is one of the few metals that exists in a pure form. It is not found chemically combined with other elements. It can be used straight from the ground.

Gold has been mined in Wales for thousands of years because it can easily be extracted from the surrounding rock. Pure Welsh gold forms in seams in the rock, when the rock is crushed, or eroded naturally by the weather, the gold is released.

**Questions**

7   Which properties do the non-metals, graphite and silicon, share with metals?

| Melting point | 1063 °C |
|---|---|
| Boiling point | 2970°C |
| Density | 19 g/cm$^3$ |

Table 4  The properties of gold

**Questions**

8   What small-scale method was traditionally used to separate pieces of gold from small pieces of crushed rock?

Fig 3.9  Gold is one of the most valuable elements

Fig 3.10  Gold straight from the ground

A mixture of gold and crushed rock is easy to separate, because gold has a much higher density than the surrounding rock.

24 carat gold is pure and is very expensive. Cheaper gold has other, less expensive metals such as copper mixed in with it to form an alloy. For example, 24 g of 18-carat gold only contains 18 g of gold.

Gold is such a valuable metal because it is so unreactive. It keeps its attractive, shiny appearance because it does not react with oxygen or water in the atmosphere.

Most other metals are more reactive than gold so they are found in the earth as compounds, often as oxides or sulphides. To obtain the element, energy has to be supplied to break the chemical bonds that hold the compound together. For example, iron and lead have to be extracted from their ores by heating them with carbon.

## Sulphur

Sulphur is a typical non-metal:

- It has a low melting point and boiling point;
- It has a low density;
- It does not conduct electricity
- It is brittle.

Fig 3.11 Powdered sulphur

Sulphur is unreactive. It is found in the Earth's crust in a pure form and not chemically combined with other elements. It can be used straight from the ground.

Sulphur is found uncombined in volcanic regions and it occurs in large underground deposits in some parts of the world. Because it is a non-metal with a low melting point, it can be extracted from the underground deposits by melting it using pressurised hot water. The liquid sulphur is then forced up to the surface using compressed air. Under normal conditions boiling water would not be hot enough to melt the sulphur, but under pressure it can be heated above the melting point of sulphur without it boiling. The rock surrounding the sulphur has a high melting point and is not affected by the hot water.

| Melting point | 119 °C |
|---|---|
| Boiling point | 445 °C |
| Density | 2 g/cm$^3$ |

Table 5 The properties of sulphur

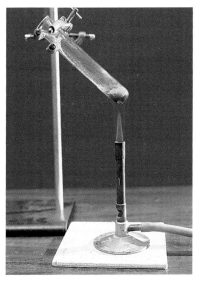

Fig 3.12 It is easy to melt sulphur in the laboratory

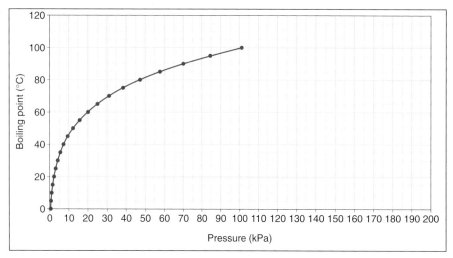

**Fig 3.13** The effect of changing pressure on the boiling point of water

**Questions**

9　Figure 3.14 shows the affect of changing pressure on the boiling point of water.

　(i)　Describe how the boiling point of water is affected by increasing pressure.

　(ii)　What is the boiling point of water at normal atmospheric pressure (101 kPa)?

　(iii)　Continue the graph to enable you to estimate the pressure needed when water is used to melt sulphur?

Much of the sulphur extracted by this method is used for the manufacture of sulphuric acid. Sulphur is also used to harden rubber and in making fireworks and matches.

Other non-metals are not as easy to obtain as sulphur. This is because, unlike sulphur, most non-metals are found combined with other elements in compounds. To extract the element, energy has to be supplied to break the chemical bonds that hold the compound together. For example, chlorine can be obtained by passing electricity through sodium chloride solution.

## Topic 3　The Structure of the Atom

Elements are made up of **atoms**. Atoms are the tiny particles from which all substances are made. Elements are special because they contain only one kind of atom.

Metals like gold have very different properties to non-metals like sulphur because their atoms have a different structure.

Atoms are made up of three smaller particles: **protons**, **neutrons** and **electrons**. The atoms of different elements have different numbers of these particles.

**Glossary**

**Atom**
The smallest particle of an element, it cannot be broken down chemically into anything simpler.

**Proton**
Small positively charged particle in the nucleus of an atom.

**Neutron**
Small particle with about the same mass as a proton but with no electric charge.

**Electron**
Very small negatively charged particle located outside the nucleus in a atom.

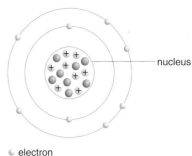

Protons and neutrons are situated in the **nucleus** at the centre of the atom. Electrons are found around the outside of the atom. It is the electrons of the atoms that determine the chemical properties of the element.

Atoms are neutral (no electric charge) because they always have an equal number of positively charged protons and negatively charged electrons.

An oxygen atom contains eight protons and eight electrons. So the **atomic number** of oxygen is 8.

A typical oxygen atom has eight neutrons, which together with the eight protons, makes a total of 16 particles in the nucleus. So the **mass number** of oxygen is 16.

nucleus

◔ electron
⊕ proton
◕ neutron

**Fig 3.14** An atom

## Glossary

**Nucleus**
The positively charged central part of an atom.

**Atomic number**
The number of protons in the nucleus of an atom. Different elements have a different atomic number.

**Mass number**
The sum of the number of protons and neutrons in the nucleus of an atom.

## Questions

**10** Copy and complete the table below. Use the atomic numbers and mass numbers given to work out the number of protons, electrons and neutrons in the atoms of the elements. The first one has been done for you.

| Element | Symbol | Atomic Number | Mass Number | Number of: Protons | Number of: Neutrons | Number of: Electrons |
|---------|--------|---------------|-------------|---------|----------|-----------|
| Carbon | C | 6 | 12 | 6 | 6 | 6 |
| Magnesium | Mg | 12 | 24 | | | |
| Fluorine | F | 9 | 19 | | | |
| Sodium | Na | 11 | 23 | | | |
| Nitrogen | N | 7 | 14 | | | |

**11** Copy and complete the table below. Work out the mass number and atomic number of these elements. The first one has been done for you.

| Element | Symbol | Atomic Number | Mass Number | Number of: Protons | Number of: Neutrons | Number of: Electrons |
|---------|--------|---------------|-------------|---------|----------|-----------|
| Aluminium | A1 | 13 | 27 | 13 | 14 | 13 |
| Phosphorus | P | | | 15 | 16 | 15 |
| Silver | Ag | | | 47 | 61 | 47 |
| Hydrogen | H | | | 1 | 0 | 1 |
| Zinc | Zn | | | 30 | 35 | 30 |

Because atoms from different elements have different numbers of protons, electrons and neutrons they behave in different ways. Knowing the structure of the atom helps us to predict the way in which the element will behave. Unlike the atoms of sulphur and gold, the atoms of many elements are chemically reactive and they combine with the atoms of other elements to form compounds.

## Topic 4  Compounds

A compound is a pure substance formed when the atoms of two or more elements join together. Compounds have different properties to the elements that they are made from. For example water, a liquid at room temperature, is made from the reactive gases oxygen and hydrogen.

Compounds can be simple substances like carbon dioxide, or much larger and more complex substances like the proteins, carbohydrates and fats that make up living things.

The **chemical formula** shows which elements are present in the compound. The symbols for the elements are put together and the numbers in the formula show the number of atoms of each element present. For example, the formula for calcium carbonate is $CaCO_3$. Calcium carbonate contains the elements calcium, carbon and oxygen. The number of atoms of each element is in the ratio 1:1:3, in other words for every atom of Ca there is one atom of C and three atoms of O.

**Glossary**

**Chemical formula**
Gives the symbol for the elements and the number of each type of atom present.

**Questions**

12 Copy and complete the table below with the names of the elements and the ratio of the number of atoms present in the compounds. The first one has been done for you.

| Compound | Formula | Elements present | Ratio of the number of atoms |
|---|---|---|---|
| Iron oxide | $Fe_2O_3$ | Iron and oxygen | 2:3 |
| Sodium chloride | NaCl | | |
| Ammonia | $NH_3$ | | |
| Sulphuric acid | $H_2SO_4$ | | |
| Potassium nitrate | $KNO_3$ | | |

## Case Study | Limestone

Calcium carbonate ($CaCO_3$) is an example of a compound used straight from the ground. It occurs in a pure form in rocks such as limestone and marble. Both types of rock were formed from the shells of creatures that lived in the seas millions of years ago.

Fig 3.15 Limestone rocks

Limestone is an important industrial chemical that is used to make calcium oxide (quicklime used for purifying steel and making cement), calcium hydroxide (slaked lime is used to reduce the acidity of lakes and soil) and sodium carbonate (used to make glass). Several million tonnes of limestone are mined in the UK each year.

Large quantities of rock are blasted from the quarry face using dynamite. The rock is transported using giant earth moving equipment to be crushed and sorted ready for the next stage in the process. Blocks of limestone are used for building. Smaller pieces are required for road stone and making concrete.

Fig 3.16  A limestone quarry has a major impact on the environment

### Questions

13  Visit http://www.peakdistrict-education.gov.uk/ to find out more information about limestone and limestone quarrying.
  a)  What is the most important use for limestone mined in the Peak District?
  b)  What steps are taken to reduce the environmental impact of a quarry?

Limestone is made up of a compound, but it is easy to extract. Most other compounds are more difficult to extract from the earth than calcium carbonate. They are usually found in an impure form mixed with other chemicals and they have to be separated from this mixture before they can be used.

## Topic 5  Ionic Bonding

The elements in a compound are **chemically bonded** together. There are two types of chemical bonding, **ionic** and **covalent**. Calcium carbonate is an example of an ionic compound. An ionic compound is produced when atoms of a metal form bonds to atoms of a non-metal.

The atoms of metals tend to lose electrons to form positively charged **ions**. For example sodium atoms lose one electron to form sodium ions ($Na^+$); magnesium atoms lose two electrons to form magnesium ions ($Mg^{2+}$); and aluminium atoms lose three electrons to form aluminium ions ($Al^{3+}$).

### Glossary

**Chemical bonding**
The attractive force that holds the elements together in a compound.

**Ionic**
A type of chemical bonding that involves the transfer of one or more electrons from one atom to another to form ions.

**Covalent**
A type of chemical bonding that involves the sharing of electrons between atoms.

**Ion**
An atom or group of atoms that has a positive or negative electric charge as a result of the loss or gain of electrons.

Table 6 shows a range of positively charged ions formed when the atoms of metals lose electrons.

The atoms of non-metals tend to gain electrons to form negatively charged ions. For example chlorine atoms gain one electron to form chloride ions ($Cl^-$); and oxygen atoms gain two electrons to form oxide ions ($O^{2-}$).

A range of negatively charged ions is shown in Table 7. Some of these ions contain more than one element.

When metals form chemical bonds with non-metals there is a transfer of electrons from the atoms of the metal to the atoms of the non-metal, forming positively charged ions and negatively charged ions.

| Element | Positively charged ion |
|---------|------------------------|
| Potassium | $K^+$ |
| Silver | $Ag^+$ |
| Sodium | $Na^+$ |
| Barium | $Ba^{2+}$ |
| Calcium | $Ca^{2+}$ |
| Copper | $Cu^{2+}$ |
| Lead | $Pb^{2+}$ |
| Magnesium | $Mg^{2+}$ |
| Aluminium | $Al^{3+}$ |
| Iron | $Fe^{3+}$ |

**Table 6**  Metal ions

| Name | Symbol |
|------|--------|
| Chloride | $Cl^-$ |
| Hydroxide | $OH^-$ |
| Nitrate | $NO_3^-$ |
| Carbonate | $CO_3^{2-}$ |
| Oxide | $O^{2-}$ |
| Sulphate | $SO_4^{2-}$ |

**Table 7**  Non-metal ions

## The Formation of Sodium Chloride

When sodium reacts with chlorine there is a transfer of one electron from a sodium atom (Na) to a chlorine atom (Cl), forming a sodium ion ($Na^+$) and a chloride ion ($Cl^-$). An ionic compound called sodium chloride is formed.

BEFORE ELECTRON TRANSFER

| Sodium atom |
| --- |
| Na |
| 11 protons (11+) |
| 11 electrons (11–) |

**Elements**
The atoms are not charged because they have an equal number of protons and electrons

| Chlorine atom |
| --- |
| C1 |
| 17 protons (17+) |
| 17 electrons (17–) |

AFTER ELECTRON TRANSFER

| Sodium ion |
| --- |
| $Na^+$ |
| 11 protons (11+) |
| 10 electrons (10–) |

**Ionic compound**
Positively charged ions have more protons than electrons
Negatively charged ions have more electrons than protons

| Chloride ion |
| --- |
| $C1^-$ |
| 17 protons (17+) |
| 18 electrons (18–) |

$$Na^+Cl^-$$

The formula for sodium chloride can be written as $Na^+Cl^-$ or more simply as NaCl.

## The Formation of Magnesium Oxide

When magnesium reacts with oxygen there is a transfer of two electrons from a magnesium atom (Mg) to an oxygen atom (O), forming a magnesium ion ($Mg^{2+}$) and an oxide ion ($O^{2-}$). An ionic compound called magnesium oxide is produced. The formula for magnesium oxide can be written as $Mg^{2+}O^{2-}$ or more simply as MgO.

**Questions**

14 Copy and complete the following table to show the number of protons, electrons and neutrons in
   a) magnesium atoms,
   b) magnesium ions,
   c) oxygen atoms,
   d) oxide ions.

| Element | Symbol | Atomic Number | Mass Number | Number of: | | |
| --- | --- | --- | --- | --- | --- | --- |
| | | | | Protons | Neutrons | Electrons |
| Magnesium atom | Mg | 12 | 24 | | | |
| Magnesium ion | $Mg^{2+}$ | 12 | 24 | | | |
| Oxygen atom | O | 8 | 16 | | | |
| Oxide ion | $O^{2-}$ | 8 | 16 | | | |

## Writing Ionic Formulae

Brackets have to be included when writing ionic formulae if the charges on the ions in the formula don't balance. For example the formula for iron oxide should be written as $(Fe^{3+})_2(O^-)_3$ or more simply as $Fe_2O_3$

### Questions

15 Work out the names of the following ionic compounds:
  a) $Ca^{2+}O^{2-}$
  b) $K^+OH^-$
  c) $Ba^{2+}(Cl^-)_2$
  d) $Cu^{2+}CO_3^{2-}$
  e) $(Na^+)_2SO_4^{2-}$

16 Write the ionic formulae for the following ionic compounds:
  a) Silver nitrate
  b) Copper sulphate
  c) Barium carbonate
  d) Calcium chloride
  e) Aluminium oxide

There are strong forces of attraction between the positive and negative charges holding an ionic compound together, so these compounds usually have high melting points and boiling points. Ionic compounds form crystals containing a **giant ionic structure**.

Ionic compounds contain charged particles, when the ions can move the material will conduct electricity. This happens when an ionic compound is melted or dissolved in water.

### Glossary

**Giant ionic structure**
A crystal structure held together by the forces of attraction between positive and negative ions.

## Topic 6 Covalent Bonding

A covalent compound is formed when the atoms of non-metals form chemical bonds with each other. The atoms share their electrons, forming **molecules** with strong covalent bonds between the atoms. The force of attraction between molecules is weak, so covalent compounds usually have a low melting point and a low boiling point. There are no charged particles so covalent compounds cannot conduct electricity.

Some examples of covalent compounds together with their formulae are shown in Table 8.

### Glossary

**Molecule**
A group of two or more atoms joined together.

Some non-metallic elements are made up of molecules consisting of pairs of atoms:

| | |
|---|---|
| Bromine | $Br_2$ |
| Chlorine | $Cl_2$ |
| Fluorine | $F_2$ |
| Hydrogen | $H_2$ |
| Nitrogen | $N_2$ |
| Oxygen | $O_2$ |

**Table 8** Covalent compounds

| Name | Formula |
|---|---|
| Water | $H_2O$ |
| Hydrogen chloride | HCl |
| Ammonia | $NH_3$ |
| Carbon dioxide | $CO_2$ |
| Methane | $CH_4$ |
| Ethene | $C_2H_4$ |

Table 9 shows the position of the covalent bonds between the atoms in the molecules of some covalent compounds. Each line represents a single covalent bond.

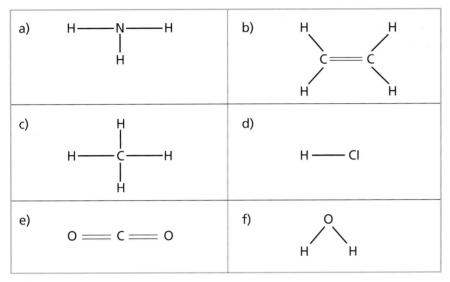

Table 9

**Questions**

17 Name the covalent compounds labelled a) to f) in Table 9.

18 Name the compounds in the table that contain double covalent bonds.

## Organic or Inorganic?

Organic compounds contain the element carbon, they usually have covalent bonding and they can be obtained from living organisms. Crude oil is a good source of organic compounds because it was formed from the remains of organisms that lived millions of years ago. Methane ($CH_4$) and ethene ($C_2H_4$) are examples of organic compounds that can be obtained from crude oil.

Not all carbon-containing compounds are classified as organic. The oxides of carbon are classified as inorganic. For example, calcium carbonate ($CaCO_3$) is an example of an **inorganic** compound containing the element carbon.

Inorganic compounds can have either covalent bonding or ionic bonding. Ammonia ($NH_3$) and hydrogen chloride (HCl) are examples of inorganic compounds with covalent boning. Calcium carbonate ($CaCO_3$) is an example of an inorganic compound with ionic bonding.

**Glossary**

**Organic**
The group of carbon compounds that come from living things. Polymers and many pharmaceutical products are organic compounds.

**Inorganic**
The group of substances that includes all the elements and the compounds that are not classified as organic. Metals, ceramics and fertilisers are inorganic compounds.

| Organic | Inorganic |
|---|---|
| Compounds containing carbon. Mostly formed from living organisms. | Substances not classified as organic. |
| Usually covalent (formed from only non-metal elements) e.g. methane, $CH_4$. | Can be ionic e.g. calcium carbonate, $CaCO_3$. |
| | Can be covalent e.g. ammonia, $NH_3$. |

The type of bonding in a compound affects its physical and chemical properties. A summary of the characteristics of compounds with ionic and covalent bonding is shown in Table 10.

| Ionic | Covalent |
|---|---|
| Formed when metals bond with non-metals | Formed from non-metals |
| Made up of ions | Made up of molecules |
| High melting point | Usually low melting point |
| Conduct electricity when melted or dissolved in water | Do not conduct electricity, even when melted or dissolved in water |
| e.g. NaCl and MgO | e.g. HCl and $H_2O$ |

**Table 10** Characteristics of compounds with ionic and covalent bonding

You need to know the names and formulae of the following 20 chemical compounds:

| Compound | Formula | Compound | Formula |
|---|---|---|---|
| Ammonia | $NH_3$ | Barium chloride | $BaCl_2$ |
| Carbon dioxide | $CO_2$ | Sodium chloride | NaCl |
| Methane | $CH_4$ | Calcium carbonate | $CaCO_3$ |
| Water | $H_2O$ | Copper carbonate | $CuCO_3$ |
| Hydrochloric acid | HCl | Sodium carbonate | $Na_2CO_3$ |
| Sulphuric acid | $H_2SO_4$ | Potassium nitrate | $KNO_3$ |
| Calcium oxide | CaO | Silver nitrate | $AgNO_3$ |
| Iron oxide | $Fe_2O_3$ | Barium sulphate | $BaSO_4$ |
| Lead oxide | PbO | Copper sulphate | $CuSO_4$ |
| Sodium hydroxide | NaOH | Sodium sulphate | $Na_2SO_4$ |

**Table 11** Chemical compounds

## Questions

19 a)  Fourteen of the compounds in Table 11 are ionic.

   HCl and $H_2SO_4$ are covalent but, being acids, they form ions when added to water.

   Name the other four covalent compounds listed in the table.

b)  Nineteen of the compounds in the table are inorganic. Name the organic compound listed in the table.

| Compound | Electrical conductivity | Melting point (°C) | Boiling point (°C) |
|---|---|---|---|
| X | Does not conduct electricity when molten | 1610 | 2230 |
| Y | Conducts electricity when dissolved in water or when molten | 801 | 1413 |
| Z | Does not conduct electricity when molten | −182 | −162 |

Table 12

## Questions

**20** Some properties of three compounds X, Y and Z are given in Table 12. Classify the compounds as either ionic or covalent.

## End-of-Section 1 Questions

**1** Chemical elements are the simplest kind of substance.

a) Copy and complete the table below.

| Name | Symbol | Metal or non-metal |
|---|---|---|
| Barium | | Metal |
| | C | Non-metal |
| Iron | Fe | |
| Magnesium | | Metal |
| Nitrogen | N | |
| | O | Non-metal |
| Potassium | | Metal |
| | Si | Non-metal |
| Sodium | | Metal |
| Sulphur | S | |

b) Choose one element from the table that is:
   (i) A reactive gas.
   (ii) Obtained straight from the ground.
   (iii) The second most common metal in the Earth's crust.
   (iv) The second most commom non-metal in the Earth's crust.

**2** Some information about the element helium is given below.

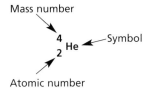

Mass number

$^{4}_{2}$ He — Symbol

Atomic number

a) Why is H not used as the symbol for helium?

b) Work out the number of protons, neutrons and electrons in an atom of helium.

c) Draw a diagram to show how these particles are arranged in an atom of helium.

**3** Chemical compounds are made up from two or more elements joined together.

a) Copy and complete the table below.

| Name | Formula | Inorganic or organic | Type of bonding |
|---|---|---|---|
| | $NH_3$ | | Covalent |
| Potassium nitrate | | Inorganic | Ionic |
| Methane | | Organic | |
| | $CaCO_3$ | Inorganic | |

b) Chose one compound from the table that:
   (i) Is known as a fossil fuel.
   (ii) Is a rock used straight from the ground.
   (iii) Has a high melting point.
   (iv) Has a low boiling point.

| Section 2 | **Pure Substances and Mixtures** |
|---|---|

Section 2 is divided into three topics:

1   Obtaining pure substances from the Earth
2   Chemical Analysis
3   Making useful mixtures

Your Unit 1 portfolio should include evidence that you have carried out qualitative analysis. You need to:

★ Separate mixtures by evaporation, distillation and chromatography to determine their composition.

★ Carry out qualitative chemical tests for $Na^+$, $K^+$, $Ca^{2+}$, $Cu^{2+}$, $Pb^{2+}$, $Fe^{3+}$, $Cl^-$, $SO_4^{2-}$ and $CO_3^{2-}$ ions and draw conclusions from your results.

In the Unit 2 written examination you will be expected to:

★ Describe how some substances are separated before use.

★ Classify materials as pure substances or mixtures.

★ Give examples of useful mixtures and explain why they are useful.

★ Explain the composition of a solution, suspension, gel, emulsion, foam and aerosol.

## Topic 1   Obtaining Pure Substances from the Earth

Useful chemicals must be obtained from the natural raw materials that are found in the atmosphere, the earth and the sea.

A few **elements** can be found in an uncombined form. Oxygen can be separated from the atmosphere. Gold and sulphur are easily extracted from the ground because these elements are not **chemically bonded** to other elements to form **compounds**.

The vast majority of chemical substances are found as compounds. Limestone and marble are unusual in that they consist of almost pure calcium carbonate. Most other **minerals** contain a mixture of compounds from which the useful chemical must be separated. For example, sodium chloride (salt) is separated from rock salt; petrol is separated from crude oil.

Compounds containing useful metals are called **ores**. Once the ore has been separated from the surrounding rock, the metal can be extracted by heating it with carbon. (See Chapter 4, Section 1 for the extraction of iron and lead using this method.)

**Glossary**

**Element**
A pure substance that cannot be broken down into simpler substances.

**Chemical bonding**
The force of attraction that holds the elements together in a compound.

**Compound**
A pure substance made up of two or more elements joined together.

**Mineral**
A substance that is valuable for mining.

**Ore**
A rock that is mined because it contains enough mineral to be worth extracting.

## Questions

1   Information about how some useful chemicals can be obtained is summarised in the table below. Copy and complete the table. Use information from the previous section to help you.

| Useful chemical | Type of chemical | How is the chemical found? | How is the chemical extracted? |
| --- | --- | --- | --- |
| Oxygen | Element | As an element mixed in the air | Fractional distillation of liquid air |
| Gold | | | |
| Sulphur | | | |
| Iron | Element | As a compound – iron oxide, mixed with other rock | Ore is separated from other rock then heated with carbon |
| Lead | | As a compound – lead sulphide, mixed with other rock | |
| Calcium carbonate | | | |
| Sodium chloride | | In underground deposits mixed with other rock | Separated from rock salt by solution, filtration and evaporation |
| Petrol | Mixture | Part of a liquid mixture found trapped underground in rocks | Separated from crude oil by fractional distillation |

# Sodium Chloride

Sodium chloride is an **ionic** compound that is made up of equal numbers of $Na^+$ and $Cl^-$ ions. The pure compound forms white crystals that are soluble in water. The **solubility** of sodium chloride in water depends on temperature.

## Glossary

**Ionic**
A type of chemical bonding that involves the transfer of one or more electrons from one atom to another to form ions.

**Solubility**
The amount of solute that will dissolve in a given amount of solvent.

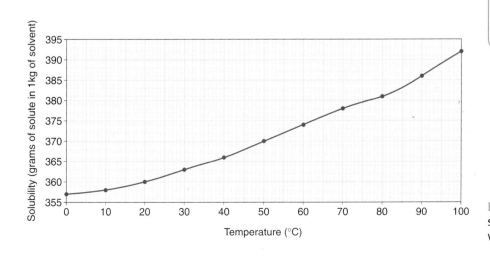

Fig 3.17 Variation of the solubility of sodium chloride with temperature

Sodium chloride, commonly known as salt, is essential for good health, but too much in the diet can lead to high blood pressure and an increased risk of heart attacks. The compound is used in the food industry as a flavouring and a preservative. There are vast amounts of sodium chloride dissolved in the ocean and salt can be obtained directly from the evaporation of seawater.

**Fig 3.18** Not a successful method of extraction in the UK!

Salt obtained directly from seawater is not pure. Although $Na^+$ and $Cl^-$ are the most abundant ions, there are many other ions present as well.

| Ion | Symbol | Percentage by mass of salt dissolved in seawater |
|---|---|---|
| Chloride | $Cl^-$ | 55.0 % |
| Sodium | $Na^+$ | 30.6 % |
| Sulphate | $SO_4^{2-}$ | 7.7 % |
| Magnesium | $Mg^{2+}$ | 3.7 % |
| Calcium | $Ca^{2+}$ | 1.2 % |
| Potassium | $K^+$ | 1.1 % |
| Hydrogencarbonate | $HCO_3^-$ | 0.4 % |
| Bromide | $Br^-$ | 0.2 % |

**Table 13** Ions found in sea water

**Questions**

2   Figure 3.18 shows the variation of the solubility of sodium chloride with temperature.

a)   Describe the effect of increasing temperature on the solubility of sodium chloride.

b)   How much salt will dissolve in 1 kg of water at 20 °C?

**Questions**

3   Sodium chloride ($Na^+Cl^-$) is the most common ionic compound present in the salt obtained from seawater. Name, and write the chemical formulae for, four other ionic compounds present in sea salt.

Rock salt is an impure form of sodium chloride mined from underground deposits. These deposits are the remains of seas that dried up thousands of years ago. Salt solution can be obtained directly from the underground deposits by solution mining.

## Solution mining

Water is pumped down into the underground deposits to dissolve the salt. The surrounding rock is insoluble so it does not dissolve in the water. The resulting salt **solution** is then pumped to the surface. Salt solution (brine) can be used directly by the chemical industry for the manufacture of many useful chemicals including chlorine, hydrogen, sodium hydroxide and sodium carbonate.

Sodium chloride crystals can be obtained from the salt solution by evaporation. However, the process is expensive because energy is needed to heat the brine. Lowering the pressure can reduce this cost.

### Questions

4   Refer to Figure 3.14 on page 16. How does a lower pressure affect the boiling point of water? How does this save money?

5   Refer to Figure 3.18. What mass of salt can be disolved by 1 kg of water at 100 °C?

As water evaporates away, the salt solution becomes more concentrated and crystals begin to form. Figure 3.17 on page 107 shows that even hot water can only dissolve a certain amount of salt.

The crystals produced can be separated from the solution by **filtration**.

It is also possible to collect the pure water as it evaporates from the solution. This process is known as **distillation**. A simple laboratory distillation apparatus is shown in Figure 3.19.

### Glossary

**Solution**
A solid, liquid or gas (the solute) dissolved in a liquid (the solvent).

**Filtration**
Separation of a solid from a liquid using filter paper, or a sieve with holes too small for the solid to pass through, but large enough for liquid molecules to pass through.

**Distillation**
A method of separation based on the fact that a substance with a low boiling point will vaporise and separate from a substance with a higher boiling point. The vapour is cooled, condensed and collected as the distillate.

**Fig 3.19** Distillation of salt solution produces pure distilled water.

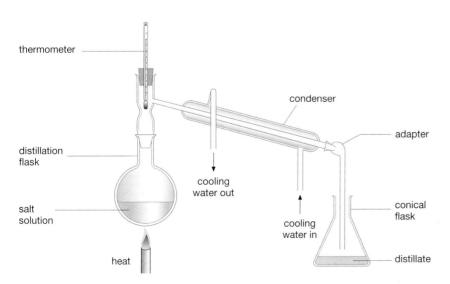

- thermometer
- condenser
- adapter
- distillation flask
- cooling water out
- salt solution
- cooling water in
- conical flask
- heat
- distillate

The salt, with its high boiling point, remains in the flask. Water, with a low boiling point, evaporates and passes into the water-cooled condenser.

### Questions

6   What temperature reading would the thermometer show during distillation?

## Practical Work | The Purification of Rock Salt in the Laboratory

Rock salt is a mixture of sodium chloride (NaCl) and insoluble compounds such as silicon dioxide ($SiO_2$). Rock salt is used on the roads in winter. It causes ice to melt and provides better grip for vehicles.

Rock salt can be purified in the laboratory using water as a solvent. Water dissolves the soluble salt but not the insoluble silicon dioxide. Filtration removes the insoluble material form the salt solution. Evaporation removes the solvent leaving pure salt crystals behind.

Fig 3.20 Grinding rock salt

Fig 3.21 Dissolving rock salt

1  Grind the rock salt to a powder using a pestle and mortar. This helps the salt to dissolve more quickly.

2  Mix the ground up rock salt with distilled water. Now heat the solution over a Bunsen burner. Stir the solution to help the salt dissolve more quickly.

3  Filter the solution through filter paper. This will remove the insoluble material. You are now left with a pure salt solution.

4  Heat the salt solution over a Bunsen burner, or a steam bath until all the solvent has been removed. You are left with crystals of salt.

### Questions

7  The salt obtained from this experiment does not contain any silicon dioxide, but it is unlikely to be 100 % pure sodium chloride. Explain why it is likely to contain other ionic compounds.

Fig 3.22 Filtering the solution

Fig 3.23 Dry salt crystals

# Petrol

Petrol is an important fuel obtained from crude oil. Crude oil is a mixture made up of **organic** compounds called **hydrocarbons**. These hydrocarbons are the remains of living things. Millions of years ago some organisms died and became covered with sediment. Away from the air, they did not decay naturally. The chemicals within them became changed over time as they were affected by heat and pressure from the surrounding rocks. The result is a natural mixture called crude oil. This oil can now be extracted by drilling down into the rock.

Crude oil is a valuable raw material containing many useful chemicals. So it is worth the expense and danger of extracting it from, amongst other places, under the North Sea.

**Glossary**

**Organic**
The group of carbon compounds that come from living things.

**Hydrocarbon**
An organic compound containing the elements carbon and hydrogen only.

**Fig 3.24** Extracting crude oil from the rocks beneath the North Sea

**Fig 3.25** An oil refinery

Oil extracted from rocks below the seabed is brought ashore by pipeline. Petrol and other useful mixtures are separated from the crude oil in an oil refinery.

**Questions**

8   A well-managed oil refinery is a safe place to work, but there are many hazards and risks involved.
   a)  Make a list of five potential hazards that would apply to a large chemical operation like an oil refinery.
   b)  What can be done to ensure the safety of employees at the oil refinery?

Petrol is separated from crude oil by distillation, but the simple distillation that works so well for salt and water does not work for crude oil. Instead of just two different compounds with very different boiling points, there are hundreds of different compounds within crude oil with boiling points spread over a range of temperatures. Fractional distillation must therefore be used. A **fractionating column** is used to separate the liquids into fractions. Each fraction boils over a fixed range of temperatures and contains molecules with a similar number of carbon atoms.

**Glossary**

**Fractionating column**
A column packed with inert material to create a large surface area on which rising vapour can evaporate and condense. The vapour that reaches the top of the column contains compounds with the lowest boiling points.

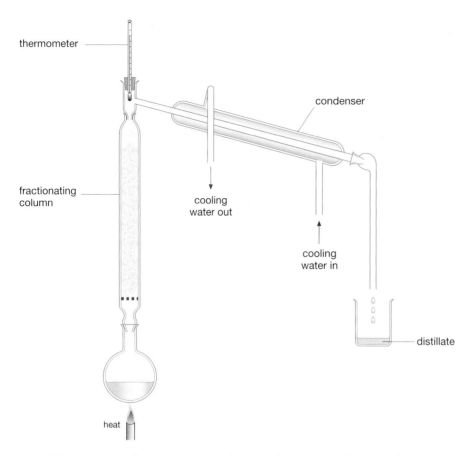

**Fig 3.26** Apparatus for carrying out fractional distillation in the laboratory

In the petrochemicals industry, large-scale fractional distillation takes place in steel towers. In a continuous process, crude oil is fed in at the bottom, heated and vaporised. As the vapours rise they cool. The compounds with the lowest boiling temperatures rise to the top to condense, forming the fraction with the smallest molecules. The compounds with the highest boiling temperatures condense at the bottom, forming the fraction with the largest molecules.

Table 14 Some fractions of crude oil

| Fraction | Boiling range | Number of carbon atoms in the molecules |
|---|---|---|
| Refinery gas | Less than 25 °C | 1 or 4 |
| Petrol | 25 to 75 °C | 5 to 7 |
| Naphtha | 75 to 190 °C | 6 to 10 |
| Kerosene | 190 to 250 °C | 10 to 16 |
| Gas oil | 250 to 350 °C | 14 to 20 |
| Residue | Greater than 350 °C | Greater than 20 |

Petrol, and the other fractions with small molecules, make good fuels. They easily turn into a gas, they are easy to ignite, and they burn with a clean flame.

**Questions**

9   What type of chemical bonding holds the carbon and hydrogen atoms together in the hydrocarbon molecules present in crude oil and petrol?

**Fig 3.27** Petrol – a useful mixture

Examples of some of the compounds that might be found in crude oil, together with their boiling points are given in the table below.

| Name | Formula | Boiling point (°C) |
|---|---|---|
| Methane | $CH_4$ | −162 |
| Butane | $C_4H_{10}$ | 0 |
| Hexane | $C_6H_{14}$ | 69 |
| Decane | $C_{10}H_{22}$ | 174 |

**Table 15** Some compounds found in crude oil

### Questions

10 a) How is the boiling point of a hydrocarbon related to the number of carbon atoms in the molecule?

b) Which of the molecules in Table 15 might be found in petrol?

c) In which fraction would you find decane?

The fractions with the lowest boiling points make the best fuels. The fractions with high boiling points have low **volatility** and high **viscosity** and they do not make good fuels. These chemicals provide **feedstock** for the refinery. They are converted into more useful chemicals such as ethene ($C_2H_4$). Ethene is an important raw material for the plastics industry.

### Glossary

**Volatility**
A liquid with a low volatility does not turn into a gas easily because it has a high boiling point.

**Viscosity**
A liquid with a high viscosity is thick like treacle.

**Feedstock**
The raw material for an industrial process.

### Questions

11 Separation depends on using differences in the properties of the chemicals being separated. What differences in properties are used to separate the following? Describe the method used in each case.
a) Sulphur from the surrounding rock;
b) Sodium chloride from the surrounding rock;
c) Sand from salt solution;
d) Sodium chloride from water;
e) Water from sodium chloride;
f) Petrol from crude oil.

# Topic 2  Chemical Analysis

Materials can be classified as pure substances or mixtures. Pure substances have distinctive **physical** and **chemical properties** and tests can be used to find out whether a substance is pure. A mixture may contain two or more chemical substances and chemists use **qualitative analysis** to determine which substances are present in a mixture.

## Sampling

Tests are often carried out on a small sample that has been removed from a large batch of material. But how can we be sure that a small sample represents the composition of the whole batch? Several factors need to be considered before deciding which sampling method to use and the number of samples to be taken:

- How much material is needed for a test?
- How many tests need to be carried out to get an accurate result?
- Are the components of a mixture evenly distributed?
- Does the composition of the mixture change with time?

## Case Study | The Environment Agency

The Environment Agency is a public body whose role it is to advise and regulate air and water quality in England and Wales. As a river passes through a town or industrial area different chemicals and biological pollutants may be added to the water. Scientists take samples at several points on a river because the composition of the river water will vary along its length. Sampling takes place at these points at regular time intervals because the composition of river water can vary with time. Samples are returned to the laboratory and the presence of pollutants can be detected using standard chemical and biological tests.

**Fig 3.28** Testing water quality

## Questions

12 Visit http://www.environment-agency.gov.uk/
Search the website to find the answers to the following questions.
   a) (i)   What kind of pollution affects our rivers?
      (ii)  How does the Environment Agency deal with pollution problems?
   b) Where is the Environment Agency located? Is the organisation sited in one spot or is it spread over several locations in the UK?
   c) What careers are available in this organisation?
   d) Are employees of this organisation major users of science?

## Questions

13 What sampling methods do you think would be used in each of the following situations?
   a) The viscosity of a batch of salad cream must be within certain maximum and minimum limits before it can be sent to the bottling plant.
   b) The pH of a solution must be monitored during an industrial manufacturing process.
   c) An environmental group would like to measure the air quality in a street in a busy town.

# Tests for Purity
## Melting point and boiling point

A pure substance has a definite melting point and boiling point. Measuring the melting point of a solid or the boiling point of a liquid can be used to identify an unknown substance, or to determine whether a known substance is pure. A slightly lower melting point shows the presence of an impurity in a solid. A slightly higher boiling point shows the presence of an impurity in a liquid. For example, water as a pure compound will melt at exactly 0 °C and boil at exactly 100 °C. When salt is dissolved in water the mixture freezes below 0 °C and boils above 100 °C.

# Chromatography
### Paper chromatography

Paper chromatography will separate a mixture containing two or more substances. The sample is placed on filter paper and a solvent soaks through the paper carrying the components of the mixture with it. Different substances are carried different distances along the paper – the most soluble substance is carried the furthest. The distance moved by an unknown substance can be compared with the distance moved by a known pure substance.

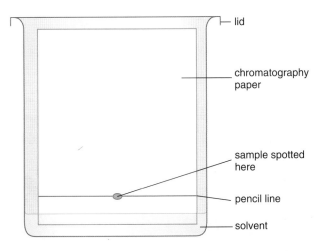

Fig 3.29 The apparatus for paper chromatography

Fig 3.30 Paper chromatography can be used to separate a mixture of dyes

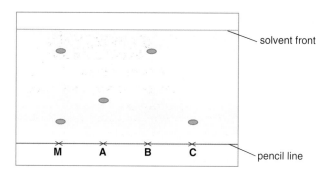

Fig 3.31

**Questions**

14 Which of the pure substances labelled A, B and C in Figure 3.31 are present in mixture M?

### Gas-liquid chromatography

Gas-liquid chromatography (GLC) works in the same way as paper chromatography but it separates a mixture of gases. The gas-liquid chromatograph consists of a long heated tube filled with an **inert** support coated in a liquid. The vaporised sample is carried along the tube by an inert carrier gas such as nitrogen. Gases that dissolve in the liquid are held back. Other gases pass through the tube quickly. The gases are detected as they come out of the end of the tube and a recorder marks the position of each gas on a trace.

**Glossary**

Inert
Unreactive.

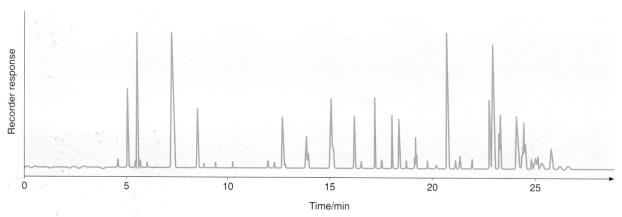

**Fig 3.32** A gas-liquid chromatogram of a sample of petrol. Petrol is a mixture of many different hydrocarbon molecules

Gas-liquid chromatography can be used in forensic science to separate and analyse the components of a fuel mixture that has been used to start a fire. The trace can be matched to one produced by a second sample of fuel mixture owned by the suspected arsonist.

**Practical Work** | **Chemical tests**

The distinctive chemical behaviour of ions and molecules can be used to identify them. You will carry out the chemical tests described below in order to determine the identity of a pure substance or to determine which substances are present in a mixture.

*continued* ➤

Tests will be described to identify the presence of the following ions and molecules.

| Positive ions | Negative ions | Molecules |
|---|---|---|
| $Na^+$ | $Cl^-$ | $H_2$ |
| $K^+$ | $SO_4^{2-}$ | $O_2$ |
| $Ca^{2+}$ | $CO_3^{2-}$ | $Cl_2$ |
| $Cu^{2+}$ | | HCl |
| $Pb^{2+}$ | | $NH_3$ |
| $Fe^{3+}$ | | $CO_2$ |

**Questions**

15 Name all the molecules and ions listed opposite.

## The Flame Test

Coloured light is produced when the ions of some metal elements are heated in a hot Bunsen burner flame. It is the behaviour of the electrons that produces the light, so ions with different numbers of electrons produce light of a different colour.

### Procedure for carrying out a flame test

- Use a platinum wire that has been cleaned by heating in a Bunsen burner flame, dipping into concentrated hydrochloric acid and heating again.

- Dip the clean wire into clean hydrochloric acid then into a small portion of a powdered metal chloride.

- Hold the wire in the edge of a hot Bunsen burner flame and note any colour produced in the flame.

### Results

| Compound used | Chemical formula | Metal ion present | Flame colour |
|---|---|---|---|
| Sodium chloride | $Na^+Cl^-$ | $Na^+$ | bright yellow |
| Potassium chloride | $K^+Cl^-$ | $K^+$ | lilac |
| Calcium chloride | $Ca^{2+}(Cl^-)_2$ | $Ca^{2+}$ | brick red |
| Copper chloride | $Cu^{2+}(Cl^-)_2$ | $Cu^{2+}$ | green with blue streaks |

## Coloured compounds

The presence of some metal ions can be identified by the colour of their compounds.

- Compounds containing $Cu^{2+}$ ions are usually blue or green.
- Compounds containing $Fe^{3+}$ ions are usually yellow or brown.
- Simple compounds containing $Na^+$, $K^+$ and $Ca^{2+}$ ions are usually white.

Fig 3.33 Name the metal ion present in this flame test

*continued* ➤

**Practical Work** | **Chemical tests** continued

# Chemical tests in solution

Ionic compounds have distinctive reactions when solutions containing their ions are mixed with chemical reagents. The first step is to make a solution of the ionic compound in water.

## Procedure for making a solution of a compound for use in qualitative chemical tests

- Always use distilled water. Tap water contains small amounts of dissolved ions that can affect the chemical tests.

- Use only a small amount of the compound. If you add too much, only some of the compound dissolves and the rest looks like an insoluble **suspension**.

- Use finely ground compound as this helps it to dissolve more quickly.

- Shake or stir to help the compound dissolve more quickly.

- Heating the water helps to dissolve some compounds that are not very soluble in cold water.

- For a fair comparison use the same amount of compound and the same amount of water each time.

- An insoluble compound will produce a cloudy suspension.

- A clear solution of the ionic compound dissolved in water can be divided into smaller portions and each portion used for a separate chemical test.

The solubility of the ionic compound and the colour of the solution can help to identify the ions present.

| Ionic Compound | Negative ion present | Solubility in water | Exceptions |
|---|---|---|---|
| metal chloride | $Cl^-$ | soluble | silver and lead chlorides are insoluble |
| metal sulphate | $SO_4^{2-}$ | soluble | barium and lead sulphates are insoluble |
| metal carbonate | $CO_3^{2-}$ | insoluble | sodium and potassium carbonates are soluble |

Table 16

## Safety

**REMEMBER**

**Take care when handling copper compounds and lead compounds.**

**Copper compounds are harmful and irritants.**

**Lead compounds are harmful.**

## Glossary

**Suspension**
Lumps of insoluble material make the solvent cloudy.

## Questions

16 a)   Collect the labels from several different bottles of mineral water. Find out which ions are dissolved in the mineral water.

b)   Does mineral water from different regions contain different types of ions and different amounts of these ions?

c)   Can you account for the differences?

*continued* ➤

## Practical Work — Chemical tests continued

### Procedure for chemical tests in solution

| Positive ion | Test | Observation |
|---|---|---|
| $Ca^{2+}$ | add drops of sodium hydroxide solution | white **precipitate** |
| $Cu^{2+}$ | add drops of sodium hydroxide solution | blue precipitate |
| $Pb^{2+}$ | add drops of sodium hydroxide solution | white precipitate is produced at first, but this dissolves again when more sodium hydroxide solution is added |
| $Fe^{3+}$ | add drops of sodium hydroxide solution | brown precipitate |

Table 17 Tests for positively charged ions.

| Negative ion | Test | Observation |
|---|---|---|
| $Cl^-$ | add a few drops of dilute nitric acid followed by a few drops of silver nitrate solution | white precipitate |
| $SO_4^{2-}$ | add a few drops of dilute hydrochloric acid followed by a few drops of barium chloride solution | white precipitate |
| $CO_3^{2-}$ | add a few drops of dilute nitric acid or dilute hydrochloric acid | bubbles of carbon dioxide gas are given off |

Table 18 Tests for negatively charged ions

**Glossary**

**Precipitate**
Insoluble suspension produced when two solutions are mixed.

**Safety**

REMEMBER

**Sodium hydroxide solution is corrosive.**

**Dilute nitric acid is an irritant.**

**Barium chloride solution is harmful.**

irritant

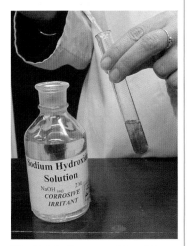

Fig 3.34 Can you identify the positive ion present in this test?

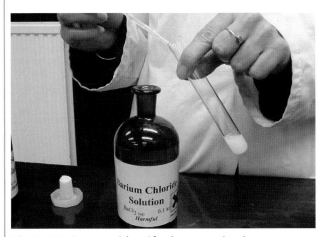

Fig 3.35 Can you identify the negative ion present in this test?

*continued* ➤

**Practical Work** | **Chemical tests** continued

### Questions

**17** A white ionic compound dissolves in water to form a colourless solution. When drops of dilute sodium hydroxide solution are added to a portion of the solution a white precipitate is formed, but the precipitate does not dissolve in excess sodium hydroxide solution.

When dilute nitric acid and silver nitrate solution are added in turn to a second portion of the solution a second white precipitate is formed.

a) Name the positively charged ion present in the compound.
b) Name the negatively charged ion present in the compound.
c) Write the chemical formula for the compound.
d) Predict the colour produced when a small sample of this compound is placed in the edge of a hot Bunsen burner flame.

**Fig 3.36** Which gas could be present in this test?

## Tests for gases

Gases are made up of small covalent molecules. Some gases can be identified by their chemical reactions.

| Gas | Test | Positive result |
|-----|------|-----------------|
| Hydrogen | lighted splint | gas ignites with a squeaky pop |
| Oxygen | glowing splint | splint relights |
| Chlorine | damp blue litmus paper | paper turns white (bleach) |
| Hydrogen chloride | damp blue litmus paper | paper turns red (acidic) |
| Ammonia | damp red litmus paper | paper turns blue (alkaline) |
| Carbon dioxide | bubble gas through limewater | limewater turns milky |

**Table 19** Tests for gases

### Safety

REMEMBER

**Only test small quantities of gases.**

**Hydrogen is flammable.**

**Hydrogen chloride is corrosive.**

**Ammonia is toxic and corrosive.**

### Questions

**18 a)** Which of the gases listed in Table 19 are elements?

b) Which of the gases listed in the table are compounds?

# Instrumental Analysis

Chemical tests can be used to identify a pure substance, or to show the presence of certain ions or molecules in a mixture. Modern instrumental methods give greater accuracy and sensitivity than simple chemical tests. Examples of these techniques are infrared spectroscopy and mass spectrometry. Both techniques can identify the presence of a compound in a very small amount of material.

## Infra-red spectroscopy

Covalent bonds absorb infra-red radiation. The infra-red spectrometer produces a spectrum that shows which covalent bonds are present in an organic compound. The spectrum can be matched against those of known compounds in order to identify the organic compound present.

Ethanol (alcohol) is an organic compound that absorbs infra-red radiation. Infra-red spectroscopy can be used to measure the amount of ethanol in a driver's breath and so determine whether he or she has drunk sufficient alcohol to put them over the legal limit for driving.

## Mass spectrometry

The mass spectrometer bombards a sample with electrons to produce a mixture of positive ions. The ions are separated in a magnetic field and the resulting mass spectrum can be matched to one of thousands of spectra held on a computer database to identify the compound present.

A mass spectrometer can be linked to a chromatograph so that a component of a mixture, for example a banned substance in the blood of an athlete, can be identified by mass spectrometry once it has been separated and detected by chromatography.

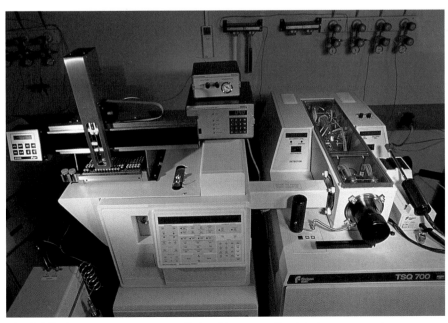

**Fig 3.37** A mass spectrometer linked to a gas-liquid chromograph

# Topic 3  Making Useful Mixtures

Raw materials obtained from the earth are separated to obtain useful chemicals. Some chemicals are used as they are. For example, salt is used for flavouring food and petrol is used as fuel for cars. Other chemicals are mixed together in a controlled way to make useful mixtures.

**Fig 3.38** Most of the products sold in the supermarket are mixtures

Mixtures can contain solids, liquids or gases. The form of the mixture depends on the solids, liquids and gases in it and how they are mixed together. The products you use may be in either a solution, suspension, gel, emulsion, foam or aerosol. All of these mixtures have some liquid present and usually one substance finely dispersed in another. Examples and descriptions of the six different types of product mixtures are given in Table 20.

| Form of mixture | Description | Example |
|---|---|---|
| Solution | a mixture of chemicals dissolved in a liquid | cola |
| Suspension | a liquid mixed with small lumps of solid that are not dissolved in the liquid | toothpaste |
| Gel | a liquid trapped inside a solid structure | hair gel |
| Emulsion | two liquids mixed together but not dissolved | salad cream |
| Foam | bubbles of liquid filled with gas | shaving foam |
| Aerosol | very small liquid particles mixed with a gas | deodorant spray |

**Table 20** Types of product mixtures

The labels on commercial products describe what the product is used for and give instructions on how to use it. The total mass or volume of the mixture is given, together with a list of the substances that the product contains. Safety considerations and hazard warnings are indicated if appropriate. The exact quantities of the chemicals in the mixture and the method of manufacture are not usually revealed to the public. However, these details are essential to the production process when a consistent mixture must be produced every time. Most large companies have their own quality control laboratory to monitor the quality of the ingredients and the composition and properties of the product.

## Solution

Cola contains a gas and several different solids dissolved in water. All the ingredients are soluble so the drink is clear with no suspended particles.

Fig 3.39

> *Fizzy Cola*
>
> Carbonated Soft Drink
>
> BEST SERVED CHILLED
>
> **3 Litres**
>
> Ingredients: Carbonated water, colouring, phosphoric acid, sugar, preservative, flavouring.

Fizzy drinks contain carbon dioxide gas which escapes from the solution when the bottle is opened. This gives the drink its bubbly appearance and adds to the taste experience. The drink contains sugar and flavouring to improve the taste, preservative to prevent the growth of microorganisms, and colouring to give the drink the distinctive brown colour of cola.

## Suspension

Toothpaste contains a liquid mixed with large amounts of insoluble solid to form a paste. The insoluble solid cleans the teeth as the brush rubs it against them.

Not all toothpastes are the same. They all do the same job, but other added ingredients like colourings and flavourings are designed to appeal to different consumers. Some toothpaste has added fluoride to help young people grow strong and healthy teeth.

**Questions**

19 a) Which ingredient would need to be changed in a 'diet' cola drink?

b) Why is cola best served chilled?

123

> ## Toothpaste
> ### Strengthens teeth and freshens breath
> ## 100 ml
> ### Gives maximum cavity protection
>
> DIRECTIONS FOR USE:
> Brush thoroughly at least twice a day.
> Children under 7 should use a pea-sized amount
> for supervised brushing to minimise swallowing.

**Fig 3.40**

### Questions

20 Why is it important that all the ingredients of toothpaste are rigorously tested to make sure that none of them are harmful, toxic or an irritant?

## Gel

> ## Hair Styling Gel
> ### Extra firm
> ## 300 ml
>
> ❖ Holds without stickiness
> ❖ Washes out without leaving a residue
>
> DIRECTIONS:
> Apply evenly through towel-dried hair.
>
> WARNING:
> Avoid contact with eyes. If this happens, rinse thoroughly
> with warm water.

**Fig 3.41**

Gel contains liquid trapped inside a solid structure that is made up of large covalent molecules. Hair gel feels wet and sticky at first, allowing hair to be shaped and styled. It dries out as the liquid evaporates away, leaving behind the solid still holding the hair in position.

### Questions

21 Which of the following points would the manufacturer consider to be important when producing a new hair gel?

- Colour
- Smell
- Shape and colour of container
- Style and colour of label
- Price
- Effectiveness of product
- Purity of ingredients
- Quality control

## Emulsion

Oil and water do not mix; they usually form two separate layers. Salad cream contains oil and water mixed together with other ingredients, such as the protein from egg yolk. The other ingredients help to keep the oil and water mixed together in the form of an emulsion.

**Questions**

22 Why is it important to shake this product before using it?

> *Salad Cream*
> **Traditional recipe**
> 650 g
> Shake before use
>
> INGREDIENTS: Vinegar, vegetable oil, water, sugar, mustard, salt, egg yolk.
>
> No artificial colours, flavours or preservatives.

Fig 3.42

## Foam

Using a razor directly on the skin is painful and may result in cuts and irritation. Fats and other organic chemicals are used to lubricate the shave and moisturise the skin. This liquid mixture would be messy to use and difficult to apply as a thin coat, so gas is used to create a foam. Foam is mostly gas with a thin coating of liquid around the bubbles. It is light, easy to apply and easy to wash away after the shave.

> *Shaving foam*
> **Suitable for sensitive skin**
> 250 ml
>
> DIRECTIONS FOR USE:
> Wet face with warm water. Shake can before use. Hold container upright and release the desired amount of foam onto the fingertips. Smooth evenly onto the face. Shave and rinse.
>
> CAUTION
> PRESSURISED CONTAINER
> Protect from sunlight and do not expose to temperatures exceeding 50 °C.
> Do not pierce or burn the container even after use.
> Do not spray on a naked flame.
> No smoking – keep away from sources of ignition.
> Use in well ventilated areas.
> Do not spray near eyes or onto sore or broken skin.
> Keep out of reach of children.

Fig 3.43

The gas used to make the foam must have the right properties. Its boiling point must be high enough so that it turns to a liquid when under pressure in the container, but low enough for it to turn to a gas when the pressure is released and it is sprayed out of the container. Butane is ideal because it boils at approximately 0 °C, it is not toxic, and unlike the gases used in the past, it does not cause damage to the ozone layer.

## Aerosol

Fig 3.44

Aerosols need even more butane gas than foam. The gas is used to create a spray of fine droplets of liquid. It is ideal when a small amount of liquid product needs to be delivered quickly and evenly onto an area of skin.

> *Deodorant Bodyspray*
> **Long lasting protection with a distinctive
> masculine fragrance**
> 150 ml
>
> DIRECTIONS: Hold can 15 cm from the body and spray.
>
> CAUTION: Extremely flammable. Use only as directed. Do not spray near eyes or face. Keep out of reach of children.
>
> **Pressurised container**: Protect from sunlight and do not expose to temperatures exceeding 50 °C. Do not pierce or burn, even after use. Do not spray on a naked flame. Keep away from sources of ignition – no smoking during or shortly after use. Use in well ventilated places, avoid prolonged spraying.

## Questions

24  Which hazard symbol should be displayed on the product label of this deodorant?

25  Find out which form of mixture is used in each of the following products:
a)  Paint
b)  Aftershave
c)  Tomato ketchup
d)  Hair styling mousse

## End-of-Section 2 Questions

1  Name a method that could be used to seperate the pure substance from the mixture.

   a)  Salt from salt solution.

   b)  Sand (silica) from a mixture of sand and salt solution.

   c)  Water from salt solution.

   d)  Gold from pieces of rock.

   e)  Ethanol (boiling point 78 °C) from a mixture of ethanol and water.

   f)  A red dye from a mixture of coloured inks.

2  A series of chemical test were carried out on a chemical compound, compound **X**.

   ●  Compound **X** is a white powder which is soluble in water.

   ●  When a sample of compound **X** is held in the edge of a Bunsen burner flame it produces a lilac coloured flame.

   ●  When a solution of compound **X** is mixed with dilute hydrochloric acid, bubbles of carbon dioxide gas are produced.

   a)  Write the name and symbol for the positive ion present in compound **X**.

   b)  Write the name and symbol for the negative ion present in compound **X**.

   c)  Name and write the chemical formula for compound **X**.

3  Classify the following chemicals as pure substances or mixtures.

   a)  Rocksalt

   b)  Sodium chloride

   c)  Water

   d)  Crude oil

   e)  Petrol

   f)  Methane

4  Useful products are usually mixtures of solids, liquids or gasses.

   Copy and complete the table below.

| Name of product | Type of mixture | Description |
|---|---|---|
| Lemonade | Solution | |
| Shaving gel | | A liquid trapped inside a solid structure |
| Natural orange juice | | A liquid mixed with small lumps of solid that are not disolved in the liquid |
| | Emulsion | Liquids mixed together but not dissolved |

## Section 3  Properties and Uses of Materials

Section 3 is divided into four topics:

1 Metals

2 Polymers

3 Ceramics

4 Composites

Your Unit 1 portfolio should include evidence that you have investigated the way in which materials behave. You need to:

★ Compare the thermal conductivities of materials.

★ Compare the densities of materials.

★ Compare the strengths of materials of different sizes, shapes and composition.

In the Unit 2 written examination you will be expected to:

★ Classify materials as metals, polymers, ceramics and composites.

★ Describe the uses of these materials and their advantages and disadvantages over naturally occurring materials

★ Know the characteristic properties of metals, polymers and ceramics.

★ Use sources of data to find the physical properties of materials.

★ Explain the properties of composites in terms of the properties of their components.

★ Explain the effect of plasticisers on polymers.

★ Select materials for a particular product given a specification for the product.

If you are entered for the Higher Tier examination paper you need to be able to:

★ Relate the properties of metals to a simple model of metallic structure.

★ Explain the effect of alloying on the properties of metals.

★ Relate the properties of polymers to a simple model of long polymer chains entangled with one another.

★ Explain the effect of cross-linking, side chains and chain length on the properties of polymers.

★ Explain the properties of giant molecular and giant ionic structures.

★ Relate the properties of ceramics to simple models of giant structures and explain the effects of firing clay.

## Topic 1  Metals

Metals have a wide variety of uses and each use depends on one or more of the characteristic properties of the metal.

Metals are useful because they have the following properties:

- Good electrical **conductivity**
- High strength
- **Malleability**
- High density
- Shiny appearance
- Hardness
- Good thermal conductivity

Fig 3.45  Electrical copper wire

Fig 3.46  Steel car bodies

Copper is used for electrical wiring because it is flexible, it can be drawn out into thin strands with a uniform cross section and it has very good electrical conductivity.

Iron, in the form of steel alloy, is used to make car bodies because it is strong and malleable.

Fig 3.47  Silver jewellery

Fig 3.48  Lead diving weights

Silver is used to make jewellery because it is shiny. It is also relatively unreactive so it maintains its attractive appearance.

Lead is used to make weights for scuba divers because of its high density and it's resistance to corrosion.

No two metals are the same. Their atoms have different structures so their properties are slightly different. The trick is to select the metal with the right properties for a particular use.

| Metal | Density (g/cm³) | Melting temperature (°C) | Electrical conductivity $10^{-8}$ ($\Omega^{-1}m^{-1}$) |
|---|---|---|---|
| Aluminium | 2.70 | 660 | 0.382 |
| Copper | 8.92 | 1083 | 0.593 |
| Iron | 7.86 | 1535 | 0.100 |
| Lead | 11.3 | 327 | 0.046 |

Table 21  Properties of some common metals

## Questions

1   Use the data in Table 21 to explain why:
a)  Copper is a good choice for making electrical wiring
b)  Lead is a good choice for making diving weights
c)  Aluminium is used to make light weight cups and plates
d)  Iron is a good choice for making car engines

## Structure and Bonding in Metals

Understanding the bonding between metal atoms and the way in which the atoms are arranged in a metal crystal enables us to explain the properties of metals.

Millions of metal atoms are closely packed together in layers to form a crystal structure that is described as a **giant metallic structure**. Metals have a high density because their atoms are packed closely together. The layers of atoms can slide over each other so metals can bend and stretch.

Metal atoms tend to lose electrons to form positively charged ions. The negatively charged electrons that are lost can move freely around the outside of the positive ions. Metals are strong and hard because there are strong forces of attraction between the positive ions and the surrounding negative electrons. The movement of the free electrons explains the good electrical conductivity of metals.

## Glossary

**Giant structure**
Many thousands of particles held together by strong forces of attraction.

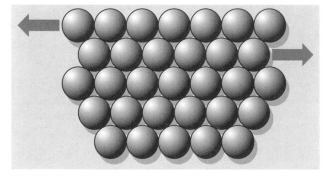

Fig 3.49  Atoms packed together in layers. The layers can slide past each other.

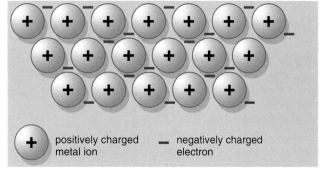

+ positively charged metal ion    − negatively charged electron

Fig 3.50  Metallic structure – positive ions in a sea of negative electrons

## Case Study    Lead

Lead is a metal element with many important uses. Unlike gold it is rarely found as the element because it reacts with non-metal elements to form compounds. Lead compounds, usually lead sulphide, have to be dug from the earth and separated from other rock before the lead can be chemically extracted from the ore. (See Chapter 4 for details.)

Over 400 000 tonnes of lead is produced in the UK each year. About 50 % of this comes from recycled lead from scrap batteries, lead piping and lead sheeting. The rest comes from imported lead extracted from lead ore.

Some of the uses of lead include:

- Storage batteries,
- Pigments,
- Lead pipes,
- Lead sheet for roofs,
- Protective outer casing for underground electric cables,
- Lead alloy, for example solder.

**Fig 3.51** An important use of lead – the lead-acid battery.

## Questions

2   Lead can be used outdoors because it does not corrode in air or water.

   Which of the uses of lead listed above depend on this property?

3   Lead has some similar properties to gold: it has a high density and it is quite soft. People once believed that lead could be turned into gold.

| Element | Atomic number | Mass number | Number of protons | Number of neutrons | Number of electrons |
|---------|---------------|-------------|-------------------|--------------------|--------------------|
| Lead    | 82            | 207         |                   |                    |                    |
| Gold    | 79            | 197         |                   |                    |                    |

a)  Work out the number of protons, neutrons and electrons in atoms of lead and gold.

b)  What changes would need to be made to the number of protons, neutrons and electrons in an atom of lead to turn it into an atom of gold?

*continued* ➢

**Case Study** **Lead** continued

Lead and lead compounds are toxic. Lead is no longer used to make childrens' toys and many anglers now prefer to use other materials to sink their lines.

The modern plumber no longer needs to be skilled at joining lead pipes. Although once used to carry water to homes all around the UK, lead water pipes are not fitted in modern houses and they have been removed from many older houses.

**Questions**

4   a)   Why is lead no longer user to carry the domestic water supply?

b)   Find out which material has replaced lead in the pipes of modern houses?

Fig 3.52  Lead is toxic

# Alloys

Some metals are used in their pure state as elements, but most metals in everyday use are alloys. Blending a metal element with other metals or non-metal elements modifies its properties. The properties of the resulting alloy are better suited for a particular use.

## Solder

Solder is an alloy made by mixing molten lead with tin. Like lead and tin, solder is strong and it can conduct electricity, but unlike most metals it melts at a low temperature, lower than the melting temperature of either lead or tin. It can be melted with a soldering iron and used to join the metal components in an electrical circuit, without melting these components.

Fig 3.53  Using a soldering iron

## Brass

Brass is an alloy made by adding zinc to copper. It is harder and stronger than either pure copper or pure zinc. Adding atoms of a different size to a closely packed metal structure makes it more difficult for the layers of atoms to slide over each other and this makes the metal tougher and less malleable. Brass is strong and resistant to corrosion, so it is ideal for making ship's propellers and fittings for water pipes.

Fig 3.54  Different sizes of atoms stop the layers from sliding past each other

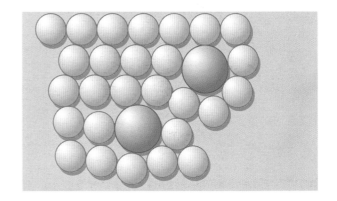

## Mild steel

Mild steel is mostly iron with a small amount of carbon added. Pure iron is quite soft and weak, adding carbon makes it much stronger. With about 0.1% carbon added the steel is strong but still quite malleable, and it can be pressed into sheets or drawn into wires. Adding more carbon makes the steel stronger, but also more brittle.

## Stainless steel

Stainless steel is expensive to make but it has a big advantage over ordinary steel in that it does not rust. It is ideal for making cutlery or fittings for boats exposed to salt water. Stainless steel contains iron mixed with about 15% chromium and 10% nickel. It is the added chromium that prevents the steel from rusting.

### Questions

5   Aluminium alloy is used for aircraft building. The alloy is mostly aluminium with about 5% copper and a small amount of other metals.
    a)  Why is aluminium a good choice for aircraft building?
    b)  Why do you think copper and small amounts of other metals are added to the aluminium?

# Topic 2  Polymers

**Polymers** are covalent compounds made up of large, long-chain molecules. Wool, silk and cotton are examples of natural polymers made by joining together many thousands of small molecules. Wool and silk are proteins formed by joining amino acid molecules. Cotton is a polymer formed by joining sugar molecules together.

Small molecules such as ethene ($C_2H_4$), obtained from the heavier fractions separated from crude oil, form the basis for the production of synthetic polymers. Thousands of ethene molecules are **polymerised** into long chain polyethene molecules.

### Glossary

**Polymer**
A long chain molecule made up of smaller molecules bound together with covalent bonds.

**Polymerisation**
A chemical reaction in which small molecules join together to make larger molecules.

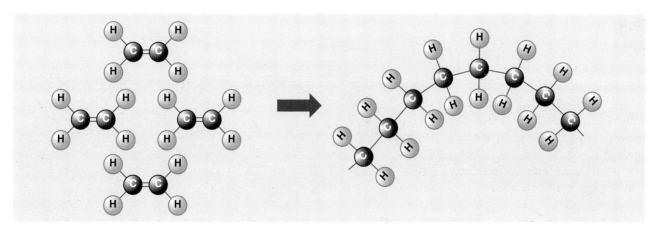

Fig 3.55  Ethene molecules join together to form polyethene

Polyethene is just one example from a whole range of synthetic polymers known as plastics. These modern materials have a great variety of properties and uses. They have replaced traditional materials in many situations around the home and workplace.

| Name of plastic | Use | Traditional material replaced by the plastic |
|---|---|---|
| Polyethene | Packaging | Paper |
| Polyester | Clothing | Cotton |
| PVC | Window frames | Wood |
| Polycarbonate | Transparent roofing | Glass |
| Formica | Kitchen worktops | Marble |

**Table 22** Examples of modern synthetic polymers and their uses

Toys are now more likely to be made from plastic than traditional materials such as wood.

Most polymers have the following general properties:

- Poor electrical conductivity (electrical insulators),
- Low density (compared with metals),
- Flexible,
- Soft,
- Low melting point,
- Poor thermal conductivity (heat insulators).

**Fig 3.56** Most modern toys are made from plastic

## Polyethene

High density polyethene (HDPE) is a typical polymer. Its structure consists of long tangled chains. The covalent bonds holding the atoms together in the chains are strong, but the forces between the chains are weak.

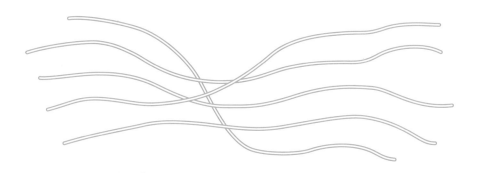

**Fig 3.57** Long entangled polymer chains

The chains can easily move past each other so this plastic is much softer and more flexible than a metal. Polyethene has a low melting point because the bonds between the chains are easily broken. Plastics do not conduct electricity because there are no free electrons.

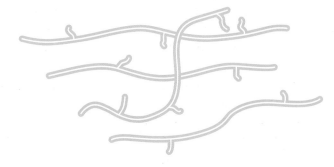

The length of the polymer chain has an effect on its properties. The longer the chains the stronger the forces between the chains. So a polymer with long chains will be stronger and less flexible than a polymer with short chains. The length of the chain can be controlled during manufacture so it is possible to produce polymers with a range of properties to suit a variety of different uses.

**Fig 3.58** Branded chains in LDPE

Because the chains in HDPE are not branched, they can pack closely together. Low density polyethene (LDPE) is less strong, less dense and more flexible than HDPE because its chains are branched. The branches prevent the chains packing closely together so the forces between the chains are weaker.

## Questions

6 HDPE and LDPE are used for different purposes depending on the strength, density and flexibility of the material required. Which type of polyethene do you think would be used in each of the following situations? Explain your answer.
a) Plastic bags
b) Insulation for electrical wiring
c) Guttering
d) Drums for industrial chemicals.

## Modifying the properties of polymers

PVC is a versatile plastic with a wide range of uses because its properties can be modified by the use of **plasticisers**. These are small molecules that are added to the polymer to reduce the forces of attraction between the polymer chains. Plasticised PVC is therefore much more flexible.

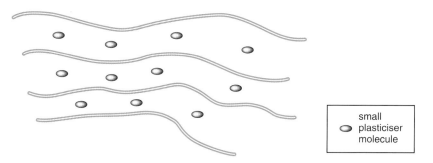

| | small plasticiser molecule |
|---|---|

**Fig 3.59** The small plasticiser molecules reduce the forces of attraction between the polymer chains

Unplasticised PVC is rigid. It is used to make bottles, pipes and window frames. Plasticised PVC is more flexible so it is used to make cables, thin film and footwear.

## Questions

7 What effect does a plasticiser have on the strength, flexibility and melting temperature of a polymer?

## Types of polymers

### Thermoplastic polymers

Polyethene and PVC are examples of thermoplastics. They soften when heated and harden when cooled. There are no chemical bonds between the polymer chains so heating just breaks the weak forces between the chains. The weak forces can reform when the polymer is cooled. This property makes these polymers ideal for processing into a great variety of useful shapes. **Injection moulding**, **extrusion** and **thermoforming** are methods used to shape thermoplastic polymers when they are soft and flexible.

### Thermosetting polymers

Bakelite is one of the oldest plastics. The polymer forms as a rigid 3-dimensional cross-linked structure rather than as separate flexible chains. There are no weak forces in the structure, only strong covalent bonds. Bakelite and other thermosetting polymers are strong and rigid, they have very good resistance to heat and provide excellent electrical insulation.

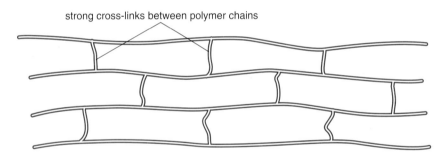

strong cross-links between polymer chains

**Fig 3.60** A cross-linked polymer. This plastic will not melt.

**Questions**

8 Which of the following uses would best suit a thermosetting plastic?
(i) Electrical plugs and sockets
(ii) Fire retardant fabric
(iii) Insulation for printed circuit boards

## Disadvantages of synthetic polymers

The use of modern synthetic polymers has revolutionised our way of life. A great variety of plastics have been developed to replace traditional materials in cars, buildings and clothing. We would find it difficult to live without them. However, our use of plastics does have some disadvantages:

● Some plastics give off toxic fumes when they burn; this can be deadly when a fire starts in an enclosed space.

- Most plastics melt easily so they cannot be used in a situation where they would be exposed to heat.

- Plastics do not decay as easily as natural materials and because they are cheap, they are often thrown away and left to pollute the environment.

## Questions

9   Summarise the effect of the following changes on the properties of a polymer.

| Change | Effect on melting temperature | Effect on strength | Effect on flexibility |
|---|---|---|---|
| Longer polymer chain | | | |
| Side chains | | | |
| Cross-linking between chains | | | |

## Topic 3   Ceramics

Pottery is the best-known example of a ceramic. The production of clay pots is by far the oldest form of materials technology, much older than the production of metals and alloys. The ceramic tiles used on a space shuttle are an example of modern ceramic technology. Modern ceramic materials have properties that could never be provided by a metal or a polymer.

**Fig 3.61** The heat-proof tiles on space shuttles are made from ceramics

Ceramics are inorganic materials with the following properties:

- Very hard and resistant to wear,
- Very high melting point,
- Electrical insulator,
- Resistant to attack by chemicals,
- Strong but brittle.

Some examples of the uses of ceramics that depend on these properties are:

- Lining for furnaces,
- Insulation on electrical components such as spark plugs,
- Crucibles – containers that can be heated strongly,
- Bricks and roof tiles for buildings,
- Cups, saucers and plates.

## Silica

Sand and many of the rocks that form the Earth's crust are made of impure silicon dioxide, $SiO_2$. Silica is a pure form of this mineral. It has a **giant molecular structure**. Silica is used to make the heat resistant tiles that protect the space shuttle from the heat generated when it re-enters the Earth's atmosphere. The very high melting point of silica can be explained by its structure.

**Fig 3.62** The ceramic case is an important part of a spark plug

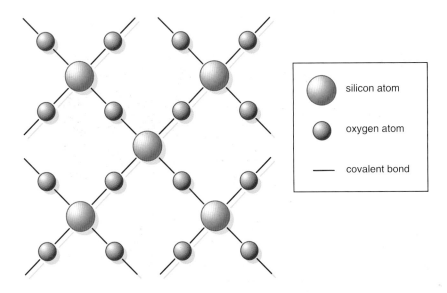

**Fig 3.63** There are strong covalent bonds between silicon and oxygen atoms

The structure of silicon dioxide consists of silicon and oxygen atoms held together by strong covalent bonds in a rigid 3-dimensional crystal **lattice**.

## Alumina

Alumina is a ceramic with extreme hardness and wear resistance. Its high melting point means that it can be used as a material for lining furnaces. The hardness of this material is explained by the strong forces of attraction between the particles in its **giant ionic structure**.

Alumina is pure aluminium oxide, $Al_2O_3$. It is an ionic compound with $Al^{3+}$ ions and $O^{2-}$ ions held together by strong ionic bonds in a giant ionic crystal lattice.

**Glossary**

**Giant structure**
Many thousands of particles held together by strong forces of attraction.

**Giant molecular structure**
A crystal structure held together by strong covalent bonds.

**Giant ionic structure**
A crystal structure held together by the forces of attraction between positive and negative ions.

**Lattice**
A regular arrangement of particles in a crystal.

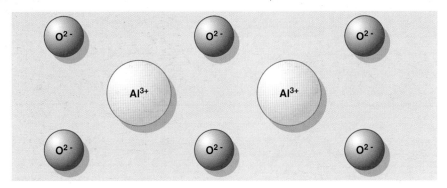

**Fig 3.64** There are strong forces of attraction between oppositely charged ions.

## Clay

Clay is found naturally in the environment. It is an important material because it is very easy to form into useful shapes. When it is heated strongly in a kiln it becomes a hard, strong and waterproof ceramic material.

**Fig 3.65** Clay is slippery when wet, but rigid when dry

Clay contains aluminium, silicon and oxygen atoms linked together in layers. Wet clay is soft and slippery because water molecules get in between the layers and allow them to slide over each other. When the clay is allowed to dry, much of the water evaporates and the clay becomes harder, but there is still some water left between the layers. When the clay is fired all of the water molecules are driven out and new chemical bonds are formed between the layers to make a very strong and rigid 3-dimensional structure.

**Questions**

10 What type of chemical bonds are likely to be formed between the layers when clay is fired?

**Fig 3.66** Ceramic pots being fired in a kiln

# Topic 4 Composites

Materials scientists are constantly trying to develop new materials with improved properties. Using two materials in combination can have great advantages. The composite will have similar properties to one of the materials, but the properties are modified by the presence of the second material.

Plasticised PVC is an example of a composite material. The plasticiser makes the PVC more flexible and allows it to be used for a wider variety of applications.

## Fibreglass

**Fig 3.67** Many modern boats are made from fibreglass

Fibreglass is stronger and lighter than wood. It is an ideal material for making small boats.

Glass is strong but brittle. Plastic is weak but flexible. Bonding fibres of glass to plastic resin produces a new composite material that is strong like glass and flexible like plastic.

## Reinforced concrete

Concrete is a cheap and convenient building material. It is very strong when **compressed**, but it cracks when it is put under **tension**. Reinforced concrete is a composite material; the concrete is strengthened with steel rods. It combines the compression strength of concrete with the high tensile strength of steel. Therefore reinforced concrete can carry a greater load when it is strengthened with steel. Figure 3.69 shows a crushed reinforced concrete beam. The steel rods cannot normally be seen because they are hidden inside the concrete.

**Glossary**

**Compression**
A pushing and crushing force.

**Tension**
A pulling and stretching force.

**Fig 3.68** A damaged reinforced concrete structure

## Questions

11 Find out which composite materials are used to make the following:
   a) Tennis rackets
   b) Kitchen units
   c) Brake pads

## End-of-Section 3 Questions

1 Identify the type of material from the following brief descriptions:

   a) Layers of two different types of material glued together

   b) Shiny with a high density

   c) Brittle with poor electrical conductivity

   d) Lightweight and flexible

2 a) Explain why both metals and plastics make suitable materials for making small containers for fizzy soft drinks, but ceramics are not suitable for this purpose.

   b) Explain why metals and ceramic materials are used to make components for car engines, but thermoplastic polymers are not used.

   c) Explain why fibres of thermoplastic polymers are used to make clothing, but metals and ceramics are rarely used for this purpose.

3 Select the most suitable type of material for the specification described below:

   a) A lightweight and flexible component for a child's toy

   b) A container to hold molten metal

   c) A material to carry electricity over a long distances

4 Use your knowledge of the structure of materials to explain the following:

   a) Silica, $SiO_2$, has a very high melting temperature

   b) Polymers with branched chains have a lower melting temperature than polymers with unbranched chains.

   c) Metals can conduct electricity

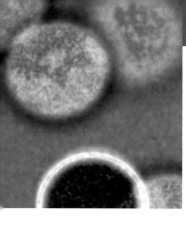

# Chapter Four

# Making Useful Products

**Chapter Four is divided into three sections:**

| | | |
|---|---|---|
| **Section 1** | **Chemical Reactions** | Applied Science GCSE Units 1, 2 and 3 |
| **Section 2** | **Chemical Calculations** | Applied Science GCSE Unit 1 |
| **Section 3** | **Controlling Chemical Reactions** | Applied Science GCSE Unit 3 |

## Section 1 — Chemical Reactions

**Section 1 is divided into five topics:**

1 Writing chemical equations

2 Different types of chemical reactions

3 Energy changes

4 Preparing chemicals in the laboratory

5 Manufacturing chemicals in industry

**When completing your assignment work you will need to:**

★ Prepare pure, dry products using three different types of chemical reaction.

★ Explain the underlying chemistry involved in each type of reaction.

★ Write balanced chemical equations to describe reactions, given the formulae of reactants and products.

★ Explain the industrial importance of each reaction.

**In the Unit 2 written examination you will be expected to:**

★ Identify examples of bulk chemicals and fine / speciality chemicals.

★ Describe how some metals may be made in a continuous process by reduction.

★ Know the meanings of the terms exothermic and endothermic.

**If you are entered for the Higher Tier examination paper you need to:**

★ Know that energy is required to break bonds and that energy is given out when new bonds form.

# Topic 1   Writing chemical equations

## Word and symbol equations

When hydrochloric acid is mixed with sodium hydroxide solution a chemical reaction occurs. Sodium chloride and water are formed.

Hydrochloric acid and sodium hydroxide are the **reactants** in this reaction. Sodium chloride and water are the **products**. Chemists write a simple description of this reaction called a **word equation**.

hydrochloric acid + sodium hydroxide → sodium chloride + water

Reactants                              Products

If we know the chemical formulae of the reactants and products we can write a **symbol equation** for the reaction.

| Reactants | | Products | |
|---|---|---|---|
| **Name** | **Formula** | **Name** | **Formula** |
| hydrochloric acid | HCl | sodium chloride | NaCl |
| sodium hydroxide | NaOH | water | $H_2O$ |

**Table 1**

$$HCl + NaOH \rightarrow NaCl + H_2O$$

The symbol equation shows which chemicals are involved in the reaction. It also shows the number of atoms involved and what happens to them during the reaction. No new atoms are made during a chemical reaction. Chemical bonds are broken between the atoms in the reactants and new chemical bonds are formed between the same atoms in the products. The number of each type of atom is the same on both sides of the equation.

### Questions

1   Give the number and type of atoms involved in the reaction between hydrochloric acid and sodium hydroxide.

When sulphuric acid is mixed with sodium hydroxide solution a chemical reaction occurs. Sodium sulphate and water are formed.

| Reactants | | Products | |
|---|---|---|---|
| **Name** | **Formula** | **Name** | **Formula** |
| sulphuric acid | $H_2SO_4$ | sodium sulphate | $Na_2SO_4$ |
| sodium hydroxide | NaOH | water | $H_2O$ |

**Table 2**

The word equation shows the names of the reactants and products:

sulphuric acid + sodium hydroxide → sodium sulphate + water

### Glossary

**Reactant**
Any chemical which is reacting in the reaction.

**Product**
Any chemical which is made during a reaction.

**Word equation**
A description of a reaction using the chemical names in *words* of all the chemicals which are reacting, and all those that are produced.

**Symbol equation**
A description of a reaction using the fomula of the chemicals that are reacting and being produced.

The symbol equation for this reaction is more complicated:

$$H_2SO_4 + x\ NaOH \rightarrow Na_2SO_4 + y\ H_2O$$

The number of atoms in the reactants does not match the number of atoms in the products. To make it work we have to write a **balanced symbol equation** by putting numbers in front of some of the formulae.

$$H_2SO_4 + 2\ NaOH \rightarrow Na_2SO_4 + 2\ H_2O$$

In this example $x$ and $y$ both equal 2.

You need to know the names and formulae of the following chemical compounds:

| Compound | Formula | Compound | Formula |
|---|---|---|---|
| Ammonia | $NH_3$ | Barium chloride | $BaCl_2$ |
| Carbon dioxide | $CO_2$ | Sodium chloride | $NaCl$ |
| Methane | $CH_4$ | Calcium carbonate | $CaCO_3$ |
| Water | $H_2O$ | Copper carbonate | $CuCO_3$ |
| Hydrochloric acid | $HCl$ | Sodium carbonate | $Na_2CO_3$ |
| Sulphuric acid | $H_2SO_4$ | Potassium nitrate | $KNO_3$ |
| Calcium oxide | $CaO$ | Silver nitrate | $AgNO_3$ |
| Iron oxide | $Fe_2O_3$ | Barium sulphate | $BaSO_4$ |
| Lead oxide | $PbO$ | Copper sulphate | $CuSO_4$ |
| Sodium hydroxide | $NaOH$ | Sodium sulphate | $Na_2SO_4$ |

**Table 3**

### Glossary

**Balanced symbol equation**
An equation, using symbols, which has equal numbers of atoms of each element on both sides of the equation.

### Questions

2   Write word and symbol equations for the following chemical reactions.
a)   Calcium carbonate turns into calcium oxide and carbon dioxide when it is heated.
b)   Barium chloride reacts with sodium sulphate to form barium sulphate and sodium chloride.
c)   Sodium carbonate reacts with copper sulphate to form copper carbonate and sodium sulphate.
d)   Sulphuric acid reacts with copper carbonate to form copper sulphate, carbon dioxide and water.

# State symbols

The **state symbol** tells us whether the compound is a solid (s), pure liquid (l) or a gas (g). A pure liquid is one not mixed with any other substance. If a substance is dissolved in water, the symbol becomes (aq), which stands for aqueous, the name for a solution.

| State | Symbol |
|-------|--------|
| Solid | (s) |
| Pure liquid | (l) |
| Gas | (g) |
| Dissolved in water | (aq) |

**Table 4**  State symbols

Each chemical is shown by its formula and state symbol.

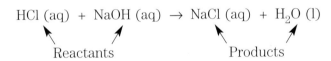

$$NaCl(s) = \text{solid sodium chloride}$$

formula     state symbol

The full reaction can be described using formulae and state symbols.

$$HCl\ (aq)\ +\ NaOH\ (aq)\ \rightarrow\ NaCl\ (aq)\ +\ H_2O\ (l)$$

Reactants                    Products

a) Copper carbonate is a solid

b) Water is a liquid

c) Copper sulphate solution

d) Calcium carbonate reacts with acid to give off carbon dioxide gas

**Fig 4.1**

## Questions

3   Which states are these chemicals in?
a)   NaCl (s)
b)   $CO_2$ (g)
c)   $H_2SO_4$(aq)
d)   $C_2H_5OH$ (l)

4   Write the state symbol for these chemicals:
a)   water at room temperature
b)   ice
c)   methane gas
d)   table salt for putting on chips (solid sodium chloride)
e)   a solution of hydrochloric acid
f)   aqueous copper sulphate

# Topic 2 Different Types of Chemical Reactions

Chemical reactions can be used to prepare new products in the laboratory and on a large scale in industry. Some examples of the different types of chemical reactions that can be used are:

- Precipitation
- Neutralisation
- Condensation
- Decomposition
- Reduction

## Precipitation

A **precipitation** reaction is any reaction where you start with two or more solutions and end up with a solid. You can tell from a chemical equation if you've got a precipitation reaction because the state symbols on the left hand side of the chemical equation will all be (aq) and the right hand side will have one (s). The solid produced is called the **precipitate**. Below are some examples of precipitation reactions.

*Example 1·*

sodium chloride + silver nitrate → silver chloride + sodium nitrate
solution        solution        solid        solution

$$NaCl\ (aq) \quad + \quad AgNO_3\ (aq) \rightarrow \quad AgCl\ (s) \quad + \quad NaNO_3\ (aq)$$
white precipitate

This reaction is used as a test for chloride ions ($Cl^-$).

*Example 2*

Barium chloride + sodium sulphate → barium sulphate + sodium chloride
solution        solution        solid        solution

$$BaCl_2\ (aq) \quad + \quad Na_2SO_4\ (aq) \quad \rightarrow \quad BaSO_4\ (s) \quad + \quad 2NaCl\ (aq)$$
white precipitate

This reaction is used as a test for sulphate ions ($SO_4^{2-}$).

These reactions are important for detecting particular ions in solution, as precipitates make the reaction mixture go cloudy. Precipitates often have colours as well, which makes them easy to identify. Precipitation is also an important way of creating products which are easy to separate, as the solid can be filtered off.

---

**Glossary**

**Precipitation**
A reaction which produces a solid from solutions.

**Precipitate**
A solid that forms during a reaction between solutions of chemicals.

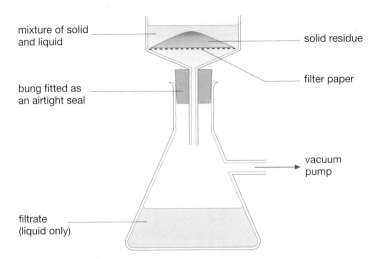

mixture of solid and liquid

solid residue

filter paper

bung fitted as an airtight seal

vacuum pump

filtrate (liquid only)

**Fig 4.2** Filtration under reduced pressure

Precipitates are compounds which are **insoluble** in water. As the percipitation reaction occurs an insoluble compound is formed. This cannot dissolve in water, so it forms solid particles. The solid is formed very quickly, so the particles of solid produced are very small. The particles make the solution cloudy, or can be seen as a powder which collects at the bottom of the test tube.

> **Glossary**
>
> **Insoluble**
> Cannot be dissolved in water.

## Questions

**5** Which compound in this reaction is the precipitate?

$$BaCl_2 \text{ (aq)} + Na_2SO_4 \text{ (aq)} \rightarrow BaSO_4 \text{ (s)} + 2NaCl \text{ (aq)}$$

**6** Which of these reactions can be called precipitation reactions?

a) $KI \text{ (aq)} + AgNO_3 \text{ (aq)} \rightarrow AgI \text{ (s)} + KNO_3 \text{ (aq)}$
b) $MgSO_4 \text{ (aq)} + BaCl_2 \text{ (aq)} \rightarrow BaSO_4 \text{ (s)} + MgCl_2 \text{ (aq)}$
c) $HCl \text{ (aq)} + LiOH \text{ (aq)} \rightarrow LiCl \text{ (aq)} + H_2O \text{ (l)}$

## Neutralisation

**Acids** react with **bases** to make an ionic compound called a salt, and water is produced. The solution formed is neutral (pH7), and the reaction is called **neutralisation**.

Below are some examples of neutralisation reactions:

*Example 1*

Hydrochloric acid will neutralise calcium oxide, a base.

$$2HCl(aq) + CaO(s) \rightarrow CaCl_2(aq) + H_2O_{(l)}$$

> **Glossary**
>
> **Acids**
> Substances that react with bases or carbonates in solution. They have a pH below 7.
>
> **Bases**
> Metal oxides or metal hydroxides that react with acids.
>
> **Neutralisation**
> When an acid reacts with a base to produce a neutral solution.

*Example 2*

Hydrochloric acid will neutralise sodium hydroxide, an **alkali.**

$$HCl \ (aq) \quad + \quad NaOH \ (aq) \quad \rightarrow H_2O(l) + \quad NaCl \ (aq)$$

*Example 3*

Acids will also react with carbonates.

$$H_2SO_4 \ (aq) \quad + \quad CuCO_3 \ (s) \quad \rightarrow \quad H_2O \ (l) \quad + \quad CO_2 \ (g) \quad + \quad CuSO_4 \ (aq)$$

**Questions**

**7** Using the table on page 144, name the salts formed in each of the three equations above.

## Uses of neutralisation reactions

Acids and alkalis are often irritants or corrosive, depending on their **concentration**. Neutralisation reactions are very important as they can turn either acids or alkalis into harmless chemicals that can easily be disposed of.

Many industrial processes create large quantities of waste material which is acidic or alkaline, that need to be disposed of safely. They use neutralisation reactions to do this.

Neutralisation is also important as a method for making many important chemicals. These chemicals are known as salts. As the salt is the only product produced, apart from water, it will be pure but in solution. The water can be removed easily by evaporation.

Neutralisation is also important for use in chemical analysis. It can be used as part of volumetric analysis (**titration**) to find out the concentration of unknown solutions (see Section 2).

## Condensation reactions

**Condensation** is the name given to a reaction between organic compounds that produces water as one of the products.

*Example*: manufacture of nylon

$$Diaminohexane + hexanedioylchloride \rightarrow nylon + water$$

This reaction is easily identified as a condensation reaction as water is one of the products.

Condensation reactions can be used to make a variety of modern materials, including many types of polyester used for clothes.

**Esterification** is a type of condensation reaction that occurs between an organic acid and an alcohol.

The compound made by the esterification reaction is called an ester. These often have sweet fruity odours. Esters are often used in perfumes and as flavourings in food. They occur naturally in ripening fruit.

*Example*: the preparation of ethylethanoate

ethanoic acid + ethanol → ethyl ethanoate + water

## Decomposition

A decomposition reaction occurs when a substance is broken down (decomposed) into two or more substances. Heat is normally used to make this decomposition take place.

*Example*:

$$\text{Calcium carbonate} \xrightarrow{\text{heat}} \text{calcium oxide + carbon dioxide}$$

$$CaCO_{3(s)} \xrightarrow{\text{heat}} CaO_{(s)} + CO_{2(g)}$$

Limestone is a pure form of calcium carbonate. The above reaction is carried out on a large scale to produce quicklime (calcium oxide).

Calcium oxide is added to water to produce slaked lime (calcium hydroxide), an alkali that can be used to neutralise acids. Slaked lime is often used in agriculture to neutralise acidic soils.

$$CaO_{(s)} + H_2O_{(l)} \rightarrow Ca(OH)_{2(aq)}$$

**Questions**

8   Write word equations and symbol equations to show how slaked lime can neutralise
a)  sulphuric acid
b)  hydrochloric acid

Hint: The salts formed are calcium sulphate ($CaSO_4$) and calcium chloride ($CaCl_2$).

## Reduction reactions

Metals are extracted from their ores by **reduction**. The metal oxide is heated with carbon. The carbon acts as a reducing agent to remove the oxygen, leaving behind the pure metal.

*Example:*

lead oxide + carbon → lead + carbon dioxide

$$2PbO_{(s)} + C_{(s)} \rightarrow 2Pb_{(s)} + CO_{2(g)}$$

Reactions involving reduction also involve **oxidation** and are known as redox reactions.

Combustion is an example of an oxidation reaction.

*Example:*

carbon + oxygen → carbon dioxide

$$C_{(s)} + O_{2(g)} \rightarrow CO_{2(g)}$$

## Displacement reactions

The displacement of elements from their compounds is a type of redox reaction.

Iron will displace copper from copper sulphate solution.

iron + copper sulphate → copper + iron sulphate

$$Fe + CuSO_4 \rightarrow Cu + FeSO_4$$

Metal ions gain electrons to form metal atoms – this is reduction.

$$Cu^{2+} + 2 \text{ electrons} \rightarrow Cu$$

Chlorine will displace bromine from sodium bromide solution.

chlorine + sodium bromide → bromine + sodium chloride

$$Cl_2 + 2NaBr \rightarrow Br_2 + 2NaCl$$

Non-metal ions lose electrons to form non-metal atoms – this is oxidiation.

$$2Br^- \rightarrow Br_2 + 2 \text{ electrons}$$

# Summary of reactions

| Type of reaction | Use | Characteristic features of the reaction type |
|---|---|---|
| Precipitation | <ul><li>identification of ions in solution (forensic work and analysis)</li><li>making new compounds</li></ul> | <ul><li>a solid forms as a suspension</li><li>reaction mixture goes cloudy</li></ul> |
| Neutralisation | <ul><li>removing acid or alkali waste</li><li>making salts (ionic inorganic compounds)</li></ul> | reaction mixture changes from high or low pH to pH 7(neutral) |
| Condensation | making nylon and esters | <ul><li>water is formed</li><li>reaction between organic compounds</li></ul> |
| Decomposition | producing lime (CaO) from limestone, used in making cement | requires heat and produces two or more products |
| Reduction | extracting metals from their ores | <ul><li>shiny metals are made</li><li>often needs high temperatures</li></ul> |

**Table 5**

# Topic 3  Energy changes

## Exothermic and endothermic changes

When a chemical reaction occurs there is usually a change in temperature.

When sodium hydroxide solution is neutralised by hydrochloric acid the temperature of the solution increases because heat energy is released by the reaction. This is an **exothermic** reaction.

Calcium carbonate only decomposes into calcium oxide when it is heated strongly. Heat energy is taken in during the reaction. This is an **endothermic** reaction.

Exothermic reactions:

- release energy to the surroundings
- often occur at room temperature
- are very common
- make the surroundings feel warm
- increase the temperature shown on a thermometer

Endothermic reactions:

- absorb energy from the surroundings
- rarely occur at room temperature
- are very rare
- make the surroundings feel cool
- decrease the temperature shown on a thermometer

> **Glossary**
>
> **Exothermic**
> A reaction which gives out heat.
>
> **Endothermic**
> A reaction which takes in heat.

## Questions

9  The starting temperature of a reaction is 21°C. As the reaction progresses, the temperature steadily rises, until it peaks at 36°C. Is this an endothermic or an exothermic reaction?

10  Use the data in the table below to decide if the reactions are exothermic or endothermic.

| Reaction number | Start temperature (°C) | Final temperature (°C) |
|---|---|---|
| Reaction 1 | 15 | −10 |
| Reaction 2 | 23 | 48 |
| Reaction 3 | 22 | 350 |
| Reaction 4 | 25 | 24 |

## Breaking and making chemical bonds

During a chemical reaction, some chemical bonds are broken in the reactants, and some new chemical bonds are made in the products.

Energy is taken in when bonds are broken

Energy is given out when new bonds are made

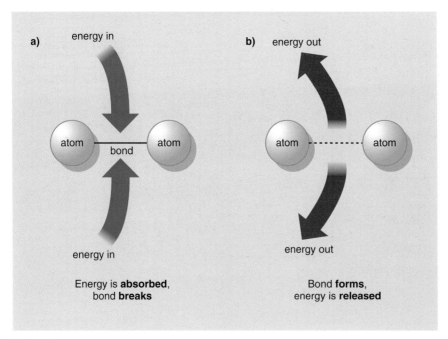

**Fig 4.3**

In an exothermic reaction more energy is given out than is taken in.

In an endothermic reaction more energy is taken in than is given out.

## Questions

**11** Methane burns in oxygen to produce carbon dioxide and water

$$\text{methane} + \text{oxygen} \rightarrow \text{carbon dioxide} + \text{water}$$

$$CH_4 + \quad 2O_2 \quad \rightarrow \quad CO_2 \quad + 2H_2O$$

a)  The methane molecule has four covalent (C – H) bonds.

The energy required to break one set of C – H bonds = 412 kJ. Calculate the energy required to break all four sets of C – H bonds.

b)  The oxygen molecule has one double covalent bond.

$$0 = 0$$

The energy required to break one set of $0 = 0$ bonds = 496kJ. Calculate the energy required to break two sets of oxygen bonds.

c)  Calculate the total energy needed to break all the covalent bonds in the reactants.

d)  The carbon dioxide molecule has two $C = O$ bonds.

$$0 = C = 0$$

The energy given out when one set of $C = O$ bonds is formed = 743kJ. Calculate the energy given out when carbon dioxide is formed.

e)  The water molecule has two O — H bonds.

The energy given out when one set of O — H bonds is formed = 463kJ. Calculate the energy given out when the water is formed.

f)  Calculate the total energy produced when carbon dioxide and water are formed.

g)  Show that the overall energy change for this reaction is 698 kJ.  Is the reaction exothermic or endothermic?

# Topic 4 Preparing chemicals in the laboratory

Chemical reactions can be used to make new products. The reaction usually produces a mixture of substances and the main product has to be separated from the **impurities**.

## Purification of the reaction mixture

The method of purification will depend on the type of mixture and the physical state of the product.

### Separating solids

If the particles of the solid are large, the compound will sink to the bottom of the reaction flask and the liquid can be removed by **decanting**.

However, if the particles are small, they will be held in suspension in the reaction liquid.

Large particles are easy to filter off. This process is called filtration.

Industry uses filtration. Filtration is very useful as it is simple and cheap. It can be used on a large scale quite easily. An example of this is the sugar beet factory in Bury St Edmunds, run by British Sugar. The factory makes granulated sugar from a vegetable called sugar beet. Large quantities of impurities must be removed during the process, which is done using filtration.

**Glossary**

**Impurities**
Any chemical which is present which is not wanted.

**Decanting**
Pouring off a liquid, leaving a solid behind.

**Fig 4.4** Sugar beet

**Fig 4.5** Filtration vats in the Bury St Edmunds Factory

Fig 4.6 British sugar make many different types of sugar from sugar beet

Very small particles of precipitate require a different method. This is called **centrifuging**. The sample is rotated in a machine at high speed. This forces the solid to collect in the bottom of the tube, while the liquid will collect at the top. The liquid is decanted, leaving the solid behind.

> **Glossary**
>
> **Centrifuging**
> A technique to collect small particles of solid at the bottom of a tube. The chemical is spun at high speed.

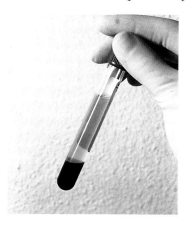

Fig 4.7 Centrifuging can be used to separate blood cells from the liquid plasma in blood

### Crystallising a product from a solution

To obtain a pure product, the water must be removed. This is easy to do as the water can be evaporated. The solid salt is left behind and can be collected. Large shallow dishes called evaporating basins are used. In industry, large pans are used which can be up to 20 m across. These give a large surface area so that the water will evaporate quickly.

Fig 4.8 Evaporating pans at the British Sugar factory

## Separating Liquids

Liquids that do not mix can be separated using a separating funnel. The liquid forms two separate layers. The liquid in the bottom layer can be run off through the tap in the funnel.

Fig 4.9  A separating funnel

### Questions

**12**

| Compound | Density (gcm⁻³) |
|---|---|
| Water | 1.0 |
| Hexane | 0.66 |

Hexane and water do not mix. Which liquid would form the bottom layer in a separating funnel?

Liquids that do mix must be separated by distillation. This method of separation depends on differences in the boiling points of the liquids and is described in Chapter 3.

### Questions

**13**

| Compound | Boiling point (°C) |
|---|---|
| Water | 100 |
| Ethanol | 78 |

Which liquid will form the greatest proportion of the distillate if a 50:50 mixture of ethanol and water is separated by distillation?

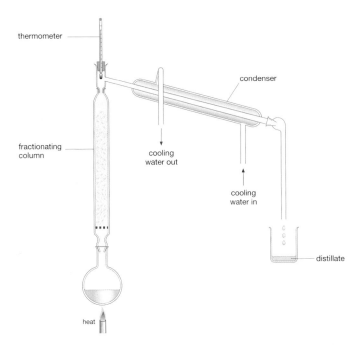

**Fig 4.10** Fractional distillation will give a better separation when the boiling points are close

# Drying the pure product

The method of drying the product will depend on the state of the product. There will be a different procedure for solids to that used for liquids.

## Drying a solid

Solids can be dried in two ways:

1  Solids which are difficult to break down are **stable**. They can be dried using an oven. The typical temperature for the oven setting would be 80–100 °C. The temperature must not be any higher, or there is a risk that the solid could break down into unwanted substances.

2  Some products cannot even withstand temperatures of 80 °C. These are often organic chemicals. A different method is needed for these unstable molecules. The sample is put into a **dessicator**. A dessicator is a sealed glass container which has a drying agent at the bottom.

The drying agent is a chemical which will absorb moisture from both the atmosphere and any substance near to it which is wet.

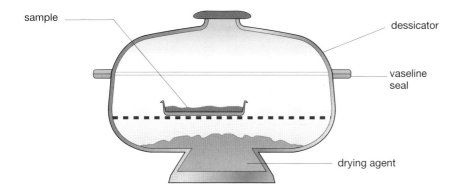

sample

dessicator

vaseline seal

drying agent

**Fig 4.11** A dessicator is used to dry unstable chemicals

The sample is left in an open sample tube inside the dessicator for a week or so. Throughout this time, the sample tube and sample must be weighed regularly. When two weighings which are **consecutive** (one after the other) give the same mass, the sample is dry.

## Drying agents

You can see drying agents packed with some things that you can buy in high street shops. They keep the contents dry. For example in icing sugar a drying agent is blended with the sugar to make it easy to pour. Many electrical goods have small sachets of silica gel placed in the packaging to keep the goods dry.

**Questions**

**14** Find three products that contain one of the drying agents in Table 6.

| Common drying agents |
|---|
| Silica gel |
| Calcium chloride |
| Anhydrous sodium sulphate |

**Table 6**

## Drying liquids

To dry a liquid you have to add a drying agent (see Table 6) directly to the sample of liquid and stir it. As it absorbs the water, the drying agent clumps together. You must keep adding the drying agent until it stops clumping when you add it. The drying agent is then removed by filtration.

Once you have got a pure, dry product you must work out how much you have made. This is called the **Actual Yield**.

## Actual Yield

The actual yield measures the amount of product that has been made. You must weigh all the product, making sure that it is pure and dry first. The yield is usually measured in grams (g) in a laboratory.

Industry produces much larger quantities so the yields are measured in kilograms (kg) or tonnes (t).

1kg = 1000g
1 tonne = 1000kg = 1 000 000g

## Presenting Products Safely

The risk assessment for a product should include all the information on the hazards associated with that product. This information will tell you how best to store it. Some chemicals must be stored away from moisture, while others only require a secure container.

There are some standard procedures for storing any chemical:

1 The product must be put into an inert container (glass or plastic).
2 The container must have a secure lid and label.
3 The label should give:

- the chemical name of the product
- the formula of the product
- the date of preparation
- all appropriate hazard warning symbols.

You may also put your name or initials on the label. It is also good practice to put the mass of product on the label.

> ### Glossary
>
> **Actual Yield**
> The mass of a pure, dry substance produced in a reaction.

# Topic 5  Manufacturing Chemicals in Industry

Industry makes chemicals in much larger quantities than are made in the school laboratory. The quantities of chemicals that are used mean that the equipment used will be very different.

In order to be profitable the company must keep waste to a minimum. All the processes within a chemical factory will be designed to make the most chemical product in the shortest amount of time, in the least wasteful way.

**Fig 4.12** An ICI chemical factory

## Types of industrial processes

Industrial reactions occur in two types of process. These are the continous process and the batch process. The type of process must be carefully chosen to maximise the company's profits.

## Continuous process

The continuous process is suitable for chemical products where there is a high demand, which is fairly constant all year round. The reaction taking place in the plant carries on 24 hours a day, 7 days a week. It will often be continuing 365 days a year too.

Chemicals manufactured on a large scale are known as **bulk chemicals**. Examples of bulk chemicals are ammonia, sulphuric acid and polyethene.

> **Glossary**
>
> **Bulk chemicals**
> Chemicals produced in large quantities, usually by continuous processes.

### *The manufacture of ammonia (The Haber Process)*

Ammonia is made from nitrogen and hydrogen.

$$\text{nitrogen} + \text{hydrogen} \rightarrow \text{ammonia}$$
$$N_2(g) + 3H_2(g) \rightarrow 2NH_3(g)$$

The conditions for this reaction will be discussed in more detail in Section 3.

Nitrogen is obtained from the fractional distillation of liquid air, and hydrogen is obtained from natural gas (methane).

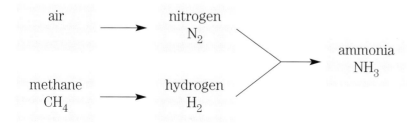

Most of the ammonia produced by this process is used in the manufacture of fertilisers. Ammonia is also used to make other useful chemicals including nitric acid and nylon.

## Questions

**15** Large quantities of ammonia are used to make ammonium sulphate and ammonium nitrate fertiliser. Ammonium sulphate, $(NH_4)_2SO_4$, and ammonium nitrate, $NH_4NO_3$, are salts made by reacting ammonia with an acid.

   a)  Name the acid used to make ammonium sulphate.

   b)  Which acid would be used to make ammonium nitrate?

### The manufacture of sulphuric acid (The Contact Process)

Sulphuric acid is manufactured from sulphur in three stages.

**1**   Liquid sulphur is burned to form sulphur dioxide.

$$\text{sulphur + oxygen} \rightarrow \text{sulphur dioxide}$$
$$S_{(g)} + O_{2(g)} \rightarrow SO_{2(g)}$$

**2**   Sulphur dioxide is oxidised to sulphur trioxide.

$$\text{sulphur dioxide + oxygen} \rightarrow \text{sulphur trioxide}$$
$$2SO_{2(g)} + O_{2(g)} \rightarrow 2SO_{3(g)}$$

**3**   Sulphur trioxide is converted into sulphuric acid.

$$\text{sulphur trioxide + water} \rightarrow \text{sulphuric acid}$$
$$SO_{3(g)} + H_2O_{(1)} \rightarrow H_2SO_{4(1)}$$

The sulphur trioxide is not combined directly with water, as this would produce a mist of acid droplets. Instead the sulphur trioxide is mixed with sulphuric acid containing some water.

Sulphuric acid is used to make many useful products including paints, detergents, dyes, fertilisers and plastics.

## Questions

**16** All three reactions in the Contact Process give out heat energy.

   a)  Name the type of chemcal reaction that gives out heat energy.

   b)  What is done to prevent the heat energy being wasted in a large scale industrial process?

### The manufacture of polyethene

Joining together thousands of small ethene molecules in a polymerisation reaction makes polyethene.

$$\text{ethene} \rightarrow \text{polyethene}$$
$$nC_2H_4 \rightarrow [-CH_2CH_2-]_n$$

Two main forms of polythene are produced:

- Low density polyethene (LDPE) which is used for packaging and electrical insulation.

- High density polyethene (HDPE) which is used to make containers, pipes and guttering.

---

**Questions**

**17 a)** What is the raw material for the production of ethene?

   **b)** Why is ethene classified as an organic compound?

   **c)** Explain the differences in the molecular structures of LDPE and HDPE.

---

# Metal Extraction

The source of all metals is the earth beneath our feet. These metals must be extracted from their ores.

The easiest and most common type of chemical extraction is reduction (see page 150) using carbon.

In rocks and minerals, the metal atoms are usually joined together with oxygen atoms.

Carbon is used to remove the oxygen. It takes the oxygen away, producing carbon dioxide (an oxidation reaction). The metal ore loses oxygen (a reduction reaction).

### Extraction of Iron

Iron is one of the most common metals in the Earth's crust. It is found as haematite ore. The ore contains high concentrations of iron oxide ($Fe_2O_3$).

Once extracted from rock the haematite ore is crushed and is then ready for processing. The process of producing iron metal occurs in a blast furnace.

The blast furnace is a huge tower, about 96m high, which can cope with the very high temperatures needed. It is lined with special bricks which will withstand temperatures of 1300°C.

**Fig 4.13** Molten iron being tapped from a blast furnace

The carbon is supplied in the form of **coke**. This is a form of coal which has been heated to remove any sulphur present. There are small holes in the pieces of coke that allow gases to get inside. The coke is tipped into the top of the furnace along with the crushed iron ore. Crushed limestone, a source of calcium carbonate, is also added at the top. The limestone is added because it reacts with the impurities in the iron ore, helping to remove them.

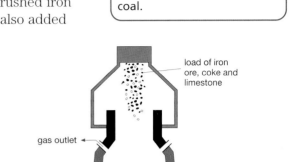

**Glossary**

**Coke**
A form of carbon made from coal.

Hot air is pumped into the blast furnace. This provides the oxygen needed to start the coke burning. As it burns, the coke produces carbon dioxide ($CO_2$). The temperature of the furnace reaches 1300°C. The carbon dioxide then reacts with more coke to produce carbon monoxide. Finally, carbon monoxide reacts with the iron oxide in the ore, removing the oxygen from it and leaving the element iron.

The heat of the furnace melts the iron, so a pool of molten (liquid) iron forms at the bottom of the furnace. Hot waste gases are removed from the top of the furnace.

The limestone reacts with any impurities, forming slag which is also molten. The slag is less dense than iron so it floats on top. A hole is opened at the base of the furnace allowing the liquid iron to flow out.

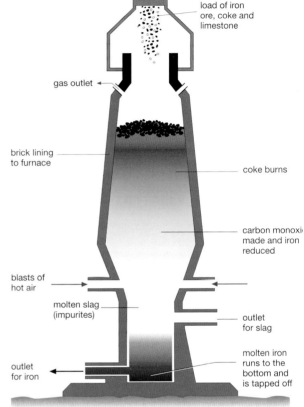

Coke burns: $C(s) + O_2(g) \rightarrow CO_2(g)$

Carbon monoxide made: $C(s) + CO_2(g) \rightarrow 2CO(g)$

Iron oxide reduced: $3CO(g) + Fe_2O_3(s) \rightarrow 3CO_2(g) + 2Fe(l)$

**Fig 4.14** A blast furnace

### Extraction of Lead

The process for extracting lead from lead oxide is very similar to iron extraction. Lead melts at a much lower temperature than iron so the furnace does not need to get so hot. Coke is used to remove the oxygen, leaving the element lead.

Lead oxide reacts with coke: $PbO + C \rightarrow Pb + CO$

Lead oxide reacts with carbon monoxide: $PbO + CO \rightarrow Pb + CO_2$

Lead is extremely toxic over long periods of time, so safety precautions must be taken to minimise the risk of inhalation of the vapour. The lead is also impure so it must be purified. Surprisingly, the main impurity is silver.

Table 7 lists the uses for iron and lead.

| Iron | Lead |
|---|---|
| • Manufacturing steel – the steel is used for making cars, bridges, tools, also used to reinforce concrete<br>• Cast iron – cookware, traditional goods<br>• Wrought iron – decorative ironwork (beds, gates) | • Flashing for roofs (bends over corners)<br>• Cable sheathing<br>• Solder<br>• Reacting to form storage batteries<br>• Reacting to form pigments/chemicals |

Table 7

## Batch processes

A batch process is suitable for the manufacture of smaller quantities of chemicals. There may be a seasonal pattern of demand, making it unprofitable to run all year round. The product may be specialised, for example medicines, and require a very complicated chemical factory. There may be a constant, but much lower demand for the product so that only a few days of operation are required to make a year's supply. These chemicals are called **fine chemicals or speciality chemicals**.

**Glossary**

**Fine or speciality chemicals**
Chemicals produced on a small scale, e.g. medicines, dyes and pigments.

### End-of-Section 1 Questions

1 Write a word and symbol equation for the reaction where copper oxide reacts with sulphuric acid to form copper sulphate and water.

2 Give the state symbols for solids, liquids and solutions.

3 What is a precipitate?

4 Name the type of reaction that always produces water as one of the products.

5 List four features of an exothermic reaction.

6 Describe how you would separate a solid from a solution.

7 Give two examples of chemicals produced by industry using the continuous process.

## Section 2 | Chemical Calculations

**Section 2 is divided into three topics:**

**1** Masses and moles

**2** Solutions and concentrations

**3** Carrying out a titration

**When completing your Unit 1 assignment work you will need to:**

★ Prepare solutions of specified concentrations.

★ Carry out titrations.

★ Carry out calculations to determine the concentration of a substance in solution.

## Topic 1 Masses and moles

It is very important that chemists know how much of each chemical they are using. So, how are chemical quantities measured?

When you use chemicals, you don't measure out 60 or even 6000 atoms or molecules. Atoms and molecules are so small that you would need billions to have an amount you could see. The only way to measure atom amounts is to take a very, very large number of them and weigh them. It is very similar to using flour – the cook doesn't measure out individual grains of flour, they just weigh it out in grams.

### Relative mass

The mass number of an atom depends on how many protons and neutrons are present in its nucleus. The **relative atomic mass** is the important number for calculating amounts of chemicals. It tells you the mass of the atom.

When chemists measure atoms, they measure 600 000 000 000 000 000 000 000 (six hundred thousand million billion) of them at a time. This is a HUGE number and difficult to say, so to refer to this number quickly, they call it a **mole**. The number has been chosen so that a mole of atoms has a mass the same as its relative atomic mass, but measured in grams.

> **Glossary**
>
> **Mole (mol)**
> One mole of a substance has the same mass as the relative mass, but is measured in grams.
>
> **Relative atomic mass (Ar)**
> The mass of an atom compared to all the other atoms, where hydrogen has a mass of one.

For example the relative atomic mass of sodium is 23. Therefore one mole of sodium has a mass of 23g. The Periodic Table gives the symbols and the relative atomic mass of all the elements.

**Fig 4.15** The Periodic Table

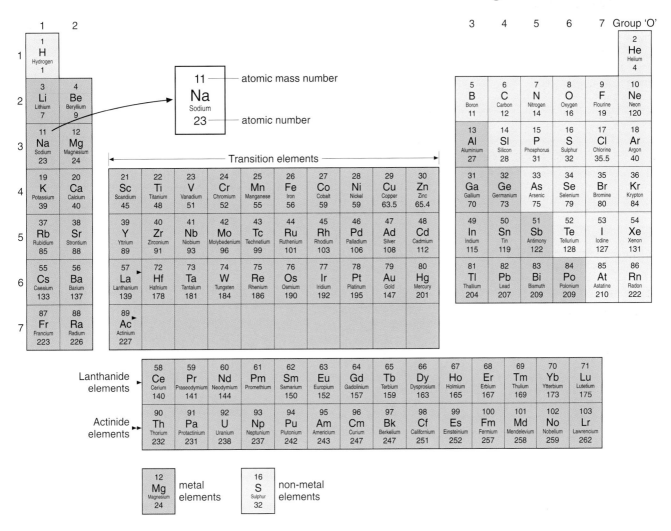

## Questions

**1** The Periodic Table also gives the atomic number of an element. What information does this give you about the atoms of that element?

**2** What is the relative atomic mass of these elements?

a) carbon (C)

b) iron (Fe)

c) lead (Pb)

d) sulphur (S)

e) chlorine (Cl)

**3**  What is the mass of one mole of these elements?

a)  aluminium (Al)

b)  calcium (Ca)

c)  silver (Ag)

d)  phosphorus (P)

e)  bromine (Br)

A molecule is made from atoms joined together, so the mass of a molecule will be the total of all the atomic masses added up, this is called the **relative molecular mass**.

*Example*

The relative molecular mass of nitrogen ($N_2$) which contains two nitrogen atoms

$$= 14 \times 2 = 28$$

Therefore one mole of nitrogen ($N_2$) has a mass of 28g.

*Example*

One ammonia ($NH_3$) molecule contains one nitrogen atom and three hydrogen atoms. So the relative molecular mass of ammonia ($NH_3$)

$$= 14 + (1 \times 3) = 17$$

Therefore one mole of ammonia ($NH_3$) has a mass of 17g.

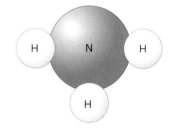

**Fig 4.16** Ammonia

**Questions**

**4**  What is the mass of one mole of the substances containing these molecules?

a)  Water ($H_2O$)

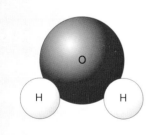

**Questions**

b) Hydrogen chloride

c) Sulphuric acid

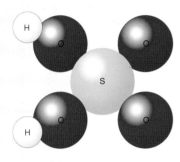

The same calculation works for ionic compounds, but because ionic compounds do not contain molecules we calculate the relative formula mass (Mr).

*Example*

Calcium carbonate ($CaCO_3$), the formula shows one calcium atom, one carbon atom and three oxygen atoms.

$$\text{Relative formula mass} = 40 + 12 + (16 \times 3)$$

$$= 100$$

Therefore one mole of calcium carbonate has a mass of 100g.

**Questions**

5  Calculate the relative formula mass of these ionic compounds.

   a)  calcium oxide (CaO)

   b)  sodium chloride (NaCl)

   c)  sodium hydroxide (NaOH)

   d)  potassium nitrate ($KNO_3$)

   e)  sodium carbonate ($Na_2CO_3$)

## Moles

Chemists measure the amount of a substance in moles. The number of moles depends on the mass of substance present and its relative formula mass.

$$\text{number of moles} = \frac{\text{mass of substance}}{\text{relative formula mass of substance}}$$

*Example*

How many moles are there in 25g of calcium carbonate ($CaCO_3$)?

$$\text{number of moles} = \frac{25}{100}$$

$$= 0.25 \text{ mol}$$

**Glossary**

**Volumetric flask**
A flask used to measure a very accurate volume.

# Topic 2  Solutions and concentrations

## Preparing solutions of known concentation

Concentration is measured in grams per cubic decimetre ($g\ dm^{-3}$) or moles per cubic decimetre ($mol\ dm^{-3}$). The cubic decimetre is the standard measure of volume, but in the laboratory we often use cubic centimetres.

$$1dm^3 = 1000cm^3$$

To prepare a solution with a known concentration we need to dissolve a known amount of a substance to make a known volume of solution.

A **volumetric flask** can be used to accurately measure the volume of the solution. These flasks come in a variety of sizes.

**Fig 4.17**  A volumetric flask

*Example*

To make a one litre solution containing 5.85g of sodium chloride (NaCl). First weight out 5.85g of pure sodium chloride, dissolve it in water, transfer it to a 1 $dm^3$ flask and make up the solution to the    mark on the flask with distilled water. Care should be taken to make sure that none of the solution is lost when transferring it to the volumetric flask.

$$\text{moles of NaCl} = \frac{\text{mass}}{\text{relative formula mass}}$$

$$= \frac{5.85}{58.5}$$

$$= 0.1 \text{ mol}$$

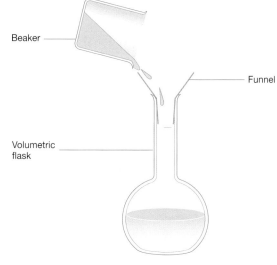

**Fig 4.18**

So the concentration of the sodium chloride solution = 0.1 mol per $dm^3$

$$= 0.1 \text{ mol dm}^{-3}$$

Changing the volume of the solution will change the concentration.

$$\text{Concentration} = \frac{\text{Moles}}{\text{Volume in dm}^3}$$

If 5.85g of sodium chloride is dissolved to make 250 $cm^3$ of solution (250 $cm^3$ = 0.25 $dm^3$)

$$\text{Concentration} = \frac{0.1}{0.25}$$

$$= 0.4 \text{ mol dm}^{-3}$$

---

**Practical Work** | **Preparing a solution of specified concentration**

**1** Weigh 5.85g of sodium chloride into a clean, dry container.

**2** Add this sodium chloride to about 100 $cm^3$ of distilled water in a beaker and stir to make sure it all dissolves.

**3** Pour the solution through a funnel into a 250$cm^3$ volumetric flask. Make sure all the solution is rinsed into the flask using distilled water.

**4** Fill the flask to within a fingers width of the line using a water bottle.

**5** Use a dropping pipette to fill the flask to the line (the bottom of the meniscus should rest on the line). **You must be accurate, so put in a drop at a time when you are very close to the line**. If you overfill the flask, you will have to start again!

**6** Once filled, put a well-fitting stopper on the flask and turn it upside down to mix the contents thoroughly. **Keep your thumb on the stopper just in case**.

**7** Label the flask with the name of the chemical in solution, its concentration and the date it was made. Your label should look something like this:

| |
|---|
| **Chemical:** Sodium chloride solution |
| **Concentration:** 0.4mol dm$^{-3}$ |
| **Made:** 3rd May 2002 |

wash bottle

**Fig 4.19**

## Questions

**6** Calculate the concentration of the following solutions in moles per $dm^3$.

a)  5.85g of NaCl dissolved to make $100cm^3$ of solution.

b)  40g of NaOH dissolved to make $250cm^3$ of solution.

c)  10.6g of $Na_2CO_3$ dissolved to make 1 litre of solution.

# Topic 3  Carrying out a Titration

Chemical equations tell you how much of each chemical in a reaction is needed and how much product is made. If the concentration of one reactant is known, we can work out the concentration of a second reactant which is not known.

This process is called quantitative analysis. It is a very important technique that is used in many industries, from forensic science laboratories to quality control departments in the chemical industry.

This procedure is called **titration**.

## Glossary

**Titration**
Technique used to find out the concentration of one solution, using another solution of known concentration.

## Practical Work   Titration

The aim of this experiment is to find the concentration of a sample of diluted drain cleaner using a solution of hydrochloric acid of known concentration.

Sodium hydroxide solution is sold as drain cleaning fluid. The companies that make drain cleaner need to check the concentration of the sodium hydroxide solution.

Sodium hydroxide will react with hydrochloric acid in a neutralisation reaction.

sodium hydroxide + hydrochloric acid → sodium chloride + water

NaOH        +     HCl →            NaCl     + $H_2O$

*continued* ➤

**Practical Work** | **Titration** continued

1  Fill the burette with hydrochloric acid and record the starting volume.

2  Measure out 25cm$^3$ of sodium hydroxide solution using a pipette and safety filler and pour into a conical flask.

   Add a few drops of methyl orange indicator and put a white tile underneath the flask to make the colour change easier to see.

3  The hydrochloric acid is added to the sodium hydroxide in the flask by opening the tap on the burette. You must go slowly and make sure that you swirl the flask to mix the contents as you add the hydrochloric acid, otherwise you might go past the colour change. The first reading is called the rough titration, because you don't know how much solution you are going to use to get the colour change. **Record the final volume when the colour change is permanent from yellow to red**.

4  Repeat the titration using another portion of the sodium hydroxide.

   This time add the hydrochloric acid from the burette more quickly, until you are within 5 cm$^3$ of the rough titration result. You must then add the solution drop by drop, **swirling continuously**, until the colour change is permanent.

**Fig 4.20**

5  Record your results in a table like this:

   Volume of sodium hydroxide in conical flask = 25 cm$^3$

|  | Rough titration | 1st titration | 2nd titration |
|---|---|---|---|
| **Burette reading when the permanent colour change is seen (cm$^3$)** | 10.05 | 0.05 | 10.00 |
| **Burette reading at start (cm$^3$)** | 0.05 | | |
| **Amount of hydrochloric acid used (cm$^3$)** | 10.00 | | |

The volume of hydrochoric acid is found by subtracting the reading obtained at the beginning from the reading obtained at the end.

Repeat the titrations until you get two results, where the volume differs by only 0.2 cm$^3$.

## Calculations to find the concentration of the sample being analysed

After carrying out the practical work, you should have a table of results similar to those in Table 8.

| Titration number | Final volume (cm³) | Start volume (cm³) | Amount used (cm³) |
|---|---|---|---|
| Rough titration | 10.05 | 0.05 | 10.00 |
| 1st accurate result | 9.80 | 0.00 | 9.80 |
| 2nd accurate result | 10.65 | 0.15 | 10.50 |
| 3rd accurate result | 9.75 | 0.00 | 9.75 |
| 4th accurate result | 9.90 | 0.10 | 9.80 |

Table 8

The second accurate result has overshot the colour change (called the **endpoint**) by some way, so cannot be used. The titration had to be repeated two more times to get results which were within $0.2\,cm^3$ of each other. The average volume of hydrochloric acid is worked out.

$$\text{Average} = \frac{9.75 + 9.80}{2} = 9.77 \text{cm}^3$$

As the results are all to 2 decimal places, the average value must also be to 2 decimal places.

As well as your results chart, you should also know the following:

- The concentration of the hydrochloric acid $= 0.10$ mol dm$^{-2}$.

- The volume of the hydrochloric acid that was used was $9.77\,cm^3$.

- The volume of sodium hydroxide solution that was used $= 25\,cm^3$.

Calculate the concentration of the sodium hydroxide solution.

$$\text{concentration of sodium hydroxide solution} = \frac{\text{concentration of} \times \text{volume of}}{\text{hydrochloric acid} \quad \text{hydrochloric acid}}{\text{volume of sodium hydroxide}}$$

$$= \frac{0.1 \times 9.77}{25.0}$$

$$= 0.039 \text{ mol dm}^{-3}$$

## Questions

7   A solution of sodium hydroxide with a concenration of 0.10 mol dm$^{-3}$ was titrated with a sample of sulphuric acid of unknown concentration. 25cm$^3$ of sodium hydroxide solution needed 22.5 cm$^3$ of sulphuric acid to be added to it from the burette before it was neutralised. Calculate the concentration of the acid using the following formula:

$$\text{concentration of } H_2SO_{4(aq)} = \frac{\text{concentration of } NaOH_{(aq)} \times \text{volume of } NaOH_{(aq)}}{\text{volume of } H_2SO_{4(aq)} \times 2}$$

## End-of-Section 2 Questions

1   What is the relative atomic mass of oxygen?

2   What is the mass of one mole of methane ($CH_4$)?

3   List all the equipment you will need to make a solution of known concentration?

4   What mistakes could be made that would cause you to start again from the beginning when making up a solution?

5   Which measurements will you need to record for a titration experiment?

6   List the three things you must know to be able to use your results to calculate the concentration of an unknown solution.

## Section 3    Controlling Chemical Reactions

**Section 3 is divided into three topics:**

1    Speeding up reactions
2    Calculating yield and cost
3    Getting the best yield

**Whan completing your Unit 3 assignment work you will need to:**

★  Describe the factors that affect how quickly a reaction occurs.

★  Calculate the mass of product that could be obtained from a specified amount of reactant (theoretical yield).

★  Calculate the percentage yield of a reaction from the theoretical yield and the actual mass of product obtained.

★  Calculate the costs of making a given amount of a product.

★  Explain that some processes are based on reversible reactions and the conditions that affect the amount of products obtained.

**Required Knowledge**

## Topic 1    Speeding up Reactions

In a reaction, molecules come close and bump into each other. If they collide with enough force, they will start a reaction. If the collision is not hard enough, the molecules bounce off each other and no reaction happens.

Each collision has an amount of energy. The energy of the collision breaks the bonds in the reactants. If the energy of the collision is big enough, the collision will break bonds and cause a reaction to happen.

Once the original bonds have been broken, new bonds can form. The new bonds make the new products.

Chemical reactions only take place:

●  if the molecules collide.
●  if the collision has enough energy.

The products that modern society relies upon are produced by a variety of chemical reactions. It is very important to control these reactions, so that the maximum yields of product are produced.

The product also needs to be produced in an acceptable time-scale. It is no good having an excellent reaction, making the best chemical ever, if it takes so long to make that people won't buy it. The longer a reaction takes the more costly it is, the more expensive the product will be.

The speed of a chemical reaction is called the **rate.** Chemical reactions that are used to make products need to be fast enough to make money for the company. While chemical reactions that cause corrosion or decay must be made as slow as possible. Chemists control the rate of reaction by first looking at the things that can affect this rate.

There are five things that can affect the rate of a reaction:

- Increasing temperature – this affects ALL reactions and makes them go faster.

- Increasing concentration – this affects reactions involving solutions and makes them go faster.

- Increasing pressure – affects reactions involving gases and makes them go faster.

- Increasing particle size – affects reactions involving solids and makes them go slower.

- Adding a **catalyst** – this can affect all types of reaction, but there may NOT be a catalyst for every reaction. If a catalyst can be found, it will make the reaction go faster.

All of these factors work by increasing the number of collisions that cause a reaction to happen.

**Glossary**

**Rate**
The speed of a chemical reaction.

**Glossary**

**Catalyst**
A chemical which increases the rate of a reaction, but is itself not used up in the reaction.

## Temperature

As the temperature of a chemical reaction increases, so the chemicals have more energy. This energy means that the molecules move faster, so it does not take as long for them to get close to another molecule. This means that more collisions can happen at the same time. Overall, the number of collisions that cause a reaction to occur increases, so the rate of the reaction increases.

## Concentration

Concentration affects reaction rate because it also controls the collision rate. An increased concentration means there are more molecules in a certain space, so the chance of the molecules colliding with the other reactants is increased. Overall this leads to an increase in reaction rate, because more collisions occur.

## Particle size

Only molecules on the outside surface of a solid particle can react. This means that collisions are restricted. When the size of the particles is increased, the surface area of the particle is decreased. As a result, fewer molecules are exposed on the surface, so the collision chances are decreased and the reaction rate is decreased.

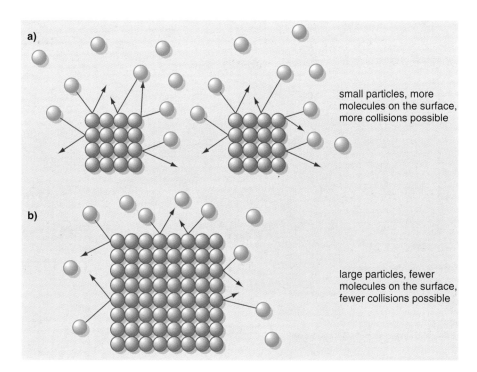

a)

small particles, more molecules on the surface, more collisions possible

b)

large particles, fewer molecules on the surface, fewer collisions possible

**Fig 4.21** Particle size affects reaction rate

Decreasing particle size results in an increase in reaction rate. This is the reason why powders of flour, sawdust and sugar can explode!

## Pressure

Pressure is only a factor in reactions where one or more of the reactants is a gas. Pressure applied from outside the vessel forces the reactant molecules into a smaller volume. This has the effect of increasing the concentration of the gas. As a result the molecules are closer together and more likely to collide, so the reaction rate increases.

High pressure is expensive to create on an industrial scale. It can also be unsafe, as any failure of equipment could lead to an explosion. Even if the reactants are stable and present no risk of fire or explosion, the high speed with which bits of metal and parts of the machinery would explode outward presents a considerable danger. Pressure is generally used ONLY when there is a clear financial and economical reason and there are no other, better or safer alternatives.

## Catalysts

Catalysts work by giving the reactants a lower energy route to the products. The lower energy required means that more molecules will have enough energy, so more molecules will be able to react. Some examples of catalysts used by industry are:

● Turning vegetable oil into solid fats for margarine by using platinum and rhodium (two metals) to attach extra hydrogen to the molecule. This is why margarines have 'hydrogenated vegetable fat' in the ingredients.

● Ammonia is made from nitrogen and hydrogen using iron as a catalyst. The ammonia is used to make fertilisers.

# Topic 2   Calculating yield and cost

In section 1, you learnt about different types of chemical reaction and how industry uses some of them. You also learnt how to measure the amount of product that was produced. This is called the actual yield.

## A reminder of actual yield

1   The product you have made must be pure and dry before you weigh it.

2   Record the mass of the sample tube BEFORE you put the sample in (weight 1).

3   Record the mass of the sample tube once you have filled it with product (weight 2).

4   Subtract weight 1 from weight 2 to get the ACTUAL YIELD.

However, it is important to know how much of the reactants has been converted into products. This can be measured by calculating the percentage yield.

Ineffective reactions mean more waste and less profit for industry.

In order to calculate the percentage yield we must first calculate the theoretical yield.

$$\text{percentage yield} = \frac{\text{actual yield}}{\text{theoretical yield}} \times 100\%$$

## Theoretical yield

The maximum amount of product that could be made is called the **theoretical yield**. Your teacher may tell you what the theoretical yield is for your reaction. It is also possible to work out the theoretical yield using the chemical equation. An example is given below.

### Calculating theoretical yield and percentage yield

When iron is added to copper sulphate solution, copper is displaced from the solution.

$$\text{iron + copper sulphate} \rightarrow \text{copper + iron sulphate}$$
$$\text{Fe} + \quad \text{CuSO}_4 \quad \rightarrow \quad \text{Cu} \quad + \quad \text{FeSO}_4$$

In an experiment 0.56g of iron displaced 0.52g of copper.

**1**  Moles of iron used $= \dfrac{\text{mass of iron}}{\text{relative atomic mass}}$

$$= \frac{0.56}{56}$$

$$= 0.01 \text{ mol}$$

**2**  The equation shows that the theoretical yield of copper will be the same number of moles, 0.01 mol.

**3**  The actual yield of copper = 0.52g

$$\text{moles of copper} = \frac{\text{mass of copper}}{\text{relative atomic mass}}$$

$$= \frac{0.52}{64}$$

$$= 0.0081 \text{ mol}$$

> **Glossary**
>
> **Theoretical yield**
> The maximum mass of a chemcial that it would be possible to make if the reaction was perfect.

**4**   The percentage yield = $\dfrac{\text{actual yield}}{\text{theoretical yield}} \times 100\%$

$= \dfrac{0.0081}{0.01} \times 100\%$

$= 81\%$

## Questions

**1**   Work out the percentage yield for a reaction in which the actual yield of product was 2.35 g, and the theoretical yield is 2.80 g.

**2**   Calculate the percentage yield for a reaction in which the actual yield of product was 375 g and the theoretical yield is 435.3 g.

**3**   A chemist uses a sample tube which weighs 4.68 g. He finds that the combined weight of the tube and his sample is 12.54 g. The theoretical yield is 12.50 g. What is the percentage yield of this reaction?

**4**   0.63g of lead was extracted from 4.5g of lead oxide by reduction.

$$PbO + C \rightarrow Pb + CO$$

a)   Calculate the relative formula mass of lead oxide.

b)   Calculate the number of moles of lead oxide.

c)   Calculate the theoretical yield of lead (from the equation this is the same as the number of moles of lead oxide).

d)   Calculate the actual yield of lead in moles.

e)   Calculate the percentage yield.

## Why might the percentage yield be different from the theoretical yield?

If the reaction worked with perfect effectiveness, 100% of the reactants would convert to products. However, there will always be some chemical loss when the reaction mixture is transferred between items of equipment. Drops of liquid will get left behind in beakers or measuring cylinders. It is very difficult to transfer solids between one container and another without losing any of them.

As well as the practical difficulties of getting a complete reaction, some reversible reactions just will not give 100%. The reasons are complicated, but the effect is to reduce the amount of product you can make.

In general, the more steps a reaction uses, the lower the percentage yield will be, as the effects add up. In industry, chemicals are pumped round the factory to try to prevent waste caused by the transfer of chemicals. If possible, the factory will carry out as much of a reaction in one large container as it can. The biggest cause of waste in industry comes from unwanted reactions using up the product, a kind of chemical 'decay', and reactions that can't give 100%. Losses are often also caused by products that remain in filtering and separating systems.

## Costing a reaction

The difference between laboratory preparations and industrial manufacturing is a question of scale. In industry, any waste is an unacceptable cost and must be minimised. In the laboratory, it is more important to find methods that work, and which can be adapted and modified to improve their efficiency. After all, if you can't produce the product in the first place, waste is immaterial.

Industry must cost every reaction to make sure that waste is kept to the minimum. Laboratories must also keep an eye on cost, as there is no point discovering a reaction which is too expensive for anyone to use.

Once the chemical equation for a reaction is known, it can be used to work out the cost of making a known amount of product. There are four things that are needed to be able to work out the cost of making a specified amount of product. These are:

● the chemical equation for the reaction;

● the masses of the reactants and products;

● a cost for a specified amount of each of the reactants. This is often the cost per 100 g, as this can be recalculated to give the cost per gram.

● Other costs such as equipment and fuel.

*Example*:

Using the earlier example of making calcium oxide, calculate the cost of making 56 g of calcium oxide.

chemical equation: $CaCO_3$ (s) $\rightarrow$ CaO (s) + $CO_2$ (g)
mass of calcium carbonate needed = 100 g
calcium carbonate sells for $2.50 per 1 kg

**Step 1 – Work out the cost per gram of each reactant. Calcium carbonate has a cost of $2.50 per kg.**

$$\text{cost per g} = \frac{2.50}{1000}$$
$$= \$0.0025 \text{ per g}$$

**Step 2 – Multiply the mass of each reactant by its cost per gram.**

total cost for calcium carbonate = cost per g × mass
$$= 0.0025 \times 100$$
$$= \$0.25$$

**Step 3 – Find the total cost by adding up all the costs of the reactants.**

In this reaction, calcium carbonate is the only reactant, so the total cost is $0.25 for making 56 g of calcium oxide.

## Topic 3  Getting the Best Yield

In most common reactions, when you add the reactants together, the reaction starts. At first there are no product molecules, but they gradually build up until all the reactant molecules are used up.

However, there are some reactions where the products can react with each other to re-form the reactants. Both reactions (called the **forward** and **backward** reactions) continue until the concentration of every chemical builds up. Eventually it reaches a point where product is being produced at the same rate as reactant is being produced.

**Reversible reactions** are unusual reactions because they can adjust to the conditions surrounding them. If chemists carefully control the conditions, they can make the reversible reaction work to their advantage. One example of this is the production of ammonia.

$$N_2 + 3H_2 \rightleftharpoons 2NH_3$$

> **Glossary**
>
> **Forward reaction**
> The reaction which is making product.
>
> **Backward reaction**
> The reaction which removes product.
>
> **Reversible Reaction**
> The rate of the forward reaction equals the rate of the backward reaction

## Ammonia production

Ammonia is produced using the Haber process. Nitrogen is reacted with hydrogen to make ammonia ($NH_3$). The reaction is reversible, which means that the ammonia can also break down into the two gases used to make it. This is not very helpful if you make money from selling ammonia However, the amount of ammonia made can be increased by controlling the conditions of temperature and pressure. In addition, removing the ammonia as it forms helps to keep losses to the smallest amount possible.

To make the maximum amount of ammonia, the temperature should be low and the pressure kept high. However, low temperatures mean slow reaction rates and high pressures are expensive and dangerous. Industry has to use a compmise, where the temperature is high enough to make the ammonia quickly, and the pressure is low enough to be safe, but high enough to be profitable. This means that in factories producing ammonia, the temperature is at 450 °C and the pressure is between 200 and 250 atmospheres.

Reversible reactions are often complicated to use, but they may be the only way to make some chemicals. In the case of ammonia, the world depends very heavily on the fertilisers that are made from ammonia, which makes the compromises worthwhile.

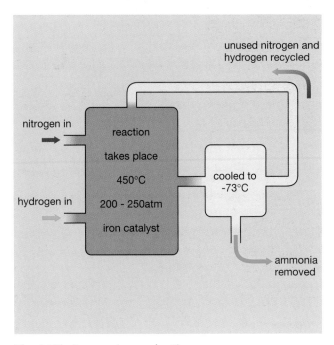

**Fig 4.22** Ammonia production

---

### End-of-Section 3 Questions

1 List five things that can speed up the rate of a reaction.

2 Name one industrial process that uses a catalyst to speed up the reaction.

3 Why is it important for industry to calculate the percentage yield of their reactions?

4 Why might the percentage yield be different to be theoretical yield.

5 To make 8 g of copper a chemist heats 20 g of copper oxide with 20 g of charcoal in a crucible.

$$2CuO_{(s)} + C_{(s)} \rightarrow CO_{2(g)} + 2Cu_{(s)}$$

Copper oxide costs £5.00 per 100 g and charcoal costs £0.30 per 100 g. What is the cost of making 8 g of copper? What other costs might be involved?

6 What is a reversible reaction?

# Chapter Five

# The Importance of Energy and its Use in Instruments and Machines

**Chapter Five is divided into four sections:**

**Section 1**    **Energy Resources**    Applied Science GCSE Unit 2

**Section 2**    **Energy Efficiency**    Applied Science GCSE Unit 2

**Section 3**    **Heating Systems at Work**    Applied Science GCSE Unit 1 & 2

**Section 4**    **Instruments and Machines**    Applied Science GCSE Unit 3

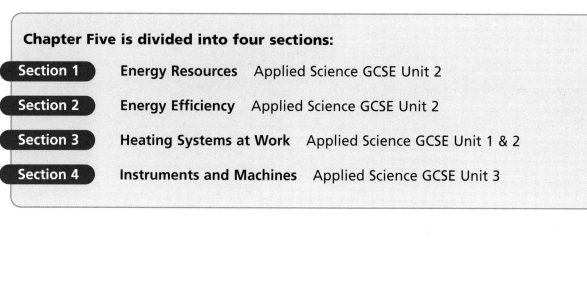

## Section 1    Energy Resources

**Required Knowledge**

Section 1 is divided into three topics:

1   Forms of energy      3   Non-renewable energy resources
2   Renewable energy sources

**In the Unit 2 written examination you will be expected to know:**

★   That fossil fuels (natural gas, oil, coal) are useful energy resources.

★   The problems of using fossil fuels (global warming, limited deposits).

★   That nuclear fuels and renewable energy resources (wind, solar, HEP, wave, tidal) may be used as alternatives to fossil fuels.

★   The problems of using nuclear fuels (problems of radioactive emissions, disposal of waste), and of using renewable sources (unreliability and possible effects on the environment).

★   How, in processes of energy transfer, energy is conserved but tends to spread out and become less useful.

★   How electricity is generated from the burning of fossil fuels.

★   The relative costs of various energy resources (natural gas, mains electricity, batteries).

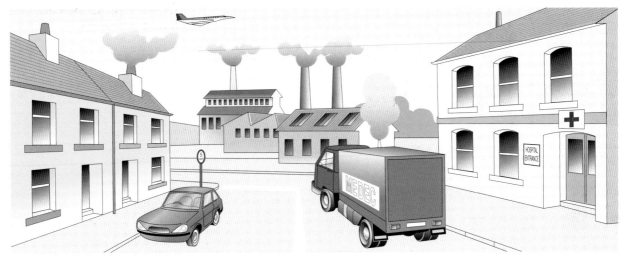

**Fig 5.1** Factories, homes, hospitals and transport use large amounts of energy

Energy is an essential part of our lives. As the world has become more industrialised, our need for energy has increased. Factories, homes, offices, shops, hospitals, cars, planes and other forms of transport all use huge amounts of energy to operate. As our use of machines increases, our use of energy increases too.

# Topic 1  Forms of Energy

Energy comes in many forms:

- kinetic
- sound
- thermal
- light
- potential – chemical
            – gravitational
            – elastic
            – atomic & nuclear
- electrical

## Using Energy

Energy cannot be made or destroyed, it just changes from one form to another. When we talk about using energy, what we really mean is that we have made the energy change from one form to another, or we have moved the energy from one place to another.

If energy can't be lost, why do we worry about running out of energy? The reason for this is because, when energy is transformed it becomes more spread out and therefore less useful. The main problem is that energy changes almost always produce heat, whether you want it or not. This heat usually just spreads out into the surroundings, making the surroundings slightly warmer. It is impossible for us to capture this heat energy again, and use it to produce some form of energy that would be more useful to us.

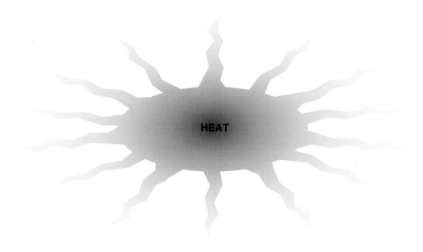

**Fig 5.2** Heat spreads out into the surroundings

HEAT

## Energy Resources

There are two types of energy sources, **renewable sources** and **non-renewable sources**.

## Renewable energy resources

These are sources of energy that will not run out. Examples of renewable sources include, solar, wind, wave, tidal, hydroelectric and biomass energy, and wood burning.

**Fig 5.3** Renewable energy sources

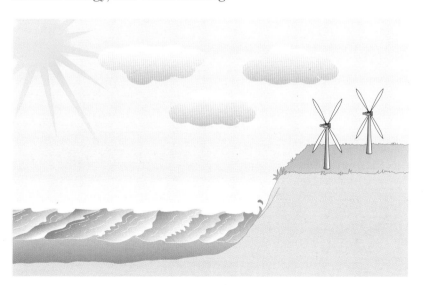

## Non-renewable energy resources

These are sources of energy that will run out. Some, such as coal and oil, are in short supply already, others will last for thousands of years or more before they are in danger of being used up. Examples of non-renewable sources include, fossil fuels (coal, natural gas and oil) and nuclear fuels.

At the moment, we meet most of our energy needs by using non-renewable fuels, especially fossil fuels. As fossil fuels become used up and our use of energy gets even greater, we will need to start using renewable energy sources much more than we do now. We also use fossil fuels for other purposes, not just producing energy. The most important example of this is using oil to manufacture plastics. It would be sensible to conserve the oil we have left for uses such as this.

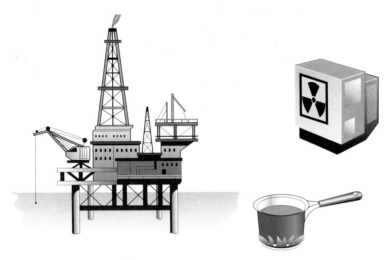

**Fig 5.4** Non-renewable energy sources

# Topic 2  Renewable Resources

**Advantages**:

- Are always going to be available
- Are usually cheaper than non-renewable sources
- Usually produce less chemical pollution than non-renewable sources

**Disadvantages**:

- Are less reliable than non-renewable sources, because they rely on nature. Scientists and engineers are working on ways to store the energy produced by renewable sources more effectively so that unreliability becomes less of a problem.

- Can have a negative effect on the environment. To produce large amounts of useful energy, systems that use renewable sources usually need to be on a large scale. This means that they may upset ecosystems and take up a lot of land that is currently used for other purposes. They can create an eyesore in the local area. Some systems for using renewable energy can be very noisy.

## Wood

Wood is burned to produce heat energy. The chemical potential energy of the wood is changed to thermal energy. This heat energy can then be used to create electricity.

**Advantages**:

- Wood can be grown in many areas of the world.
- Wood is easily transported from one place to another.
- Wood is renewable, trees can easily be replanted to replace those cut down.

**Disadvantages**:

- Wood only produces a small amount of energy when burned. To replace the energy produced by fossil fuels we would need to burn a huge amount of wood. This would mean huge areas of land would be needed to grow enough trees.

**Fig 5.5** A wood burning boiler at Shenstone Lodge School

- When wood is burned carbon dioxide is produced. This increases levels of carbon dioxide in the atmosphere and adds to the greenhouse effect, increasing global warming.

- Burning wood produces smoke which pollutes the local area.

## Solar Power

Solar power can be used in one of two ways:

### Solar Panels

Heat energy from the Sun can be used to heat up water in solar panels. This water can then be used to run central heating and hot water systems in homes, schools and offices.

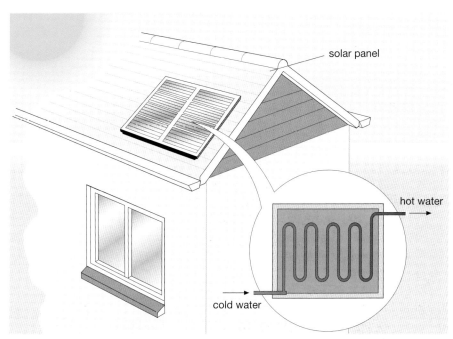

**Fig 5.6** Solar panels are used to heat water

**Advantages**:

● Renewable.
● No chemical pollution.
● Very low cost of heating water once installed.
● Can be used to produce a reasonable amount of hot water in most parts of the world.
● Very simple equipment.

**Disadvantages**:

● Unreliable, if there is little Sun you will not get very hot water. The hot water produced can be stored and used a few hours later, but this is not as efficient as using the hot water straight away, as the water will lose heat while it is being stored.

● Solar panels take up a lot of space.

● Solar panels are expensive to install.

### Solar Cells

Light energy from the Sun is turned directly into electrical energy.

**Advantages**:

● Renewable.
● No chemical pollution.
● Light is changed directly into electricity with very little waste heat.
● Simple equipment with no moving parts so little energy is lost.

**Disadvantages**:

● Unreliable, if there is little Sun, little electricity will be produced. No electricity will be produced at night. There are ways of storing electricity made during the daytime to be used at night, but this is less efficient than using the electricity straight away.

● Very large areas of solar cells are needed to produce useful amounts of electricity.

● The surface has to be kept very clean to work effectively.

● Expensive to install.

## Water Power

There are three main ways of getting useful energy from moving water. These are wave power, tidal power and hydroelectric power. In all three cases the **kinetic energy** of the moving water is used to generate electricity.

### Wave power and tidal power

The kinetic energy of water moving up and down in waves, or moving in and out with the tides, is used to generate electricity.

> **Glossary**
>
> **Kinetic energy**
> Energy that something has through moving.

**Advantages**:

● Renewable.
● Cheap way of producing electricity.
● No chemical pollution.

**Disadvantages**:

● The amount of electricity produced depends on how strong the waves and tides are. Tides are more reliable than waves .

● Very large areas of the coastline would have to be used to produce a useful amount of electricity.

● Shipping could not always use areas of the coast being used for wave or tidal power production.

● Can only be used in countries with a large coastline.

● Involves moving parts so useful energy is lost due to friction.

**Fig 5.7** The Limpet wave power station on the island of Islay in Scotland

## Hydroelectric power (HEP)

Water is held in a reservoir. Here it has **gravitational potential energy**. The water then falls, changing its energy to kinetic energy as it does so. This kinetic energy is then used to generate electricity.

**Advantages**:

● Renewable.

● Cheap way of producing electricity once the power station is built.

● No chemical pollution.

● Usually reliable as long as there is a reasonable supply of water. Some HEP stations re-use the fallen water by pumping it back up into the reservoir.

● The reservoirs can be used to supply drinking water as well as being used to generate electricity.

> **Glossary**
>
> **Gravitational potential energy**
> Energy that something has because of its position.

**Disadvantages**:

● Large areas of land may need to be flooded to form reservoirs to hold the water.

● Can only be used in areas where there are suitable valleys that can be dammed to form reservoirs.

● Expensive to build.

● Involves moving parts, so useful energy will be lost due to friction.

● Most HEP systems rely on the reservoirs being refilled by rainfall so they cannot be used if water levels are very low due to a drought.

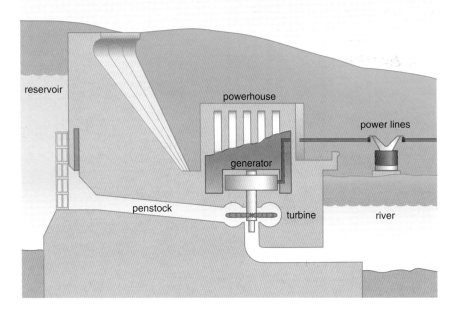

**Fig 5.8** Hydroelectric dam

## Wind Power

Wind turbines use the kinetic energy of the wind to generate electricity.

**Advantages**:
● Renewable.
● Cheap way of generating electricity.
● Can be built anywhere where there is enough space and wind.

**Disadvantages**:

● Unreliable, will not work if there is no wind and cannot be used if the wind is very strong.

● Very tall so they can cause visual pollution.

● Only work well in exposed areas.

● Large numbers of wind turbines are needed to produce a useful amount of electricity.

● Can be noisy.

● Involve moving parts, so useful energy will be lost due to friction.

● Normally built on open ground in the countryside where they can cause damage to the ecosystem when being constructed.

**Fig 5.9** Wind turbines

**Questions**

**Questions**

1   A family is building a house on an exposed hillside in the north of Scotland, and want to generate their own electricity. They are trying to decide between using solar cells or their own wind turbine. Write down three advantages and three disadvantages of each of these systems for the family.

2   You are a member of an environmental group. A company wishes to set up a tidal powered electricity generating system on a beautiful stretch of coast with a lot a rare wildlife living nearby. Write down three reasons why you would be in favour of and three reasons why you would be against the tidal power system.

# Topic 3  Non-renewable Resources

The two most important types of non renewable energy sources are nuclear fuels and fossil fuels.

## Nuclear Fuels

These are materials that can be made to undergo nuclear reactions. These nuclear reactions produce heat energy that can then be used to generate electricity. Nuclear fuels give out dangerous radiation all the time, so they have to be used very carefully.

Once the radioactive fuels have been used, they are still radioactive, this radioactive waste has to be dealt with safely.

**Advantages:**

● There is a big enough stock of nuclear fuels to provide us with all the energy we need for many thousands of years.

● Huge amounts of energy can be made from very small amounts of nuclear fuel.

● No chemical pollution.

**Disadvantages**:

● Radioactive emissions are highly dangerous.

● There is a chance that an uncontrolled nuclear reaction could cause a huge explosion.

● Nuclear waste can remain radioactive for many thousands of years and it needs to be disposed of carefully and safely.

## Fossil fuels

These fuels have been formed from the remains of plants or animals. Fossil fuels take millions of years to form. Coal, oil and natural gas are fossil fuels. There is a limited amount of fossil fuels in the Earth's crust. When these are used up, no more fossil fuels will be formed for millions of years.

**Fig 5.10** Chernobyl nuclear power station after it exploded in 1986

Fossil fuels are concentrated sources of energy. Their **chemical potential energy** is released by burning them in oxygen. The heat energy produced can be used to generate electricity. Most of our electricity is produced by burning fossil fuels in power stations.

**Advantages**:

- Very concentrated source of energy.
- We already have a large number of fossil fuel power stations.
- Fossil fuels are easy to transport.
- Fossil fuel power stations can be built almost anywhere.

**Disadvantages**:

- Non renewable, with very limited stocks remaining.
- Carbon dioxide is produced when fossil fuels are burned adding to the greenhouse effect and global warming.
- Smoke and fumes are produced when fossil fuels are burned which pollutes the local area.
- Burning fossil fuels produces sulphur dioxide which causes acid rain.
- Extracting fossil fuels can be difficult and dangerous.
- Oil has a vast number of other important uses, such as making plastics. Using oil as a fuel means that there is less oil available for these other uses.

**Glossary**

**Chemical potential energy** Energy that something has because of its chemical structure.

**Questions**

**3** What do we mean by fossil fuels?

**4** Name three types of fossil fuels.

**5** Give three reasons why we should cut down on our use of fossil fuels.

---

**End-of-Section 1 Questions**

**1** Write down two advantages of generating electricity using renewable energy sources rather than by using fossil fuels.

**2** What do we mean by the term 'renewable'?

**3** Write down and explain two advantages of using nuclear fuels, rather than fossil fuels, to generate electricity.

**4** Imagine that you work for the Government and have been asked to draw up plans for a renewable energy power station somewhere in the UK. What type of renewable energy would you choose? Explain your answer.

**5** Why is wood classed as a renewable energy source?

**6** Britain makes most of its electricity from three types of power station: nuclear, fossil fuel and hydroelectric.

a) Write down one advantage and one disadvantage of each of these types of power station.

b) Write down one way in which all three types of power station are similar.

c) Write down one way in which the method of generating electircity in hydroelectric power stations is different from the other two types mentioned.

**7** Some people believe that nuclear power stations are too dangerous to use.

a) Write down three reasons why people think they are too dangerous.

b) Other people argue that the fossil fuel power stations are just as dangerous.

What are the dangers involved in using fossil fuels to produce electricity?

## Section 2 | **Energy Efficiency**

Section 2 is divided into four topics:

**1** Energy efficiency

**2** Improving efficiency

**3** Heat transfers

**4** Getting warm and keeping cool

**In the Unit 2 written examination you will be expected to know:**

★ The meaning of the term 'efficiency' when applied to simple energy transfers in mechanical and electrical appliances.

★ The advantages to the user, and to society, of making and using devices with high efficiency, by considering the benefits of low energy lamps compared to filament lamps.

★ How heat losses by conduction, convection and radiation may be minimised.

★ About and explain the use of heat exchangers to enable waste energy to be captured and recycled.

★ About the relative merits of water and anti-freeze in terms of their heat capacities and appreciate why both have a role to play as coolants.

**Required Knowledge**

# Topic 1 Energy Efficiency

Electricity is a very convenient and useful way of transferring energy. Most industries, shops and public services use huge amounts of electricity. Because of this, we need to produce electricity on a very large scale.

Electricity is generated from a **primary** source of energy. In most power stations, the primary source is chemical energy from fossil fuels. Other power stations use nuclear fuels as their primary source of energy. The gravitational potential energy of falling water is used as the primary energy source in hydroelectric power stations.

## Electricity production in power stations

### Fossil fuel power stations

The fossil fuel is burned in oxygen (air). The heat produced is used to boil water and turn it into steam. This steam is then used to turn a turbine which rotates a generator. The generator then produces electricity.

In fossil fuel power stations the main energy changes are:

chemical potential ⟶ thermal ⟶ kinetic ⟶ electrical
(in fuel)    (when fuel burns)   (as steam turns a turbine)

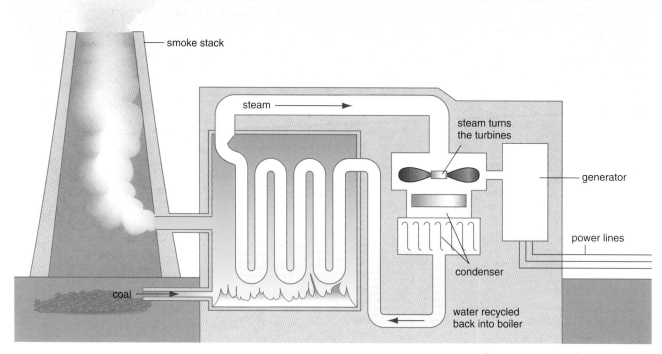

**Fig 5.11** A coal fired power station

Other forms of energy are produced and wasted during each of the energy changes. Thermal energy is produced at every energy change, sound is produced whenever movement takes place. The wasted thermal and sound energy both spread out into the surroundings so they are not very useful to us. There is always a lot of wasted energy in fossil fuel power stations. The amount of electrical energy generated is much less than the amount of chemical energy originally stored in the fuel. Fossil fuel power stations are not very efficient. This makes electricity generated by fossil fuel power stations expensive.

## Nuclear power stations

Nuclear fuel undergoes a controlled nuclear reaction. This produces heat which is used to boil water and turn it into steam. The rest of the process is exactly the same as for fossil fuel power stations, with the steam turning a turbine which rotates a generator, producing electricity.

Nuclear power stations are more efficient than fossil fuel power stations because more of the energy stored in the nuclear fuel is turned into electrical energy. However a large amount of energy is still lost to the surroundings.

## Questions

1   Draw an energy flow diagram to show the energy changes in:
    a) a nuclear power station.
    b) a wind powered electricity generator.
    c) a hydroelectric power station.

Generating electricity from a primary source is not usually very efficient. This means that electricity is more expensive (per Joule) than the primary source of energy, such as natural gas. Batteries are a more expensive source of electricity than mains electricity.

When we use a source of energy for a particular task, we have to think about how suitable the source is for that task, as well as the relative cost of the source. For example, we use batteries rather than mains electricity to power a video camera that we want to use to record a fieldwork visit to the beach, because we need a portable power source.

## Calculating Efficiency

Efficiency is defined as 'the percentage of the input energy that is converted to useful output energy'.

$$\text{efficiency} = \frac{\text{useful energy output}}{\text{total energy input}} \times 100\%$$

*Examples*:

In one second, 60 Joules of electrical energy are supplied to a light bulb. Only 15 Joules of light energy are produced in that time. What is the efficiency of the light bulb?

$$\text{efficiency} = \frac{\text{useful energy output}}{\text{total energy input}} \times 100\%$$

$$\text{efficiency} = \frac{15}{60} \times 100\%$$

$$= 25\%$$

**Don't forget the % sign**

**You must show all working clearly**

If the light bulb was 70% efficient, how many Joules of light energy would it give out in one second?

$$\text{useful energy output} = \text{efficiency} \times \text{total energy input}$$

$$= \frac{70}{100} \times 60$$

$$= 42 \text{ Joules}$$

**Don't forget the units**

An energy change, like generating electricity, can be made more efficient by keeping the energy losses as small as possible. By doing this, we make sure that more of the input energy is available as useful output energy.

**2** Why do we heat methanol with an electric heater rather than with a bunsen burner?

**3** Why do many householders choose to heat their houses with natural gas rather than with electric heaters?

**4** Think of an example where we choose to use mains electricity rather than batteries to power a device. Explain the reason for this choice.

# Topic 2  Improving Efficiency

There are a number of ways of increasing energy efficiency, these include:

- **Cutting down how much waste heat is produced**.
  Because waste heat is usually produced by friction between moving parts, reducing friction or reducing the number of moving parts help reduce the amount of waste heat produced. As friction also produces sound, this will help reduce wasted sound energy as well.

  Low energy light bulbs are more efficient than filament bulbs because they do not rely on heating something up to produce light. In filament bulbs, the filament has to be heated to a very high temperature until it glows white. Not all of the heat energy is converted into light, most of it stays as heat. This leads to a typical filament bulb being only about 30 % efficient.

- **Cutting down on the amount of unwanted heat transfer**.
  A lot of the useful heat that we produce does not stay where we want it. Conduction, convection and radiation cause the heat to move to areas where it is not wanted. By reducing conduction, convection and radiation, the heat energy can be kept where it is needed.

  This can be achieved, for example, by using insulation to keep heat inside buildings.

- **Improving useful heat transfer**.
  We can make use of good conductors to move heat more efficiently to the areas where we want it. For example a good conductor of heat is used as the base of a saucepan so that the heat produced by the cooker hob can travel easily into the food being cooked within the pan.

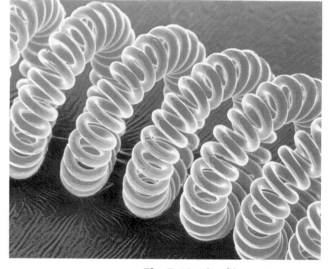

**Fig 5.12** The filament in a filament light bulb is heated to a very high temperature

Heat exchangers can also be used to capture wasted thermal energy and move it to the places where it is needed. Refrigerators use a heat exchanger to take away the heat from the inside of the fridge.

## Heat Exchangers

In a heat exchanger, unwanted heat energy is removed from one area and transferred to an area where it can be used. Waste energy is captured and recycled. Heating the inside of a car using unwanted heat produced by a car engine is a good example of a heat exchanger.

The car cooling system takes heat energy from the engine to stop it overheating. This heat energy is then released into the car to keep the passengers warm.

5   A hotel manager wants to find a use for the waste heat energy extracted from the hotel bedrooms by the air conditioning units on hot days.
    a) Suggest a possible use for the heat.
    b) Explain how you would get the heat energy from the bedrooms to the places where you want to use it.

6   Most methods of generating electricity involve using devices that have moving parts.
    a) Why is a lot of waste energy produced by machines that have moving parts?
    b) In what form(s) is this waste energy produced?
    c) Suggest two ways of reducing the amount of waste energy produced.
    d) Name one form of generating electricity that does not involve using devices with moving parts.

## Controlling Thermal Energy

Unwanted or uncontrolled heat energy is the biggest cause of low efficiency. Heat is produced in all energy changes. Usually this heat is unwanted and just spreads into the surroundings. This heat cannot easily be captured or converted into another, more useful form of energy.

If the transfer of heat can be improved more heat could be transfered to where we want it and less heat allowed to escape into the surroundings.

Before this is possible, we need to understand how heat energy moves from one place to another.

# Topic 3  Heat Transfer

There are three ways that heat can move from one place to another, in other words there are three **transfer mechanisms**. These are: **conduction**, **convection** and **radiation**.

These three mechanisms of heat transfer are all very different from each other. Before we can control heat transfer effectively, we need to know which of the three mechanisms we are trying to control.

## Conduction

This is when heat is passed from molecule to molecule through a material. The molecules with heat energy become more active, as they vibrate they bump into each other and pass the heat energy on. Because molecules need to be close together for this to happen, conduction works best in solids. Gases are poor conductors because the molecules are so far apart.

**Glossary**

**Transfer mechanisms**
Transfer mechanisms are conduction, convection and radiation.

**Conduction**
The transfer of heat energy through a material by vibration or movement of free electrons.

**Convection**
The transfer of heat energy in a liquid or gas, caused by differences in density.

**Radiation**
The transfer of heat energy through space.

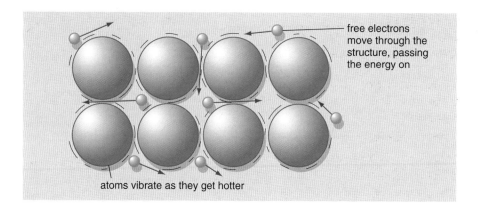

free electrons move through the structure, passing the energy on

atoms vibrate as they get hotter

**Fig 5.13** Energy is conducted by vibration and electrons moving through the material

**Free electrons** also help heat conduction. Metals have electrons that are free to move. The hotter the metal, the more energy these electrons have, and the quicker they move throughout the metal. The electrons also bump into each other, passing the energy on. This is why metals are better conductors of heat than non-metals are.

Conduction is a very slow process compared with convection and radiation. Poor conductors of heat, such as wood and plastic, are called insulators.

## Using conduction

Heat can travel easily through good conductors. Good conductors can therefore be used to move heat from one place to another. For example, the casing of a central heating radiator has to be made of a good conductor so that the heat energy carried by the hot water inside the radiator, can travel easily through the radiator casing and into the room.

Good insulators can be used when it is necessary to keep heat inside an object, or when we want to stop heat entering something. For example, clothes are made out of good insulators so that the heat in our body does not escape easily. The outsides of refrigerators are made out of good insulators to stop heat from the surroundings getting into the fridge and warming up the food inside.

> **Glossary**
>
> **Free electrons**
> The electrons in metals that are free to move through the metal.

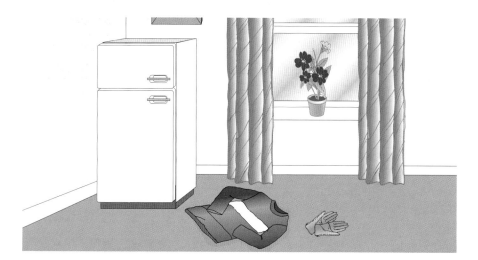

**Fig 5.14** All these things are good insulators

## Questions

**7** Some of the following items should be made out of good conductors, others should be made out of good insulators. Sort the items in the list into two lists, one list of items that should be made from good conductors, and the second list of items that should be made from good insulators.

**slippers**    **handle of a saucepan**    **blankets**    **curtains**
**outside of an oven**    **baseplate of an iron**    **electric cooker ring**
**filament of a light bulb**    **carpet**    **teapot**

**8** In both hot and cold countries, the outsides of houses should be made out of good insulators.
 a) Explain why houses should be built out of good insulators in cold countries.
 b) Explain why houses should be built out of good insulators in hot countries.

**9** Both glass and air are poor conductors of heat. Use these facts to explain why very little heat is lost by conduction through double glazed windows.

**10** Sally says that a hot water bottle should be made from a good conductor of heat. Imran says that Sally is wrong, hot water bottles should be made out of good heat insulators.

 Explain why both Sally and Imran are partly correct.

## Convection

In convection, molecules with heat energy move through the material, carrying the heat energy with them. Because the molecules have to move around, convection cannot happen in solids, where the molecules are fixed in one position. Convection only occurs in liquids and gases.

Convection usually transfers heat faster than conduction does.

When a liquid or a gas is heated it expands. This makes the heated part less dense, so it rises above the more dense, colder parts of the liquid. This heated part then gradually loses its energy, becomes cooler and more dense, and falls back downwards. Other parts of the liquid that have been heated will now be less dense and will rise. A cycle of rising and falling will be set up, these are called **convection currents**. In convection currents, hot fluids rise and cold fluids fall.

This is NOT the same as saying 'heat rises', which is wrong. When heat is transferred by either conduction or radiation it does not rise. It is equally likely to travel in any direction, depending on which materials it has to travel through.

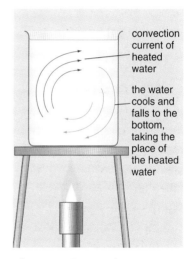

**Fig 5.15** Convection currents in a beaker of water

convection current of heated water

the water cools and falls to the bottom, taking the place of the heated water

### Glossary

**Convection current**
A cycle of rising and falling fluids caused by convection.

## Using convection

Good use can be made of convection currents to move heat energy upwards from a heat source. For example, a single electric heater uses convection to heat a whole room.

The fact that cold air falls is used in fridges. A single cooling unit near the top of a fridge can cool the entire fridge.

### Questions

**11** Use what you know about convection to explain the following:

a) The heating element of an electric kettle is placed near the bottom of the kettle.

b) Air conditioning units, used to cool down rooms, are placed high up on the walls of the room.

c) If you are caught in a smoke filled room you are advised to crawl, rather than walk, out of the room.

**12** A simplified diagram of a hot water tank is shown below. Cold water enters the tank through pipe A. The heater then heats up the water. Hot water leaves the tank through pipe B.

a) Copy the diagram and draw arrows to show the convection currents in the water when the heater is switched on.

b) Explain the following:

i) Pipe A has to be at the bottom of the tank.

ii) Pipe B has to be at the top of the tank.

c) Describe what would happen if a plumber connected the pipes wrongly so that the cold water came in through pipe B and the heated water left the tank through pipe A.

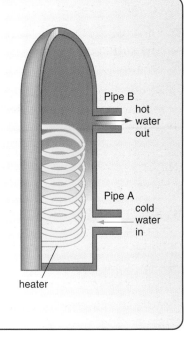

Pipe B
hot water out

Pipe A
cold water in

heater

## Radiation

All surfaces that are hotter than their surroundings give out heat radiation. The hotter the object is the more radiation it emits. Unlike conduction and convection, radiation does not involve moving particles. Instead this heat energy travels in the form of waves of **infra-red** radiation. When these waves hit a surface they are either absorbed or reflected. Any surface that absorbs radiation gets hotter, and the more it absorbs the hotter it gets. Surfaces that reflect radiation, do not absorb any heat.

In real life, most surfaces will absorb some of the heat radiation that falls on them and reflect the rest.

There are three factors that decide how much heat radiation a surface will absorb:

- the colour of the surface,
- the surface area,
- how cool the surface is.

Good absorbers of heat radiation are black and dull, have large surface areas, and are much cooler than their surroundings.

Light, shiny surfaces are good reflectors of heat radiation. Most of the heat radiation that falls on them will be reflected away, so they will not become much hotter.

Objects that are already hot will not absorb heat energy as easily as cooler objects.

Some objects are better at emitting heat radiation than others. Good emitters of heat radiation lose heat easily so they will become cold more quickly than poor emitters.

### Glossary

**Infra-red**
Heat radiation that travels at the speed of light.

There are three factors which decide whether an object will be a good emitter of heat radiation:

- the colour of the surface,
- the surface area,
- how hot the surface is.

Good emitters of heat radiation, are dark and dull, have a large surface area, and are much hotter than their surroundings.

Light, shiny surfaces do not emit heat radiation well. They retain their heat energy better than good emitters do.

Heat radiation travels best through materials where the molecules are well spread out. Infra-red radiation travels better through gases, than through liquids or solids. Radiation is the only way heat energy can travel through a vacuum.

Getting heat energy from the Sun is a good example of heat radiation. Radiation from the Sun travels across space to the Earth. When it reaches the atmosphere some of the radiation is reflected back into space. The rest is absorbed by the atmosphere and heats the Earth.

**Fig 5.16**

## Questions

**13** Which would be better at keeping tea hot, a dull brown teapot or a shiny white teapot? Explain your answer.

**14** An Eskimo decides to paint the outside of his igloo black. Explain why this is not a good idea.

**15** Explain why it is usually better to wear light coloured clothes, rather than dark coloured clothes, in hot weather.

**16** John has one radiator in his bedroom. He says that his bedroom would be warmer if he painted the walls white. Saira says that he is wrong. She thinks he should paint the walls black. Who do you think is right? Explain your answer.

**17** The cooling system in a car uses water in cooling pipes to remove heat from the car's engine. This heat then warms up the water in the cooling pipes. The water has to cool down again by losing some of its heat, before it is pumped back to the engine.
   a) Give two reasons why the pipes in the cooling system are painted black.
   b) Suggest how the heat energy given out by the cooling pipes could be put to use, rather than just wasted.

# Topic 4  Getting Warm and Keeping Cool

How easily something heats up or cools down doesn't just depend on how good the material is at carrying heat. It also depends on the **specific heat capacity** of the material.

The specific heat capacity of a material tells you how many Joules of energy are needed to change the temperature of one kilogram of the material by one degree Celsius.

Materials with high specific heat capacities are difficult to heat up. They take in a lot of heat energy before getting hot themselves. These materials are also good at storing heat. They cool down slowly, giving out a lot of heat energy to their surroundings before becoming cool themselves.

## Glossary

**Specific heat capacity**
The number of joules required to change the temperature of one kilogram of material by one degree Celcius.

Water has a very high specific heat capacity. It takes a lot of heat energy to warm the water up, but once hot the water cools down slowly.

Metals have low specific heat capacities. This is why metals get hot easily and cool down quickly. Not all metals have the same value of specific heat capacity. The specific heat capacity of aluminium is about three times greater than the specific heat capacity of brass.

The main uses of materials with high specific heat capacities include:

● **Cooling systems**

For example, the cooling system in a car that prevents the engine overheating. The cooling system needs to take in a lot of heat energy from the engine to keep it as cool as possible. If the water in the cooling system became hot easily it would soon be too hot to take much energy away from the engine. If this happened the engine could not be cooled and it would soon overheat.

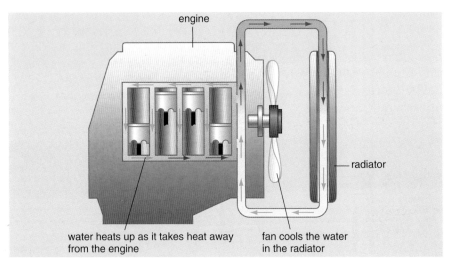

**Fig 5.17** A car cooling system uses cold water to cool the engine

● **Heat storage systems**

A good example of this is the use of electrical night storage heaters. These are basically slabs of concrete which are heated at night using low-cost, off-peak electricity. During the day, when heat is needed, the storage heaters give out their heat energy gradually and warm the surroundings. Concrete has a high specific heat capacity. If it did not, the heat would be given out too quickly, so there would be no heat energy left to give out later in the day.

The high specific heat capacity of water makes it very good to use in most heating and cooling systems. However, one of the problems with water is that it has quite a high freezing point, of 0 °C. This means that it cannot be pumped around cooling systems when it is at a temperature of zero degrees Celsius or less. This is a problem with car cooling systems. Cars still need to be driven when the outside temperature is below zero. At these temperatures the water in the car's cooling system would have turned to ice, but the engine would still need to be cooled. This problem is avoided by adding anti-freeze to the water. This lowers the freezing point of water, sometimes to as low as −15 °C. This means that the engine cooling system will still work in very cold weather.

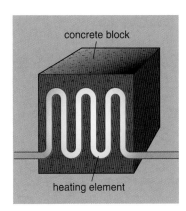

**Fig 5.18** Electrical night storage heaters use concrete slabs that are heated at night and then gradually release this heat during the day

However the problem with using anti-freeze is that it lowers the specific heat capacity of water. This means that the water will not remove heat from the engine as well as pure water would.

Another problem with water is that it has a low boiling point. In a car cooling system, the water in the system may need to get hotter than 100 °C. This problem is solved by having a pressure cap fitted on the car radiator. The extra pressure that this causes within the cooling system, raises the boiling point of the water to well above 100 °C.

## Questions

**18** Should a liquid used in a cooling system have a high or low specific heat capacity? Explain your answer.

**19** One of the reasons that water is used in the radiators of domestic central heating systems is that it has a very high specific heat capacity. Why is this an advantage?

**20** John wants to install an underground heating system under the floor in his house. He is going to use a series of pipes with hot liquid pumped through them. He cannot decide whether to use oil or water in the pipes. Use the data in the table below to comment on the advantages and disadvantages of each liquid.

|  | Oil | Water |
|---|---|---|
| specific heat capacity (J/kg/°C) | 2300 | 4200 |
| freezing point (°C) | −20 | 0 |

## End-of-Section 2 Questions

**1** Convection can only happen when fluids have room to move. Use this fact to explain why heat cannot travel easily through a double glazed window by convection.

**2** More heat is lost from the roof of an uninsulated house than from any other part of the house. Using ideas about conduction, convection and radiation, explain why this is so.

**3** Vacuum flasks have been used for many years to keep hot drinks hot an cold drinks cold. A diagram of a vacuum flask is shown below.

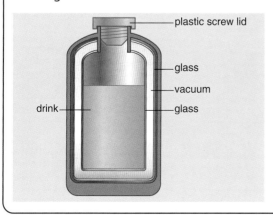

**a)** Name one feature of the flask that stops heat entering or leaving the flask by conduction. Explain how it works.

**b)** Name one feature of the flask that stops heat entering or leaving the flask by convection. Explain how it works.

**c)** Name one feature of the flask that stops heat entering or leaving the flask by radiation. Explain how it works.

**4** Loft insulation is often made from loose fibreglass with lots of small air pockets trapped between the fibres.

**a)** Explain how this trapped air makes it difficult for heat energy to be transferred by both conduction and convection.

**b)** What colour should the fibreglass be to best stop heat transfer by radiation?

**5** What do we mean by a 'heat exchanger'? Give an example of a heat exchanger being used. Explain why it is needed.

**6** Draw an energy flow diagram for each of the following methods of generating electricity:

a)  solar cells,

b)  tidal powered generator,

c)  wood burning generator.

**7** Which material is it easier to make hotter, one with a high specific heat capacity or one with a low specific heat capacity?

**8** Explain why water at 100 °C can give you a worse burn than the same mass of oil at 100 °C.

| Section 3 | **Heating Systems at Work** |
| --- | --- |

**Section 3 is devided into four topics:**

**1**  How electrical circuits work    **3**  Power

**2**  Electrical components    **4**  Paying for electricity

**Your unit 1 portfolio should include evidence that you have investigated how:**

★ The nature, length and thickness of materials influence electrical resistance.

★ Current varies with voltage in a range of devices.

**In the Unit 2 written examination you will be expected to know:**

★ The formula: **power = (voltage × current)**. And to use this formula to calculate the power of an electrical circuit.

★ How to carry out simple calculations using the formula **power = energy/time** to calculate power in watts (W) and to calculate the energy usage in kilowatt-hours (kWh) for electrical appliances.

★ How to compare the costs of using different electrical appliances.

*Required Knowledge*

## Topic 1  How electrical circuits work

Electricity is the movement of electrical charge around a circuit. Voltage and current tell you different things about what makes the charges move and how it moves arounds the circuit.

### Voltage

The charges in a material need to be given energy if they are to move around a circuit. A power supply, batteries or mains power, provide this energy. The voltage of the supply is a measure of how much energy each unit of charge is given.

The energy given to the charges has to be used up by the time the charges get back to the power supply. The charges use their energy in passing through the components in a circuit.

If there is more than one component in a **series circuit**, the energy available, and the supply voltage, will be shared between the components.

The bigger the resistance of a component, the greater the share of the available energy it uses. This means that it gets a bigger share of the supply voltage too.

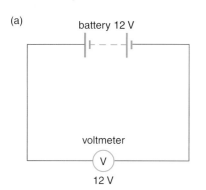

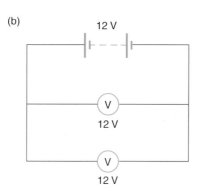

**Fig 5.19**

In a **parallel circuit**, each arm of the circuit will get the full supply of voltage (Figure 5.19).

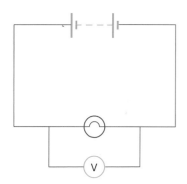

**Fig 5.20**

A voltmeter is used to measure the voltage across a component. It is placed in parallel with the component (Figure 5.20).

The symbol for voltage is V. The unit in which voltage is measured is the Volt (V). In Britain, the mains voltage is 230 Volts.

# Current

**Current** tells you how many units of charge pass a given point in a circuit in one second.

This depends on two things:

● how many charges are moving in the circuit,
● how fast the charges are moving.

The number of charges moving in the circuit is usually fixed for a given circuit. It is decided by the components in the circuit. Unless your circuit contains semiconductors, such as thermistors and LEDs, the number of charges moving in a circuit will not change unless you change the components in the circuit.

If the current in a circuit changes, it is usually because the charges are moving faster or slower. The speed of the charges depends on two things:

● the resistance of the components in the circuit,
● the supply voltage.

So, between them, the supply voltage and the resistance decide how big the current is. The greater the resistance the harder it is for the charges to get around the circuit. This means they will move more slowly and the current will go down.

The greater the voltage of the supply, the more energy each unit of charge will get. This means they will move more quickly and the current increase.

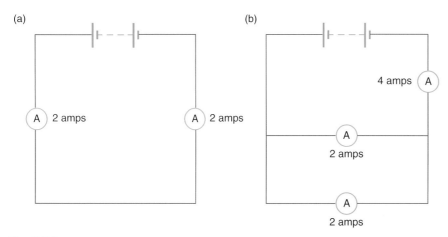

**Fig 5.21**

In a series circuit, the current is the same size everywhere (Figure 5.21a).

In a parallel circuit, the current in the main part of the circuit splits up when it comes to a junction in the circuit (Figure 5.21b). The bigger the resistance of an arm in a parallel circuit, the smaller the share of the current it will get.

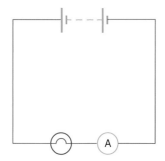

**Fig 5.22**

An ammeter is used to measure current. An ammeter is placed in series with the component you are measuring the current through (Figure 5.22).

The symbol for current is I. (Short for 'current intensity'.) The unit in which current is measured is the ampere, (A), more commonly called the amp.

## Questions

**1** Which of the four circuits below is set up correctly to measure the current through and the voltage across the bulb?

(a)
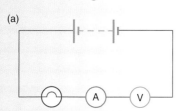

(b)
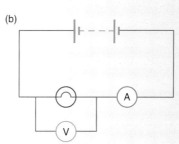

(c)
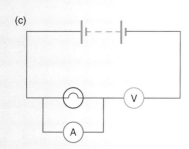

(d)
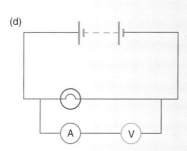

**2** Fill in the missing values in the circuit below.

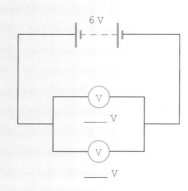

**3** Why are the electrical sockets in your home wired in parallel with each other rather than in series?

**4** Which of the circuits below would be most suitable for wiring the headlamps of a car? Explain your answer.

(a)
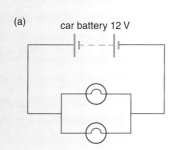

(b)
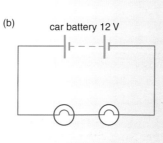

## Resistance

The **resistance** of an electrical component tells you how difficult it is for electricity to pass through it. The higher the resistance of a component in a circuit, the more it will slow down the charges moving through the circuit. The symbol for resistance is R and resistance is measured in ohms ($\Omega$).

Resistance meters can be used to measure the resistance of a component, but we often have to calculate resistance using measurements of voltage and current.

## The link between voltage, current and resistance

$$\text{resistance} = \frac{\text{voltage}}{\text{current}}$$

The equation above is called Ohm's Law. Ohm's Law is not only used to calculate resistance, it can also be rearranged to calculate current or voltage.

$$\text{current} = \frac{\text{voltage}}{\text{resistance}}$$

$$\text{voltage} = \text{current} \times \text{resistance}$$

$$\frac{V}{I \times R}$$

In symbol form these equations are:

$$R = \frac{V}{I} \quad I = \frac{V}{R} \quad V = IR$$

*Examples:*

**A**  A current of 2 A flows through a resistor when it is connected to a 6 V supply. What is its resistance?

$$R = \frac{V}{I}$$

$$R = \frac{6}{2}$$

$$R = 3 \text{ ohms}$$

Remember to show all your working clearly and don't forget to add the correct unit to your answer.

**B**  What size current will flow through a circuit when a 200 ohm resistor is connected to a 12 volt supply?

$$I = \frac{V}{R}$$

$$I = \frac{12}{200}$$

$$I = 0.06 \text{ amps}$$

**C** What sized voltage is needed to pass a current of 100 mA (milliamps), through a 2 k ohm (kilohm) resistor?

First you need to change the current to amps and the resistance to ohms.

There are 1000 milliamps in an amp, so 100 mA = 0.1 A

There are 1000 ohms in one kilohm, so 2 k ohm = 2000 ohms

$$V = I R$$
$$V = 0.1 \times 2000$$
$$V = 200 \text{ volts}$$

## Questions

5 Match up the following quantities, with their units, symbols and definitions.

| Quantities | current | resistance | voltage |
|---|---|---|---|
| **Units** | volts | amps | ohms |
| **Symbols** | R | V | I |
| **Definitions** | energy given to, or used by, each unit of charge | rate of flow of charge around a circuit | how difficult it is for electricity to travel around a circuit |

6 Calculate the resistance of a bulb that carries a current of 3 amps when it is connected to a 24 volt supply?

7 A 20 kilohm resistor is connected to a 6 volt supply in a circuit. What is the current through the resistor?

8 What is the voltage across a light bulb with a resistance of 100 ohms when a current of 200 mA flows through it?

# Factors affecting the resistance of components

There are three main factors that affect the resistance of a component:

● its length,
● its cross-sectional area,
● the material it is made from.

For some components, temperature can also affect their resistance.

## Length

The longer the component, the greater its resistance. This is because the charges have further to travel. In practice this means that connecting wires should be kept as short as possible. We sometimes forget that connecting wires have some resistance too.

## Cross-sectional area

The thicker the component, the smaller its resistance. This is because the charges have more room to move so they can move more quickly.

### *Material*

Some materials carry electricity better than others. Materials that carry electricity well are called good conductors of electricity. Materials that are poor at carrying electricity are called electrical insulators. Metals are good conductors of electricity. Good conductors offer less resistance than electrical insulators.

### *Temperature*

Passing electricity through a component always causes the component to get hotter. The amount of heat produced depends on two factors:

- the resistance of the component,
- the size of the current flowing through the component.

The greater the resistance, the more heat produced. This is why electrical devices designed to produce heat have very long, thin filaments that have a high resistance. A good example of this is a filament light bulb, where the filament has to become very hot to glow white and produce bright light.

The greater the current, the more heat produced. This is why electrical heaters use high currents.

Increasing the current has a greater effect than increasing the resistance. Doubling the resistance doubles the amount of heat produced every second. Doubling the current makes the amount of heat produced each second four times greater. Making the resistance ten times bigger makes the heat produced each second ten times greater. Making the current ten times bigger makes the heat produced each second one hundred times greater.

When conductors get warmer their resistance increases. This is because heat energy makes the atoms in the wires and components vibrate more which makes it harder for the charges (electrons) to get through the components and around the circuit. This effect is very noticeable in filament light bulbs. As the current through the bulb increases, the filament gets hotter and its resistance increases.

There is a group of materials called **semiconductors**. The resistance of a semiconductor changes as its temperature changes. When semiconductors get warmer they conduct electricity better. This is because the heat energy frees more electrons to carry current in the semiconductor. This property can be made use of in thermistors. Thermistors are used in circuits designed to detect changes in temperature, for example in electronic thermometers and automatic fire alarms.

Some semiconductors change their resistance when they are exposed to different levels of light. This is because the light energy frees more electrons to carry current in the semiconductor. This property can be made use of in light dependant resistors (LDRs). LDRs are used in circuits designed to measure or react to different light levels, for example in light level meters or in automatic lighting circuits where lights switch on automatically when it gets dark.

> **Glossary**
>
> **Semiconductor**
> A material whose conductivity is between that of a conductor and an insulator. The resistance of a semiconductor decreases as it gets hotter.

9 Apart from an automatic light switch, suggest another use for an LDR.

10 Thermistors can be used in electronic thermometers. Suggest how such a thermometer would work.

11 Why is it better to use as few connecting wires as possible in an electric circuit?

12 What type of resistor would you use as a sensor in a circuit designed to turn off your electric heater as soon as the room became warm enough.

# Topic 2  Electrical Components

There are many components that can be added to electrical circuits.

## Resistors

Resistors are usually made from long lengths of thin wire or from compressed carbon. The resistance of a good standard resistor will not be noticeably affected by temperature.

**Fig 5.23** Resistor symbol

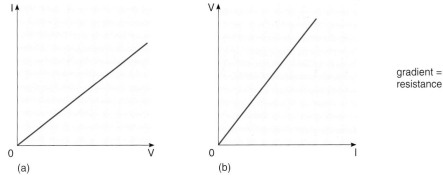

gradient = resistance

**Fig 5.24** Voltage characteristic graphs of a resistor

The graph in Figure 5.24a shows that the resistor has a constant resistance, because the graph of current against voltage is a straight line. When the graph is drawn this way around, the steeper the line, the lower the resistance. This is the technically correct way to draw a current – voltage characteristic graph.

Sometimes the graph is drawn the other way around, as in Figure 5.24b. When this is done, the gradient (steepness) of the line tells you how large the resistance is. The steeper the line, the greater the resistance.

Although this is not the technically correct way to draw this current – voltage characteristic graph, we often draw it this way because we can calculate an actual value for resistance by calculating the gradient of the line.

---

**REMEMBER**

**When you draw a graph make sure you put labels and units on both the axes. If you don't you will lose marks and no one will know what your graph is meant to show.**

---

# Filament bulb

The filament in these bulbs is a very long, coiled piece of very thin high resistance wire. The resistance of the filament changes as its temperature changes. Increasing the current through the bulb increases the temperature enough to cause a big increase in resistance.

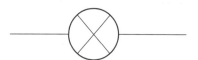

**Fig 5.25** Bulb symbol

Characteristic graphs for a filament bulb:

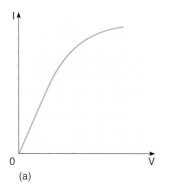

**Fig 5.26** Voltage characteristic graph of a bulb

(a)

Plotted this way round, the graph gets less steep, showing an increase in resistance.

(b)

Plotted this way round, the graph gets steeper, showing an increase in resistance.

# Thermistor

A thermistor is designed to change its resistance as its temperature changes. Thermistors are made out of semiconductors.

Voltage characteristic graphs for a thermistor.

**Fig 5.27**

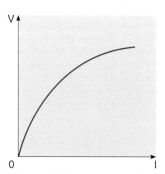

(a) Thermistor symbol (b) Plotted this way round, the graph gets steeper, showing a decrease in resistance.

(c) Plotted this way round, the graph gets less steep, showing a decrease in resistance.

# Variable Resistor

A variable resistor is used when you want to be able to change the resistance in a circuit easily. You usually need to be able to do this so you can change the size of the current flowing through the circuit. A dimmer switch and the volume control on a stereo are examples of variable resistors.

**Fig 5.28** Variable resistor symbol

# Diode (rectifier)

The function of a diode is to allow current to flow through it in one direction only. Its main use is in changing AC electricity (where the current changes its direction of travel around the circuit at regular intervals) to DC electricity (where the current flows in the same direction all the time). Diodes are usually made from semiconductors.

**Fig 5.29**

(a) Diode symbols

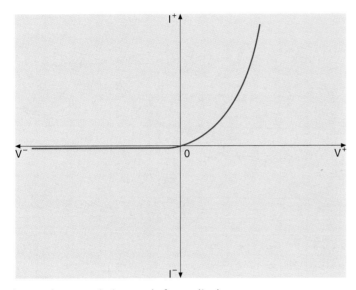

(b) Voltage characteristic graph for a diode

In the graph in Figure 5.29, the negative signs represent direction. When the signs are negative it indicates that the voltage is pushing the current the opposite way around the circuit. As the graph shows, the current only flows effectively in one direction around the circuit.  When the direction is reversed, the current is so small that it is effectively zero.

## Questions

**13** Look at the graphs below. Both graphs are drawn to the same scale. Which graph shows the resistor with the higher resistance.

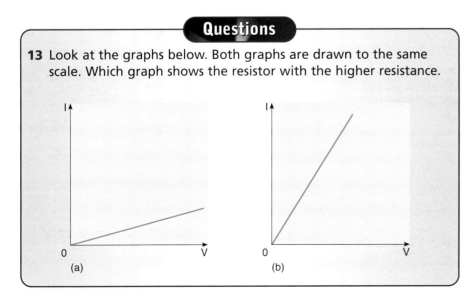

## Questions

**14** Below is the characteristic graph for a resistor. Calculate the gradient of the line in the graph. Use your answer to state the resistance of the resistor.

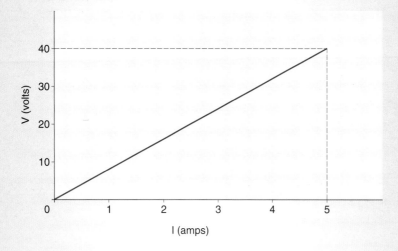

**15 a)** Draw the circuit symbols for:

    i)   a diode,
    ii)  a thermistor,
    iii) a variable resistor,
    iv) a light dependant resistor.

  **b)** What do all the resistor symbols have in common?

**16** Suggest four uses for a variable resistor.

**17** The characteristic graph for a component is shown below. Is this the graph for a thermistor or a filament bulb? Explain your answer.

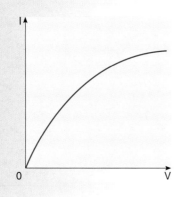

# Topic 4  Power

**Power** is a measure of how much energy is produced or used in one second, and is measured in watts (W).

To calculate power, we use the equation:

$$\text{power} = \frac{\text{energy}}{\text{time}}$$

$$P = \frac{E}{t}$$

Triangle: $\dfrac{E}{P \times t}$

1 Watt = 1 Joule of energy per second

One Watt is a very small amount of energy, so we often use the kilowatt (kW) or megawatt (MW) as units, when we are dealing with electrical energy generated in power stations, or used in household or industrial equipment.

One kilowatt = 1000 watts

One megawatt = 1 000 000 watts

To measure electrical energy, we often have to measure current and voltage and use these measurements to calculate the electrical power. To do this we use the equation below:

$$\text{power} = \text{current} \times \text{voltage}$$

$$P = I\,V$$

Triangle: $\dfrac{P}{I \times V}$

*Examples*:

**A**  A stereo uses 2000 Joules of energy in 10 seconds. What is its power?

$$P = \frac{E}{t}$$

$$P = \frac{2000}{10}$$

$$P = 200 \text{ W}$$

**B**  A radio has a power rating of 50 W. How long will it take it to use 5 kJ of energy?

First you have to change the kilojoules to joules: 1 kJ = 1000 J

$$t = \frac{E}{P}$$

$$t = \frac{5000}{50}$$

$$t = 100 \text{ seconds}$$

**C**  A 12 V bulb has a current of 2 A flowing through it. What is its power?

$$P = I \, V$$

$$P = 2 \times 12$$

$$P = 24 \text{ W}$$

**D**  How much energy would the bulb in example C use in 5 minutes?

First, change the time to seconds: 5 minutes = 300 seconds

$$E = P \, t$$

$$E = 24 \times 300$$

$$E = 7200 \text{ Joules } (7.2\text{kJ})$$

## Questions

**18** What is the power of an electric drill which uses 900 Joules of energy in 30 seconds?

**19** A power station produces electricity at the rate of 1 megawatt (1 000 000 W ). How many Joules of electricity does it produce in one minute?

**20** A 12 volt bulb operates at a power of 36 Watts. What is the current flowing through it?

**21** A battery supplies a model car with 20 000 Joules of energy. If the car operates at a power of 10 Watts, how long will the battery last?

# Topic 4  Paying for Electricity

When you pay for electricity you are paying for the amount of electrical energy you have used. The amount of electrical energy used is measured in special units called kilowatt hours (kWh). One kilowatt hour is the amount of electrical energy used by a one kilowatt appliance run for one hour. This means that a 2 kilowatt appliance run for one hour would use two kilowatt hours of electrical energy. A four kilowatt appliance run for three hours would use twelve kilowatt hours of electrical energy.

An electricity meter records how many units of electrical energy have been used. When the meter is read it is not reset to zero, it just carries on counting. This means that if you want to know how many units of electrical energy you have used between readings, you have to calculate the difference between what the meter says now and what the meter read last time a reading was taken.

**Fig 5.30**

The number of units used in the time between the meter readings in Figure 5.30 is calculated by taking reading A away from reading B.

units used = reading B – reading A

units used = 140 896 – 119 257

units used = 21 639 units

## Working out how much an appliance will cost to run

To work out how much it will cost you to run an electrical appliance, you need to know:

- how many units of electricity it will use,
- how much each unit of electricity will cost.

You can calculate the number of units of electricity you have used using the formula below :

kilowatt hours = power of appliance × number of hours it was used for

kWh = kW × h

**REMEMBER**

**One unit = one kilowatt hour**

*Examples*:

**A**  A 3 kW immersion heater is used for 2 hours. How many units of electricity does it use?

$$kWh = kW \times h$$

$$kWh = 3 \times 2$$

$$kWh = 6$$

The immersion heater has used 6 units (kWh) of electricity.

Remember: The power must be in kilowatts (not watts)

The time must be in hours (not minutes or seconds)

**B**  How many units of electricity are used by a 100 W light bulb left on for 30 minutes?

$$kWh = kW \text{ x } h$$

Now you must convert the power from watts to kilowatts and convert the time from minutes to hours before you can go any further.

$$100 \text{ W} = 0.1 \text{ kW}$$

$$30 \text{ minutes} = 0.5 \text{ h}$$

$$kWh = kW \times h$$

$$kWh = 0.1 \times 0.5$$

$$kWh = 0.05$$

The light bulb uses 0.05 units of electrical energy.

Before you can work out how much the appliances above will cost you to run, you also need to know how much one unit of electricity will cost.

The cost of one unit of electricity will depend on a number of things, for example, who your electricity supplier is and what electricity tariff you are on. Very big users of electricity, like steel works, are likely to pay less per unit of electricity than ordinary householders do. Most electricity suppliers also offer a special tariff where you can pay much less for each unit of electricity that you use overnight (off-peak rate), but slightly more than usual for each unit of electricity you use during the day (peak time rate).

running cost = number of units × cost per unit

*Examples*:

**A** How much will it cost to run a 2 kW electric oven for 4 hours if electricity costs 7p per unit?

First calculate the number of units (kWh):

$$kWh = kW \times h$$

$$kWh = 2 \times 4$$

$$kWh = 8$$

8 units of electricity have been used.

Now work out the cost:

$$cost = number\ of\ units \times cost\ per\ unit$$

$$cost = 8 \times 7$$

$$cost = 56\ p$$

**B** How much will it cost to run a 100 W light bulb for 10 hours a night, every night for a week? Electricity costs 7p an unit.

Calculate the number of units (remember to change watts to kilowatts):

$$kWh = kW \times h$$

$$kWh = 0.1 \times 70$$

$$kWh = 7$$

7 units of electricity were used.

Work out the cost:

$$cost = number\ of\ units \times cost\ per\ unit$$

$$cost = 7 \times 7$$

$$cost = 49\ p$$

As you can see, the power rating of an appliance makes a big difference to how much it costs to run. You can find the power rating of most appliances written on the appliance itself, either on a metal plate or a sticker attached to the outside of the appliance.

As a rule, appliances that produce light have a low power rating, those that produce movement have a medium power rating, and appliances that produce heat have high power ratings. This is because appliances that produce heat need to use large currents and power = current × voltage.

Appliances that can be run from batteries usually have lower power ratings than appliances that can only be run from the mains. This is because batteries produce much lower voltages than the mains supply does and, as the equation above shows, power depends on the voltage as well as the current. Remember, in Britain, mains voltage is 230 volts.

**Fig 5.31** Power rating plate

## Questions

**22** How many units of electricity are used to do the following:
   a) Run a 2 kW fire for 7 hours?
   b) Run a 5 kW immersion heater for 3 hours?
   c) Run a 500 W television for 6 hours?
   d) Run a 2 kW tumble drier for half an hour?
   e) Run a 3 kW kettle for 12 minutes?
   f) Run two 100 W light bulbs for 8 hours?
   g) Run a 700 W microwave for 5 minutes?

**23** Calculate how much it would cost to do each of the things in Question 23 if electricity costs 7 p per unit.

## End-of-Section 3 Questions

**1** Should street lights be wired in series or in parallel? Give a reason for your answer.

**2** What happens to the current in a circuit when the resistance of the circuit is doubled?

**3** What happens to the current in a circuit when the supply voltage is made 10 times bigger?

**4** What current flows through an electric oven, power 3600 watts, that is operated from the mains?

**5** Write down the units for each of the following:
   a) Current
   b) Voltage
   c) Resistance
   d) Power
   e) Energy

**6** a) Write down the equation that links resistance, current and voltage.
   b) Use the equation to calculate each of the following:
      (i) The resistance of a wire that carries a current of 3A when supplied with 12 V.

(ii) The current flowing through a 100 ohm resistor when attached to a 10 V supply

(iii) The voltage needed to pass a current 0f 2A through a heating element with a resistance of 120 ohms.

**7** For each of the following devices: a variable resistor; a thermistor, and an LDR,
   a) draw the circuit symbol,
   b) suggest two uses for the device.

**8** A current of 0.5A flows through a toy motor when it is connected to a 10 V supply.
   a) Calculate the following:
      (i) The power generated.
      (ii) The amount of electrical energy used in 5 minutes.
      (iii) The resistance of the toy motor.
   b) The motor produces only 3 J of kinetic energy each second. What is its efficiency?

| Section 4 | Useful Instruments and Machines |

Section 4 is divided into two topics:

**1** Electrical and electronic devices    **2** Mechanical machines

**When completing your Unit 3 assignments you will need to:**

★ Describe the use of electrical or electronic devices for:
  ● sensing, monitoring and controlling electro-mechanical devices or machines;
  ● generating pulses of light that are transmitted through optical fibres in communication;
  ● controlling movement;
  ● monitoring and controlling physical conditions.

★ Explain the functions of the following components in an electrical or electronic device:
  ● power source;
  ● processor;
  ● input components;
  ● output components.

★ Identify a range of components in mechanical machines used in the workplace, explain how they work, and be able to:
  ● measure the applied force and the force produced by the machine;
  ● calculate the amount the machine multiplies force;
  ● calculate the work done by the machine and its efficiency.

★ Understand the advantages and disadvantages of friction in machines.

# Topic 1 Electrical and electronic devices

This section will give you the background information to help you understand how electronic circuits work and guide you in the design of basic electronic systems. It gives basic designs for simple electronic circuits that you can build and test, but you may need to alter these circuits slightly, depending on which components you have available to use.

## Basic Electronic Systems

Electronic systems have three main parts:

**1** an **input** – this tells the system about its surroundings or tells the system what to do. The input component is a type of sensor.

**2** a **processor** – this is the active part of the system. It takes in information from the input component and decides what the output will be.

**Glossary**

**Input**
Detects a change in the surroundings.

**Processor**
Takes in the information from the input and decides what the output should be.

**3** an **output** – this is what the system does at the end.

Of course, they also need a power source.

*Examples*:

**A** A torch

**Fig 5.32**

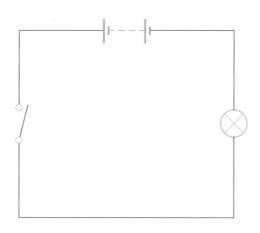

| | | |
|---|---|---|
| The INPUT is the switch which is either on or off | The PROCESSOR is the simple electric circuit that carries the electricity to the output | The OUTPUT is the torch bulb which is either on and gives out light, or is off and does not give out light |
| INPUT | PROCESSOR | OUTPUT |

**B** An automatic light switch, which turns on a street light as soon as it gets dark

**Fig 5.33**

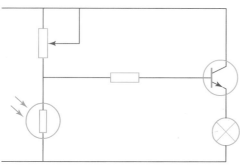

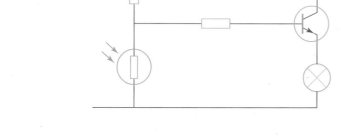

| INPUT | PROCESSOR | OUTPUT |
|---|---|---|

| LDR | transistor | lamp |
|---|---|---|
| The INPUT is an LDR which detects whether it is dark enough for the light to be turned on | The PROCESSOR is usually an integrated circuit, or a transistor, which is triggered by a signal from the input device | The OUTPUT is the street lamp which comes on if the processor decides it is dark enough and goes off again when the processor decides it is light enough |

In this system, the input component (**LDR**), converts light energy into electrical energy. The electrical signal it produces is sent to the processor. The size of this signal (the voltage) will decide whether the electrical signal sent from the processor to the output component tells the street lamp to switch on or off. The ouput component (the streetlamp) converts electrical energy to light.

However, this system is a little more complicated. The size of the current in the electronic circuit alone, is not enough to operate the output, the streetlamp. In this case, the electronic circuit will operate a switch for a second, higher power circuit, which will make the streetlamp switch on.

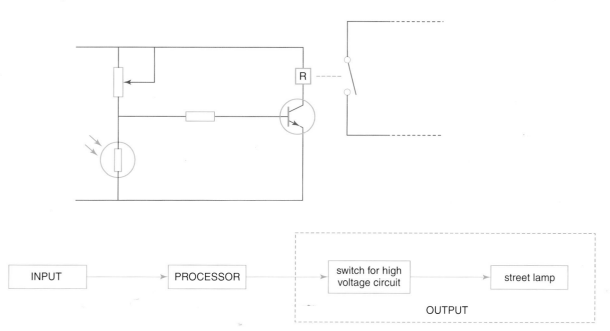

**Fig 5.34** A street lamp circuit

Electronic circuits which will only operate with low currents and voltages, are often used to trigger high powered circuits in this way. Examples include:

- Flashing headlights are detected by an LDR attached to the outside of a garage. This triggers a high voltage motor circuit which causes the garage door to open.

- A thermistor on the wall of a room triggers a circuit, which causes a mains operated heater to switch on automatically if the room is too cold.

- A moisture detector attached to the room of a house triggers a mains operated motor circuit which closes a skylight when it rains.

- A pressure pad attached to an electronic burglar alarm system, which automatically triggers a mains operated siren when someone steps on the pad.

The examples above show low voltage electronic circuits being used to switch on high voltage electrical or mechanical devices. Mechanical devices have moving parts, so they often need high voltages to have enough power to get the parts to move. Motors are the most common examples of mechanical devices operated by electronic circuits.

## Uses of Electronic Circuits

Electronic circuits can have many different uses, these include:

- sensing, monitoring or controlling physical conditions;
- sensing, monitoring or controlling machines;
- controlling movement;
- generating pulses of light to be transmitted through optical fibres.

### Sensing, monitoring or controlling physical conditions

A typical example of this is the use of a thermistor circuit to sense the temperature in a room, and automatically turn a heater on if it is too cold. The thermistor circuit will then be constantly monitoring the room temperature and will turn the heater off once the correct temperature has been reached.

**Fig 5.35** A room thermostat detects the temperature of the room and turns the heating off once the required temperature is reached

Another example of the use of an LDR circuit to sense the light level in a room. The LDR circuit turns up the lighting if it is too dark and turns the lighting down if the room becomes too bright.

### Sensing, monitoring or controlling machines

Some simple examples of this, such as the circuit used to control the automatic garage doors and the system used to close a skylight if it starts to rain, have already been mentioned.

Other examples could include:

- Monitoring the speed of a conveyor belt in a factory and automatically speeding it up or slowing it down if the speed needs to be changed.

- Sensing whether there is water left in the drum of a washing machine and unlocking the machine door if all the water has been removed.

- Shop doors opening automatically when a pressure pad senses that someone wants to come in.

### Controlling movement

This use is linked with controlling machines. For example, the conveyor belt system described above is also an example of using an electronic circuit to control movement.

Other examples could include:

● Using a thermistor circuit to automatically control the speed of a fan to keep the temperature in a room constant.

● Using a variable resistor circuit to control the speed of an electric mixer.

● Using a position sensor to make a lift stop on the correct floor.

## Generating pulses of light to be transmitted through optical fibres

Electrical signals can be converted to pulses of light. These pulses of light are then sent along **optical fibres**, which are fibres of glass or plastic. At the end of the fibre the pulses are converted back to electrical signals. Optical fibres can be used instead of sending the electrical signals from one place to another along copper wires. This is an example of a digital communications system. Modern communication systems, such as cable TV and cable telephones, use optical fibres rather than copper wires to transmit signals.

There are many advantages in sending signals along optical fibres rather than along copper wires. These advantages include:

● Optical fibres do not lose as much energy as copper wires, so the signal at the other end is stronger.

● Glass or plastic fibres do not corrode as easily as copper wire.

● There is no interference between one fibre and another so many fibres can be placed next to each other without the need for any insulation between fibres.

● Very narrow fibres can be used so they take up much less room than copper wires. They are also very much lighter than the copper wires needed to do the same job.

● Glass and plastic are much cheaper than copper.

Electronic circuits are used to produce pulses of light to represent the electrical signals that you want to transmit. Different electronic circuits are used to turn the pulses of light back into electrical signals.

Figure 5.36 shows what happens in a cable telephone system.

> **Glossary**
>
> **Optical fibres**
> Very thin strands of glass or plastic, along which large amounts of information are passed in the form of light pulses.

**Fig 5.36**

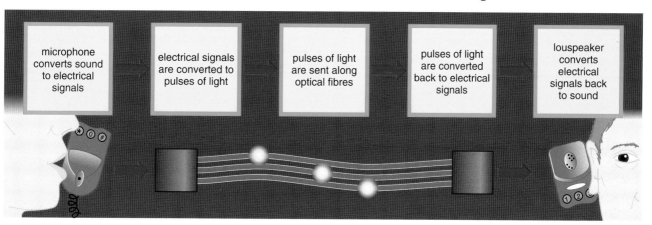

microphone converts sound to electrical signals → electrical signals are converted to pulses of light → pulses of light are sent along optical fibres → pulses of light are converted back to electrical signals → louspeaker converts electrical signals back to sound

## Questions

**1** Copy and complete the following table, putting the components below under their correct function headings:

components:

**LDR** **battery** **thermistor** **motor** **light** **bell**

**transistor** **pressure pad** **speaker** **microphone**

**power pack** **heater** **integrated circuit** **LED**

| input components | processors | output components | power sources |
| --- | --- | --- | --- |
|  |  |  |  |

**2** Suggest input and output components that could be used for the following jobs:
  a) opening the kitchen window when the room becomes too hot;
  b) turning on the lights in a room as soon as someone comes in through the door;
  c) an automatic anti-theft car alarm;
  d) a warning system for a car driver, to let you know when you are getting too close to a car when you are parking.

**3** Give an example, not already described in this chapter, for each of the following types of electronic system:
  a) sensing, monitoring or controlling physical conditions;
  b) sensing, monitoring or controlling machines;
  c) controlling movement.

**4** A telecommunications engineer is trying to decide whether to use optical fibres or copper wiring for the internal telephone system of a large hospital.
  a) What reasons might he give for choosing copper wire?
  b) What reasons would you give to pursuade him to use an optical fibre system?

## Practical Work    Making and Testing Electronic Circuits

Before you make an electronic circuit you must consider the following things:

**1  Exactly what do you want your circuit to do?**

For example, if you want a circuit to switch a warning light on when it gets cold, what temperature, or range of temperatures, do you want it to switch on at?

*continued* ➤

## Practical Work | Making and Testing Electronic Circuits continued

**2 What type of power supply do you want the circuit to work from?**

Mains powered circuits are much more complex, with far more safety considerations than low voltage battery operated circuits.

**3 What components are available?**

The choice of what to make and the final design of your circuit will depend on exactly which components you are able to use.

You also need to consider whether you want to use 'plug in' systems or individual components soldered on to circuit boards.

**4 How much time do you have?**

Making an electronic circuit always takes *much* longer than you think it will.

Don't forget, you will need to include time for fault finding, correcting faults and testing and evaluating the final product.

**5 Safety considerations.**

If your design includes making anything that works from a mains supply, there are very stringent safety regulations you MUST comply with. These regulations are continually updated. Your teacher will be able to get the latest regulations from COSH (Coalition for Occupational Health and Safety) and IEE (the Institution of Electrical Engineers).

These regulations include the following:

● Mains plugs must be correctly fitted.

● Cables to equipment should have rubber grommets where the cables enter the metal case.

● Fuses, single-pole switches and any circuit breakers used must be in the live lead.

● There must be a power indicator light to show when the device is switched on.

● The device must be properly earthed.

You must not start building a mains operated device until you have checked these regulations. You are strongly advised to make devices that work from low voltages and not mains supply.

While you are building your circuit, it is a good idea to test each component before you start and each section of your circuit as it is made, to ensure that all are working properly.

When you have finished your circuit you need to test it to see whether it matches your specifications. Does it do what you wanted it to do?

> **Safety**
>
> You must do a risk assessment before making any electronic circuit.

> **Safety**
>
> REMEMBER
>
> When you are testing capacitors, make sure the capacitor is fully discharged before you touch it. Capacitors can store large amounts of charge. Figure 5.37 shows you how to discharge a capacitor.

**Practical Work** | **Making and Testing Electronic Circuits** continued

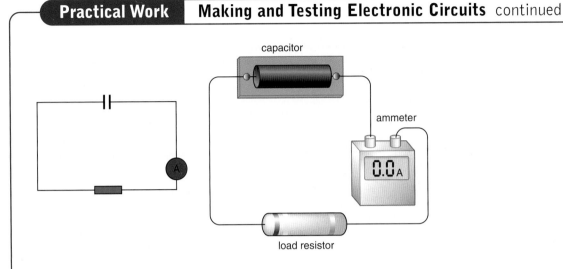

capacitor

ammeter

0.0 A

load resistor

**Fig 5.37** Discharging a capacitor

When you have tested your device, you will need to evaluate it. You will need to say how good it is for the job you wanted it to do. Even if the device does the job you wanted it to do, you may still feel that it isn't fit for its purpose. For example, your circuit might have switched on a warning light when the temperature became too cold, but your device might be too big to go where you wanted to put it. The wiring and soldering might not be secure enough for you to expect the device to work for very long. You need to think about these types of things when you are doing your evaluation, or better still, put points like size and durability into your specification.

# Topic 2  Mechanical Machines

We rely on mechanical machines to make work easier for us both at home and in the workplace. There are many different types of machines but most of them allow us to do a job using less physical force than we would need to do the same job without the machine. Many machines also allow us to get jobs done faster than we could if doing the same job by hand.

There are many different types of machines, but the most common include:

● Levers
● Pulleys
● Wheel and axle
● Ramp
● Screws
● Gears
● Hydraulic lifts

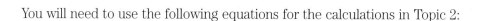

You will need to use the following equations for the calculations in Topic 2:

> moment = force applied × distance from pivot
>
> clockwise moment = anticlockwise moment
>
> $$\text{mechanical advantage} = \frac{\text{load}}{\text{effort}}$$
>
> work done = force × distance moved
>
> $$\text{efficiency} = \frac{\text{useful energy output}}{\text{total energy input}} \times 100\,\%$$
>
> $$\text{pressure} = \frac{\text{force}}{\text{area}}$$

## How machines work

Many machines use the idea that increasing the distance between where you apply a **force** and where you want the force to act, decreases the size of the force that you need to do a job.

The **Principle of moment** shows us how this works.

## The Principle of Moments

The easiest way to understand this principle is to think of a see-saw.

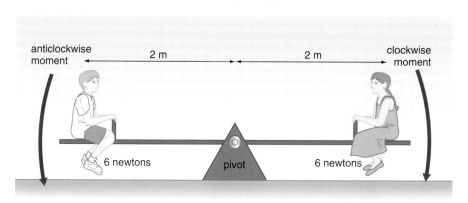

**Fig 5.38** Clockwise moment = anticlockwise moment

On each side of the see-saw there is a force of 300 **Newtons** (N) placed 2m from the pivot.

The moment is calculated by multiplying together the force exerted on one side of the pivot and the distance this force is applied from the pivot. For example, in the see-saw above, the moment on the left of the see-saw (the anticlockwise moment, because it will make the see-saw turn anticlockwise) is calculated using the following equation:

> moment = force applied × distance between force and pivot

Moments are measured in newton metres (Nm)

$$(\text{anticlockwise}) \text{moment} = 300 \times 2 = 600 \text{ Nm}$$

If the see-saw is going to balance, the moment on the right, the clockwise moment, must also equal 600 Nm.

To balance:

clockwise moment = anticlockwise moment

We can get the clockwise moment to equal 12 Nm in a number of ways. For example we could put:

300 N at a distance of 2m from the pivot

or, 1200 N at a distance of 3m from the pivot

or, 150 N at a distance of 4m from the pivot

or, 100 N at a distance of 6m from the pivot.

As you can see, if we increase the distance we need less force to balance the see-saw.

We can now look at each of the machines mentioned earlier and see how they work. Think about which ones involve increasing the distance to decrease the force.

## Levers

Levers use the principle of moments. In using a lever to move something you are increasing the distance between the force you are applying and the object you want to move. Figure 5.39 shows how this works.

**Fig 5.39**

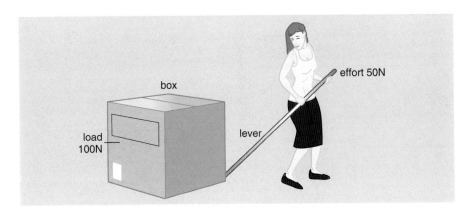

$$\text{Mechanical advantage} = \frac{\text{load}}{\text{effort}} = \frac{100}{50} = 2$$

Mechanical advantage is a measure of the output force compared to the input force. In the case of levers the output force is greater than the input force, so the mechanical advantage is greater than one.

In the example above, we have ignored friction. We have said that by doubling the distance we have halved the force needed, because we only needed to apply 50 N to lift a box weighing 100 N. In real life we would have to use more than 50 N because there would be some friction that we would have to overcome. It would be more realistic to say we need to apply a force of 60 N because of the friction involved, which means some of the energy input would be wasted. This means that the machine will not be 100% efficient.

$$\text{So, mechanical advantage} = \frac{100}{60} = 1.67$$

To calculate the efficiency of a lever system, you would need to calculate:

**1** The work done by the effort (total energy input):

$$\text{work done} = \text{size of force} \times \text{distance moved}$$

**2** The energy gained by the load (useful energy output):

$$\text{energy gained} = \text{size of load} \times \text{distance moved}$$

**3** The efficiency of the lever system.

$$\text{efficiency} = \frac{\text{useful energy output}}{\text{total energy input}} \times 100\%$$

Crowbars, wheelbarrows, scissors and some handles are all examples of levers.

## Pulleys

Pulleys make it easier to lift things because they allow you to pull downwards, so that your weight helps you. They also use the basic idea of increasing distance in order to reduce force. Figure 5.40 shows a simple pulley system.

**Fig 5.40**

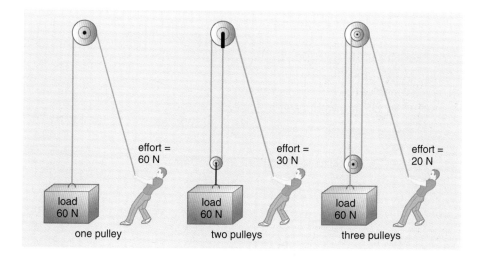

load 60 N — effort = 60 N — one pulley

load 60 N — effort = 30 N — two pulleys

load 60 N — effort = 20 N — three pulleys

The greater the number of supporting strings the pulley has, the smaller the effort needed to lift a given load. This is because the greater the number of strings, the greater the total distance moved by the pulley ropes, so the smaller the force needed.

Figure 5.40 assumes a perfect pulley system, with no **friction** and weightless ropes. However in real life, the ropes themselves have weight so you need to supply extra force to lift them. Pulley systems always produce friction. This will increase the force you need to lift a load, but it will also prevent the ropes from slipping easily. This is obviously very important when lifting heavy loads safely, for example, with a block and tackle pulley system. Figure 5.41 is a more realistic example of a real pulley system.

> **Glossary**
>
> **Friction**
> A force of resistance which opposes the movement of an object.

**Fig 5.41**

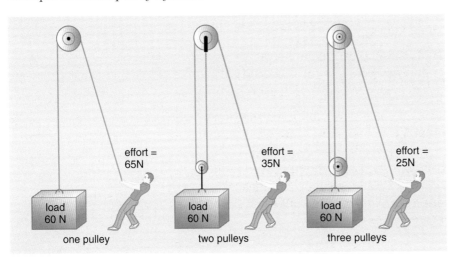

effort = 65N

effort = 35N

effort = 25N

load 60 N

load 60 N

load 60 N

one pulley

two pulleys

three pulleys

There are many examples of pulley systems, these are often in the form of block and tackle systems which are used to lift heavy objects, such as cranes on building sites.

## Wheel and axle systems

Screwdrivers, doorknobs and the steering wheel of a car are common examples of wheel and axle systems. These systems are rather like continuous lever systems. The idea behind them is that applying a small turning force on the wheel will produce a larger force on the axle. This is because the distance that the wheel moves is greater than the distance that the axle moves. Figure 5.42 is an example of a wheel and axle system

**Fig 5.42**

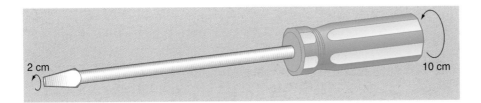

2 cm

10 cm

circumference of handle = 10 cm

circumference of blade = 2 cm

For one complete turn, the handle of the screwdriver moves 10 cm, but the blade of the screwdriver moves only 2 cm.

For a perfect, frictionless screwdriver this would give a mechanical advantage of 5 (10/2).

$$\text{mechanical advantage} = \frac{\text{load}}{\text{effort}}$$

$$\text{mechanical advantage} = \frac{10}{2} = 5$$

In real life, there would be friction, otherwise the screwdriver would slip, so the mechanical advantage would be less than 5.

## Ramps or inclined planes

Ramps, or inclined planes, are one of the simplest examples of machines. They have been used to lift heavy objects for thousands of years. A common example of their use is on the backs of delivery vans.

Again these systems are based on the idea that, by increasing the distance moved, you are reducing the force needed to move an object. The problem with ramps is that there will always be a noticeable amount of friction between the ramp and the object being moved, because their surfaces will be in contact for a long time. This means that they are always considerably less than 100 % efficient. An example to show how ramps work is given in Figure 5.43.

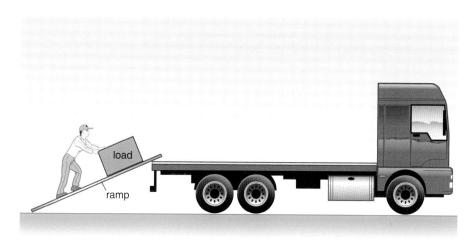

**Fig 5.43**

## Screws

We do not usually think of screws as being machines. However, you can think of a screw as being made up of an inclined plane (the thread), being wrapped around the main axis of the screw. This means that only a small force is needed to move the screw a large distance. Screw threads are used in screws, nuts and bolts, and car jacks.

## Gears

Gears involve cogs of different sizes connected together. Gears can be used to change the mechanical advantage of a machine. This is because the distance moved by the cog that the force (effort) is applied to, moves a different distance from the cog that moves the load. Gears are usually used to change the speed of rotation of an object, rather than the force applied. This is shown in Figure 5.44.

**Fig 5.44**

## Hydraulic machines

These work on a different principle from the other machines that have already been described. Hydraulic machines use liquids to move forces from one place to another. They also usually magnify the force, so that the load that can be moved by a hydraulic machine is greater than the force applied by the effort.

Hydraulic machines use the following ideas:

● Pressure is transmitted through a liquid.

● pressure = $\dfrac{\text{force}}{\text{area}}$

● Re-arranging this equation we find that –

  force = pressure × area

● This means that if we exert a fixed pressure on a larger area, we will get a larger force produced.

Figure 5.45 is an example of a hydraulic lift that shows how these principles work together in a hydraulic machine. Hydraulic lifts and hydraulic jacks are commonly used to lift large loads.

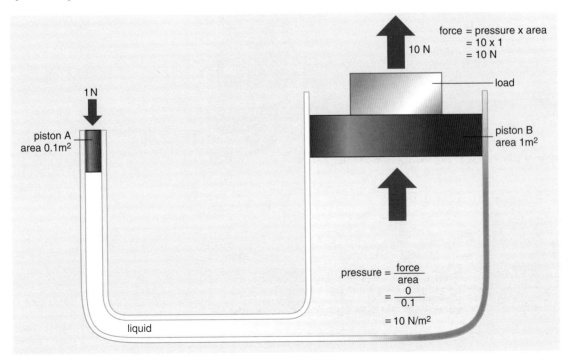

**Fig 5.45**

## Questions

**5** Write down three possible uses for each of the following machines:
  i)   a pulley,
  ii)  a lever,
  iii) a hydraulic lift,
  iv)  a wheel and axle system.

**6** Assuming there is no friction, calculate the forces needed to pull the mass in the diagram below, up the ramp shown.

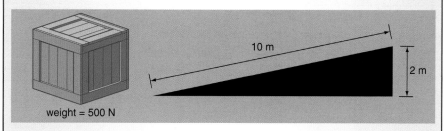

**7** Calculate the mechanical advantage of each of the systems shown below.

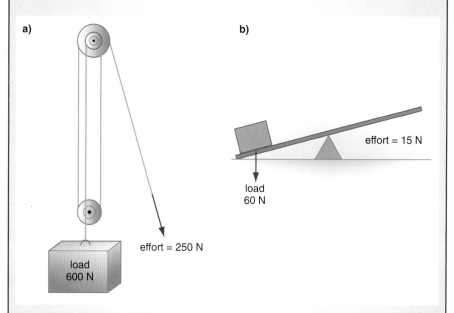

**8** Calculate the efficiency of the ramp system shown below.

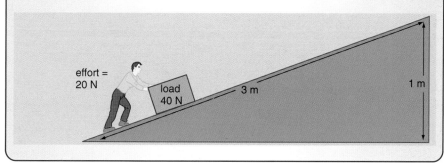

## End-of-Section 4 Questions

**1** Write down two advantages of using optical fibres rather than copper wire for networking computers.

**2** Write down two examples of each of the following:

a) Input components

b) Output components

c) Power sources

d) Processing devices

**3** Suggest suitable input and output components for the following devices:

a) A burglar alarm

b) An automatic door

c) An automatic cooling system for a bedroom

**4** a) Write down the equations you need to use to calculate the following:

(i) Mechanical advantage

(ii) Efficiency

b) (i) Calculate the mechanical advantage and the efficiency of the ramp system shown below.

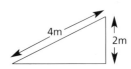

A force of 200 N is needed to pull a box weighing 500 N up the ramp

(ii) Explain why the ramp is not 100% efficient.

**5** What are hydraulic brakes? How do they work?

# Index

Page numbers in bold show that information is in an illustration or a table.